NEW CONCEPTS OF SCHEMA THERAPY

(The 6 Coping Styles)

Amir Askari

Preface by
Wendy Behary and **Jeffery Young**

Foreword by
Eckhard Roediger

New Concepts of Schema Therapy

Author
Amir Askari

Translator & Editor
Mehdi Mirkia

Psychology Editor
Golafrooz Gholamy

◆ ◆ ◆

ISBN: 9798538360130
Imprint: Independently published

For permission to use material from this text, contact by

Web: www.schematherapyiran.com

Phone: +98-9391348089

To all physicians, nurses, and medical staff around the world who devoted all they had and put their life at risk to save humans and keep them safe while fighting the Coronavirus (covid-19 disease).

ABOUT THE AUTHOR

Born in 1979 in Tehran, Iran, Amir Askari has attended the University of Mysore in India, where he has earned his master's and Ph.D. degrees in clinical psychology. He is a supervisor/ trainer and advanced degree certified schema therapist by the International Society of Schema Therapy (ISST). Amir Askari is also the founder and director of the Iranian Institute of Schema Therapy (IIST) since 2019. He is also the head of the Developmental Project of Schema Therapy (DPST) in Iran and the Middle East, which is part of the projects overseen by the Center for Advanced Studies in Mental Health (CASMH). He is currently a board member of the Iranian Clinical Psychology Association (ICPA). His studies initially began in Cognitive Behavioral Therapy and Gestalt Therapy, and eventually, he got to Schema Therapy. Amir Askari has published numerous articles in international journals and has made many speeches in different countries. Besides doing psychotherapy with disordered personality patients and also counseling and conflict resolving with the couples, he attends to teaching, doing research, writing, translating, and editing.

CONTENTS

PREFACE

Early experience becomes recorded in the archives of memory. Memory resides in a neural network of systems, occurring not only within the cerebral and limbic brain system but also actively riding the superhighway of the nervous system, becoming reenacted in muscle fiber, in the heart system, digestive track, and nervous system.

The sensory system will detect a seemingly familiar threat linked with a once lived experience and, often unknowingly, activates a distress signal. These conditions for activation can be experienced in relationship with others, and in time alone.

To quiet the internal noise of intolerable emotions/sensations, patients may spiral into challenging modes becoming detached, critical, defiant, defensive, yielding, or dismissive, in the treatment room. These moments will inform a sturdy, caring, and competent therapist—working to regulate and manage emotional intensity—of the powerfully important need to identify, validate, empathize, confront, track, and reconsolidate emotional material to ultimately meet the patient's early unmet needs and correct the longstanding biased emotional experiences.

Jeffrey Young's *Schema Therapy* is a science-based, integrative, treatment approach for personality disorders and chronic symptom disorders. Schema therapy carefully and comprehensively conceptualizes the narrative behind a patient's self-defeating life patterns; those occurring both outside and inside the treatment room. Through the use of schema therapy's highly effective blend of specific emotion focused, cognitive-behavioral, and therapy-relationship strategies – along with tools from other evidence-based schools of practice – schema therapy aims to heal the biased emotional beliefs and coping responses that have been formed in the interplay of early unmet needs and genetic predisposition; replacing *early maladaptive schemas (EMS),* corresponding coping modes, and internalized critical messages, with healthy and adaptive emotional beliefs and behaviors.

Schema therapy thoughtfully investigates the patient's emotional autobiography, appreciating how emotional scripts and messages, or *early maladaptive schemas* (EMS) get imbedded in memory and can become activated implicitly or explicitly in everyday life events, particularly in the patient's interpersonal relationships.

In our work with patients with BPD or NPD, it is not unusual to be confronted with someone who is flipping from one coping state to another, trying to stave off the oppressive and unbearable sensations emerging from a reminiscent, schema-triggering experience.

We are so pleased and grateful that our dear friend and colleague, Amir Askari decided to write this thoughtful and innovative book, *New Concepts of Schema Therapy...* This compelling new book introduces the reader, through rigorous investigations of theoretical, historical, and biological data, along with colorful metaphor and relevant case examples, to an elaboration on the maladaptive coping system. The examples are articulated in a body of material that is not only creative and resonant but immediately accessible to the clinician for grab and go use in the treatment room.

Elegantly written, Amir Askari presents the model in a comprehensive and navigable way; capturing the art of communicating self-defeating patterns of thought and behavior to patients in highly personalized and customizable ways—a hallmark strategy of the limited reparenting stance of schema therapists while assisting patients to track, confront, and weaken maladaptive coping modes.

This book is an important contribution to the clinician's resource library. *New Concepts of Schema Therapy...* offers the therapist-reader a comprehensive handbook for conceptualizing modes and engaging effective strategies for change.

We are delighted to express our confidence, our support, and appreciation for Amir Askari's *New Concepts of Schema Therapy* ... Bravo.

Wendy Behary, President (2010-2014) The International Society of Schema Therapy (ISST); Author/Expert, Schema Therapy for Narcissism

Jeffrey Young, Founder, Schema Therapy

FOREWORD

With this book, Amir Askari presents a significant contribution to the growing body of books on schema therapy. Besides John Philip Louis from Singapore, at least to my knowledge, he is the first book author from outside the western hemisphere. This fact matters because therapy is a culturally sensitive endeavor. So far, schema therapy is rooted in a humanistic western tradition. The related lifestyle and conduct rules taint our understanding of Schemas, schema-coping styles, and resulting modes. Meanwhile, schema therapy spreads out to almost all corners of the world. This requires adjustments of the model according to the population we apply schema therapy to i.e., the role of the family and resulting loyalty conflicts are significantly different in many Eastern countries compared to most western countries. This book represents a successful attempt to adjust and fine-tune the model for the work especially within an Islamic-oriented country like Iran.

While the schemas itself remained untouched, Amir Askari revisited the schema coping styles, because his intensive clinical observation revealed, that the biologically based trichotomy of schema coping stiles in terms of the fight (overcompensation), flight (withdrawal), and freeze (surrender) does not reflect the full spectrum of reactions on a schema in countries with higher normative pressure. The water finds its way and people show astonishing creativity when it comes to avoiding the pain of schema activations. Amir Askari uses a nice wording expanding the existing biologically based "wild-caught 3 f" (fight, flight, and freeze) to "6 f" by adding the socially induced (he called "farm-raised") schema coping styles "faint, farce, and fumble". He lays these new schema coping styles out in detail brought to life by a lot of practical examples and case vignettes.

The resulting spectrum of schema modes also shows much more nuances than the currently applied spectrum covers, especially among the surrendering and avoidant coping modes (while the spectrum of externalizing or overcompensatory coping modes including modes prevailing in the forensic setting is represented sufficiently in the existing descriptions). Consequently, he added 9 more coping modes playing out the new schema coping styles in social interactions as variations of the surrendering and avoidant coping modes. He describes them in detail including many clinical facets and some historical and cross-cultural background to deepen the understanding.

Since we only "see what we know", this enlarged spectrum enables therapists and clients to label and address reactions to schemas in a much more detailed and differentiated way and helps fine-tuning and customizing the case conceptualization to the clients. Finally, in the practical work, the therapist will focus on the most relevant schema-coping styles and resulting schema modes in order to keep the case conceptualization manageable. However, the choice to select from became bigger now by offering more culturally rooted schema responses. This is an important contribution creating a better fit by addressing the behavioral nuances of people, especially in Islamic cultures.

The book closes with an interesting and creative presentation of the Healthy Adult mode functioning in the shape of a manikin including a questionnaire to assess the specific skills building it up. Another substantial contribution to better understand and train this most important mode when it comes to emotional regulation and successful social functioning – finally all over the world! Altogether this book is a "must-read" for all people working either in Islamic countries themselves or with clients who migrated because the cultural bonds still remain active abroad and have to be taken into account in culturally sensitive schema therapy. Thanks to Amir Askari for using the lockdown time to write this important book. This is something that will last, even once we managed to overcome the current crisis.

Frankfurt, Germany in May 2021

Eckhard Roediger, President (2014-2016) The International Society of Schema Therapy (ISST).

THE STRUCTURE OF THIS BOOK

The primary audience of this book, "New Concepts of Schema Therapy (The Six Coping Styles)," are professional therapists who have already got themselves familiarized with schema therapy. This book aims to increase the careful consideration of the schema therapists of both their own and their patient's behaviors related to the new maladaptive coping styles. This book is divided into six chapters. The first chapter, "A Review of Maladaptive Coping Styles" points out the concepts of schema therapy while having surrender, avoidance, and overcompensation coping styles as its central focus. This chapter reviews maladaptive coping modes by giving brief descriptions as well. In the second chapter, "Getting to Know the "New" Maladaptive Coping Styles," an adaptation is being made between the sextet physiological reactions and maladaptive coping styles and the three new coping styles of indolence, mockery, and gaucherie get unveiled. In the third chapter, the indolence coping style along with its related modes, in the fourth chapter, the mockery coping style along with its related modes, and in the fifth chapter, gaucherie coping style along with its related modes are explained and expanded upon by providing examples of each newly introduced coping style. In each of these chapters (three, four, and five), a section called "opening up a new window" where some biological, social, historical, or evolutionary issues related to each coping style are discussed. Furthermore, considering the importance of personality disorders in schema therapy, a separate section is devoted to giving definitions and examples for each of the new nine coping modes and related personality disorders at the end of each chapter. The sixth chapter is dedicated to "The Healthy Adult Mode." The examples used throughout this book are taken from real individuals and events. These are the patients I had came across during years of doing schema therapy, and out of confidentiality, the names and details of them have been changed. Thank you for choosing this book, "New Concepts of Schema Therapy (The Six Coping styles)," and dedicating your time to reading it. For stating any comments, suggestions, or critiques, please use the following email address:

dramiraskari@casmh.org

You can visit the Iranian Institute of Schema Therapy's (IIST) website and get informed about the latest specialty activities of this institute:

www.schematherapyiran.com

Also, the resources of this book including the Tehran-Schema Mode Inventory (T-SMI), Tables, Figures, and Checklists are available for download at:

www.shcematherapyiran.com/resources

With Highest Regards

Amir Askari / November 2020 – Tehran

PERSONAL REMARK

Coronavirus Crisis, an opportunity for writing the present book: These days, people and the world of science have agreed on home quarantine to "buy time" for the discovery of a vaccine and the vaccination process for the Coronavirus and starting the vaccination phase. Millions of people have stayed home around the whole world, waiting with hope and optimism for scientists to discover an effective medicine for overcoming this worldwide virus finally. The reality is that since a hundred years ago and before the corona crisis, the medical and technological sciences developed so rapidly alongside each other that only a few could have thought that the global cycle of human's life would get this much punctured with the birth of an unknown virus.

A couple of days ago, I accidentally heard Antonio Guterres (Secretary-General of the United Nations) on the news warning that the outbreak of Coronavirus is the biggest challenge since World War II. Just like World War II, which initially took place in Europe and Iran got involved with it somehow, either intentionally or unintentionally, The Covid-19 crisis started in China, Wuhan but Iran was among the first countries which very soon was involved with this pandemic.

Therefore, today, April 14th, 2020, it has been seven weeks since I have been officially in total home quarantine using this mandatory opportunity to read, research, and write. Ten years in my clinical work, I have written down incidents that grabbed my attention from the therapy room in my notebooks. Also, while reading schema therapy books, I had taken notes from some lines I came across, but I never found a chance to gather and put all of them together. Now with the Iranian

Institute of Schema Therapy (IIST) being closed due to the Coronavirus pandemic, I had to stay home, and with this mandatory opportunity, I found a chance to start writing about all that I had witnessed, read, and experienced.

Also, while being in touch with my colleagues worldwide through email and phone, I realized that they were doing what exactly the great minds of psychology were doing during World War II; writing! Writing is an action through which humankind portrays his thoughts coming from his experiences. The same phenomena took place during World War II (1939 - 1945) where the world took the direction in which the schools and universities were closed, and the great thinkers who had to stay at home picked their pens, dipped them in ink, and brought them to existence extraordinary theories, articles and books. Examples among these great thinkers include Friedrich Perls (founder of Gestalt Therapy), who wrote his first book, "Ego, Hunger and Aggression," and got it published in Johannesburg in 1942. Erich Fromm laid out the foundations for Political Psychology by writing his book "Escape From Freedom" in 1941. The same year Skinner introduced Conditioned Emotional Response (CER) by giving an electric shock to mice. Next year, Ludwig Binswanger, a Swiss psychiatrist, founded Existential Psychology. The same year, 1942, Carl Rogers published his famous book on counseling and psychotherapy. The book in which he introduced his approach to psychotherapy included concepts such as non-judgmentalism and respecting the client. Next year, Abraham Maslow unveiled his hierarchy of needs in an article with the subject: "A Theory of Human Motivation." Viktor Frankl told about his lived experiences at the Auschwitz concentration camp and, by writing the book, "Man's Search for Meaning," brought Logotherapy into existence. Above all comes the formation of clinical psychology as a scientific field during World War II and due to the lack of psychiatrists. Lastly, it was at the final year of the war where the Journal of Clinical Psychology was founded, and its first issue got published the same year.

Iran was occupied by the Soviet Armed Forces in the

north and the British Army in the south. Consequently, Reza Shah (1878-1944) was first exiled to Mauritius Island and later to South Africa. As a result, the country was filled with famine, hunger, and illness, yet despite all these horrible circumstances, Iranian thinkers also found the opportunity to write a great many literary and scientific works. Therefore according to the historical experience, if the Coronavirus crisis goes on for an extended period, we can expect new achievements in psychotherapy and especially schema therapy.

Even though the medical and technological sciences have accelerated immensely, humanistic sciences, especially Philosophy, Psychology, and Sociology, have failed to make much progress. Even more, when compared with the nineteenth and twentieth centuries, these fields have gotten behind. There is a probability that just like after World War II, humanities compensate for falling behind, but this time after the Coronavirus crisis. Certainly, psychology will move toward making changes into individualistic and social theories after this crisis. For example, when it comes to Social Psychology, topics such as role-playing, conformity, persuasion, sustainable living, and group polarization will require a review. When it comes to Crisis Psychology, this time the "perceived injustice" has given its way to lack of facial masks, gloves, hygienic detergents, hospital beds, and getting vaccinated, which has become a worldwide concern instead of not receiving food, containers, tents or clothing packages which were only relevant in the context of an earthquake taking place. In Clinical Psychology, the most significant danger would probably be an increase in the suicide rate during and after the obligatory quarantine phase. Individuals who cannot adjust themselves to the long-term quarantine situation and have unresolved psychological difficulties under their belts are more prone to pathologies. Furthermore, when it comes to Family Psychology (family therapy/ couples therapy), we will witness a severe increase in divorces, domestic violence, and marital conflict rates. Concerning School Psychology (Educational Psychology), we will be faced with academic failures in students and problems in getting readapted to schooling conditions again further down the road.

Even though the issues mentioned above and many more will gradually unravel themselves in front of us, and there is no escaping from them, they contain a positive message in themselves as well. The message is "making an opportunity out of this crisis for development of humanistic sciences" in the future. Human sciences have entirely lost their ground to other sciences by failing to be as functional during the past decades. It has not been able to accelerate as well as other sciences have managed to do so. Schema therapy will face challenges (for example, the 2020 conference in Denmark being called off) and, of course, remarkable changes that would follow the challenges. This holds since the beginning of a crisis is a matter of mandatory urgency, yet putting it behind is a matter of collective wise decision making.

What has been stated in the previous paragraphs was not aimed at future telling, yet it was only meant to learn lessons from the past. As Karl Popper puts it, predicting the future is impossible because we do not know how much knowledge and capabilities we possess in the future: "no society can predict, scientifically, its future states of knowledge."

Now let us go back to May 2018, where the International Conference of Schema Therapy took place in Amsterdam. After the conference, based on the suggestion of Dutch organizers, my friends and I decided to visit the Anne Frank museum (house) in the Prinsengracht district. A rather dark multi-story house that, taking its stairs, would make us feel the sad and sorrowful experience of Anne and her family during the difficult times of the world war. Anne was only 13 years old to escape from Nazi forces in January 1942; she had to stay in a hide-out in this house for 25 months with her family and family friends. Their location was revealed to the Nazis; they got arrested and were sent to the Auschwitz concentration camp. She passed away at the age of 15 due to contracting typhoid disease in the death camp.

After returning to my hotel, I tried to picture Anne Frank's vulnerable child while having to live in that hide-out for 25 months. The pictures were hanging on the museum's walls (the house or latter being used as the hide-out) pictured a happy child. Then I tried to enter the picture of the hide-out as a good parent and tried to form a connection with the little Anna who was hiding in the closet. What I experienced most during this imagery was not the constraint condition, shortage of food, lack of hygiene, or the distress of Nazi's showing up at the door. However, it was the uncertainty of the existing situation. Therefore I came to use the term "Deadlock Stage" for describing that condition. During the deadlock stage, the individual has no idea how long she should stay in the hide-out. Are there any better options? Does remaining in the hide-out help her survive (there is a shortage of food supplies), or can she make it by showing herself to the Nazis?

It has been two and a half years since my memorable visit to Amsterdam. These days, I have stayed at home, quarantining myself (hide-out) along with the majority of the world's population; more than ever before, I get to think of Anne Frank, who had to hide in her house for 25 months. I watch people who have seriously got caught up in the dreadlock stage in an Anne Frank way on the news. They find themselves in a conflict between remaining in the difficult conditions (lack of money/ getting bored in the house) and going back to work (following health guidelines/chance of contracting the virus). During the deadlock stage, individuals have no idea how long they should remain in their home quarantine and spend their savings. At this stage, the individual can not make a self-aware decision because no matter what decision she makes, her psychological and physical survival is at risk.

History has shown that our human ancestors have probably gone through many dreadlock stages due to pervasive diseases, an abundant number of wars, and consecutive famine conditions that they experienced. Therefore there is a probability for existing genetic codes for adjusting with dreadlock and uncertainty. By giving a more detailed examination of the past dreadlocks, dividing them into two forms of short-term and long-term categories is possible. For bringing to mind a sample of a short-term dreadlock, you have to be on a winter day of 1989, where you wake your eyes up to a snowfall day, and you have no idea if you have to go to school on that day or soon you are going to hear the news on the radio of schools being closed due to the heavy snowfall!

In Chemistry, the solid particles which tend to float around in a liquid are called "suspension." Under normal conditions, the suspensions are not usually stable, and after a while, if being kept in place, they tend to settle down (just like the orange juice containing pulps). So during dreadlock suspension, those groups of individuals who were against quarantine and lockdowns from the beginning and breaking the norms (going back to work) commute in streets these days have probably settled down in hospital due to contracting the Coronavirus! Moreover, if the same group decides to stay home, they eventually have to face their suffering dreadlock in the hide-out due to their financial difficulties. It appears so that the dreadlock stage is meaningfully related to existential death anxiety, meaninglessness, and aimlessness. Therefore for some, it is easier to contract Coronavirus instead of facing existential suffering. In this book, I attend to many high-risk behaviors which are based on the new coping modes. Even Though I believe that the human psyche is yet a very complex and unknown matter, I have done my best to unravel those unknown parts of the psyche which have been out of sight and introduce them to the audience. Writing this book has not made me neglect scientific research by any means. I will conduct much practical research on the topics discussed in this book with the help of my colleagues and students soon. In the research process, besides focusing on the brain's functions on one end and the cultural effects on the other end, we ought to present simpler models of schema therapy. Models that enhance schema therapy's comprehension and provide us with more straightforward methods to teach its concepts.

ACKNOWLEDGMENTS

It is all very fortunate that despite the internet having many shortcomings in Iran, my friends and schema therapist colleagues who live around the world are very kind and responsible. They have responded to most of my questions and messages with generosity, either online or through emails. Furthermore, they have provided me with the books, articles, assessment tools, and resources in my time of need for them to help me with writing this book. Their kindness and responsibility have extended to me in other areas as well: the copyright is not recognized in Iran, and the banking system is under financial sanctions, which has made the transfer of money very challenging. These complications with the transfer of money have negatively affected the capacity to attend international workshops and conferences.

Even though many individuals have played a decisive role in writing and publishing this book, yet every book getting published in schema therapy is, without doubt, a review of the efforts and endeavors of its founder, Jeffery Young. In our last meeting in the Netherlands, I shared my ever-growing motivations for writing this book, and his valuable words and genuine smile further added to my motivation. On my behalf and behalf of my colleagues, students, and clients who have not got the chance to meet him in person, I would like to thank him and extend our levels of appreciation and gratitude for bringing extraordinary changes into our lives through the schema therapy approach.

I want to warmly thank my dearest teachers, Paul

Kasyanik, and Elena Romanova, from Schema Therapy Institute St. Petersburg (Russia). Under their supervision, I passed my standard and advanced level training in schema therapy. Indeed, their six visits to Tehran have had a significant impact on developing schema therapy in Iran. Schema therapy in Iran has witnessed a significant and increasing growth, especially during the past five years in which many individuals have played vital roles. Nevertheless, in case we are to coin the date of the beginning of schema therapy in Iran based on professional principles, schema therapy history in Iran is divided into two halves by an important event which is October 14th, 2016 (the first presence of Paul Kasyanik and Elena Romanova in Iran). Their visit to Iran consequently resulted in Iran becoming a member of the International Society of Schema Therapy (ISST) and the professional schema therapy courses with ISST protocols being conducted in Iran under their supervision. Also, Paul Kasyanik attended the opening ceremony of The Iranian Institute of Schema Therapy (October 3th, 2019) and gave a speech to 500 interested attendees in schema therapy, and Elena Romanova conveyed her congratulations through a video message.

On the other hand, in case we can witness the current development of schema therapy in Iran, the significant role of Mohammad Ebrahim Madahi is to be praised as the organizer and supporter of this approach. He has had the experience of founding different associations and institutes, founding The Psychology and Counseling Organization of Iran being among the most notable ones. He has made himself memorable in the history of Iran's psychology once more by putting the effort and supporting the licensing and registration of the Iranian Institute of Schema Therapy. Mohammad Ebrahim Madahi is currently the president of The House of Psychologists, Counselors, and Supportive Occupations in Iran, and I endlessly thank him for the efforts he has put in to develop schema therapy in our country.

I want to extend my gratitude and appreciation to my dear friend and colleague, Eckhard Roediger (Former President of International Society of Schema Therapy (ISST) and The Director of Frankfurt Institute of Schema Therapy (Germany) for all of his encouragement, support and opening up new horizons for facilitating my progress. While being the International Society of Schema Therapy (ISST) president, he took a trip to Tehran on August 26th, 2016, and gave an incredible speech on schema therapy in practice. With his permission, his book (Schema Therapy with Couples) has been translated to Farsi by my colleagues and edited by me and has now been published by Somam publishing. I hope after putting the Coronavirus crisis behind us, we have the opportunity to host him once more in Tehran for conducting specialized courses.

I want to dearly thank Golafrooz Gholamy (ISST Standard Level Certified and training and research manager at the Iranian Institute of Schema Therapy), who has been by my side during the past six years as my program manager in the Center for Advanced Studies in Mental Health (CASMH). She has put all her effort into conducting and organizing specialized training courses and seminars. During past years, she played a great role in schema therapy workshops as my co-educators and being highly creative during role-plays. Furthermore, in writing this book, she has saved me from accidental errors with her through reading and has opened up new horizons in my mind by giving me constructive suggestions.

I want to thank my friends who have influenced me, my colleagues, and my students with their trips to Iran and giving speeches. In order of their visit: Christof Loose (Writer of the book Schema Therapy with Children and Adolescents - Dusseldorf Germany), Remco van der Wijngaart (Former Vice President of International Society of Schema Therapy, Rhein-Ruhr Schema Therapy Institute, Netherlands) and John Philip Louis (Director of Singapore Institute of Schema Therapy and the writer of the book, Good Enough Parenting). Without a doubt, there are sections in this book that I have written down being inspired by the comments, experiences, and thoughts of these noble figures.

I want to thank Mehdi Mirkia (Head of The Translation Team - Iranian Institute of Schema Therapy), who, during recent years, has played a significant role in all the schema therapy seminars and professional workshops by providing consecutive translations. Now he has put the effort to translate this work from Farsi to English, and for this, I endlessly thank him and appreciate his efforts. Furthermore, besides translating this book, he has provided me with ideas, insights, and delicate points which I have put to use while writing this book.

I am thankful to David P. Bernstein (Maastricht University, Netherlands) for sending me copies of Strengths Scales, BLS, and BSS. These scales were helpful when writing the section about the healthy adult mode. Also, I want to thank Susan Simpson (Founder and Director of Schema Therapy Scotland) for sending me a copy of her new book "Schema Therapy for Eating Disorders (2020)". Reading her book was very inspiring for me in writing this work.

I am thankful to my great friends, Alireza Beygi, PhD.(Psychotherapist at Skarholmen Health center Stockholm, Sweden), Saleh Mozaffari, PhD (Senior Data Scientist, WidasConcepts GmbH, Germany), and my brother Iman Askari, PhD. (LVR Clinic Duesseldorf, Heinrich Heine University Duesseldorf Clinics, Germany) who, with their encouragement and appraisals, helped me with finishing this work and shared their valuable experiences with me along the way. I thank you from the bottom of my heart.

I want to thank Jeff Conway (Vice President of International Institute of Schema Therapy) for my supervisory training and Wendy Behary (founder and Director of The Cognitive Therapy Center of New Jersey and The Schema Therapy Institutes of NJ-NYC and DC and writer of the book Disarming The Narcissist) for her cooperation and support in writing the preface for this book.

In writing this book, I have put to use the lessons that I learned from my patients. These lessons were my patient's life and also their own lived experiences along with their knowledge and skill. Without a doubt, this book would not be as complete without them. For these lessons and experiences, I am much thankful to my patients.

I am also thankful to my students. Their enthusiasm in learning schema therapy has been my primary motivation in teaching and developing schema therapy. Not only my students in Tehran but also my students in other cities of Rasht, Ahvaz, Shiraz, Bushehr, and Mashhad too have shared with me valuable information regarding their patients along with unique and creative ideas.

Unfortunately, my father, Ali Akbar Askari, passed away last year, and this year while writing this book, my mentor Professor Jyoti S. Madgaonkar (retired professor in University of Mysore, India), passed away as well. Their presence and memory stay with me forever.

INTRODUCTION

When it comes to psychotherapy, no therapeutic approach nor theory is one hundred percent self-contained and complete. The assessment of the effectiveness of a given therapeutic approach has nothing to do with the number of therapists who utilize that approach or the positive evaluations of the quality of the research conducted in that area. It all comes down to how simple the therapist can educate her patients about the concepts of the approach in a simple, easy-to-understand manner. Furthermore, how far the patients manage to navigate their way outside the therapy room, implementing what they have learned in therapy while facing their life problems. Therefore, the abundance of therapists and the quality of research are not accurate measures for assessing a therapeutic approach. The proper assessment is thus the "beneficiary" of the given approach. Of course, this beneficiary can be easily put to review by both the therapists and the patients. I know many schema therapists who enjoy their therapy sessions more and have witnessed a significant increase in the number of patients seeking therapy from them ever since they have started to utilize schema therapy to treat their patients. I have come across many patients who show a keen interest in learning about schema therapy concepts. They believe that schema therapy has transformed their lives, and when it came to witnessing the tangible fulfilling outcomes of their therapy, the previous approaches only failed them.

When it comes to addressing and overcoming the patients' problems, putting in the effort to discover the weaknesses and shortcomings of a given therapeutic approach compared to the other approaches and comparisons among them is not much of a help. Considering how nowadays, most of the approaches take an integrative stance toward therapy, what is of utmost importance is which therapeutic theory and approach empower us more with newer and more innovative interventions. Schema therapy as an integrative approach holds in itself pure knowledge since it empowers the therapists with an extraordinary ability to examine the difficulties of the patients. The theory which makes therapy more predominant and functional is influential, and both therapist and patients agree on this feature when it comes to schema therapy.

Most people find it challenging to grasp the meanings of the concepts and findings of new sciences. It is rare to come across someone who can find his way around the concepts of Nuclear Energy, Geopolitics, and Behavioral Genetics without being a student or a professional having expertise in these fields. However, one of the goals of schema therapy is to be at the service of society by providing its concepts in an easy-to-understand manner so that the patients' minds easily comprehend them. In our everyday clinical work, we have come across patients who came to us under exceptional circumstances. We had patients who were hooked on oxygen ventilators when they visited us at the hospital. They felt they had tried everything, and nothing worked out for them. What is common among most of these patients is that they are profoundly hopeless and have accepted that no method will solve their problems. They state that schema therapy is their last hope; thus, they have prepared themselves for something unorthodox and different from other therapeutic approaches. Risk-taking, persistence, and creativity are indispensable means in our line of work. This makes us accept patients who had previously failed to solve their problems with other approaches. Schema therapy holds a supreme stance and credit due to the new power it brings to the patient's life. The power for the patient to take over the making of healthy choices in her life.

The approach which does not bring out change into vicious repeated behaviors is doomed to failure. Some of the therapeutic approaches lack the strong philosophy needed for persuading the patient to make changes in his behavior. Of course, the history of psychotherapy is filled with huge mistakes! When the therapist directly asks the patient to end alcohol abuse or high-risk sexual relationships, the patient's reaction in the best-case scenario would be: How am I supposed to do that?

Some of the patients bring questions to the therapist. Questions such as how can I quit alcohol consumption? Or how can I put an end to my extramarital relationship? There is a probability that these patients are not really after putting an end to their behaviors; instead, they want to find out how powerful the therapeutic approach is. Educating about schemas and attempts at modifying them does not necessarily result in the moderation of the schemas. While working with couples, we have witnessed many times that after the therapist has decoded and unraveled the schemas of the couples, one of them has started to utilize this newly discovered knowledge to "analyze to destruct" the other partner and gain the upper hand. The couple who face many problems and do not want to attend to problem-solving might put the newly discovered knowledge into manipulative and domineering behaviors with their other partner. Upon the unraveling of their problems related to their schemas, some of the other couples get into a deep state of despair and get so intimidated that their first decision is to seek separation. Unfortunately, when the couple does not use schema therapy to change their behaviors, the techniques become fruitless. Nevertheless, the most significant danger under these circumstances is that before this, we could predict how the patient will behave in certain situations with the aid of schema therapy. However, after the patient gained this newly discovered knowledge yet not utilizing it to bring out change into her life, we would have a difficult time knowing how she is going to behave in the future. Her future behaviors would become highly unpredictable.

Some of the techniques that transform the patients' behaviors are magnificent in the early phases of therapy, but they lose their effectiveness rather very quickly. This is because the patients gradually drop practicing and using them on a day-to-day basis. Therefore, the therapist must bring to the patient's attention that as they were practicing the new techniques initially, they have to keep practicing and using them repeatedly over a long period, thus preventing the patient from stopping their usage prematurely. On the other hand, the more awareness the patients gain, the faster their schemas and modes change and modify their course of action. This makes the patient's knowledge outdated and in vain after some time. Thus the approach which can be effective and successful in treating the patients is the one that is constantly getting updated, strengthened, and accelerates the techniques. To find out which issues are taking place with a significant acceleration in today's world, we ought to answer this question first: What is the goal of schema therapy? Is schema therapy a double-edged sword?

Patients might choose to replace some other dysfunctional behaviors with the three coping styles after realizing their coping styles for each one of their schemas. Therefore there are other coping styles that individuals tend to utilize either consciously or outside of their awareness. Each of us is born into a particular family bearing certain sets of norms and values and governed by a specific set of behavioral and emotional structures. Furthermore, our psyche has been affected by a chain of random unpleasant incidents. The school has shaped part of our sufferings, fears, and wishes despite teaching us educational material. Putting all of this behind us, our ancestral schemas happen to come out of their grave and affect our personal and marital life. Some of the schemas are indispensable parts of our family identity, which hunt us from the moment of our birth. Most couples rarely try to free themselves from the paths their parents and prior generations took based on their genograms. They fail to envision a new path leading to a better future for themselves.

In schema therapy, we do not dive into the patient's past for the sole purpose of reviewing and reminding the bitter memories of the past. However, the aim is to free the patient from the repetitive patterns by focusing on the origins in childhood. Furthermore, by developing the healthy adult in the patient, we strive to help the patient to be able to take a look around himself, make aware observations and take on a healthy path that was out of sight for his ancestors.

During past decades schema therapy has provided therapists with new forms and tools. These diverse forms and questionnaires are easy to fill and score, and of course, most of the patients utilize some of these tools for self-assessment. Furthermore, specialized books for the therapists and easier-to-understand ones for the patients are being written and published every year. This means that schema therapy is a lively and dynamic approach. We will witness the expansion of its central concepts and therapeutic interventions to address other psychological disorders soon.

CHAPTER ONE

A REVIEW OF THE MALADAPTIVE COPING STYLES

In this chapter:

- Getting to know the fight, flight, and freeze reactions
- Knowing the surrender, avoidance, and overcompensation coping styles
- A review of coping styles related to each specific schema
- Introducing the modes related to the coping styles
- The difference between coping responses and coping styles
- Two-phase coping cycle patterns in couples
- The necessity of examining the childhood origins in the process of treatment (evolution and time)

Perhaps it is safe to state that while taking into account all the vast and diverse subjects and matters in the universe, the human psyche could be the most complex matter compared to the other ones. For thousands of years, the curious minds of Greek philosophers, Persian Polymaths, Indian mystics, Egyptian priests, and Chinese physicians have been occupied with figuring out the particularity and peculiarities of this mystical and complicated structure. Scientists continue to explore and investigate this matter. Today, mental health professionals try to make their way even further into the labyrinthine hallways and corridors of the psyche utilizing psychological tools/tests, clinical experience, and scientific researches. Additionally, they try to explain and interpret the different aspects of human behavior with more precision and accuracy.

In schema therapy which is an active, dynamic and innovative therapy, by utilizing an integrative approach to psychotherapy, the aim has been set to solve the complicated puzzles of the human psyche more than before. An inspection of different schools and approaches to psychotherapy reveals that if one approach lacks the inherent nature of being theoretically expandable or misses the ability to tailor and present new therapeutic techniques and updatable interventions, after a while, it would get outdated and cease to exist. Fortunately, schema therapy possesses an organized and systematic structure and a highly flexible nature that permits it to incorporate new concepts and ideas into its model. These positive features result in more remarkable advancement of this approach, adding to its flexibility to get in line with future updates to its concepts and bring its theorists closer together.

The hallmark of schema therapy lies within its ability to clearly address and explain the reasons behind the self-defeating and other-defeating behaviors of the patients. When the patients receive an explanation for these behaviors, they become aware of their coping responses and the reasons that drove those behaviors for the first time in their life. Therefore, precisely upon gaining this awareness, we witness an initiative as a starting point in the patients' cognitive, emotional, and behavioral growth. Schema therapy which significantly expanded and built upon traditional cognitive therapy possesses a comprehensive structure based on 18 schemas and 54 maladaptive coping styles. This has contributed to the significance and appeal of this approach. Schema therapy assumes that each schema only consists of childhood memories, emotions, bodily sensations, and cognitions, and it does not consider behavioral responses as a component of each schema. In other words, behavior is not part of a given schema but is driven by it.

Young and Klosko (1993) have introduced three coping styles of overcompensation, avoidance, and surrender based on the natural psychological reactions of the fight, flight, and freeze. They believe that early in life, patients develop maladaptive coping styles and responses to adapt to schemas. These maladaptive coping styles and responses prevent the patient from experiencing intense and overwhelming emotions, usually stemming from the schemas. According to Young, these coping styles are part of healthy survival mechanisms in childhood and are considered an adaptation to threatening situations. Nevertheless, if continued in adulthood, they can further help to perpetuate the schemas. Therefore, when being utilized in the face of threats or frustrations in childhood, coping styles are usually considered adaptive. However, if continued in adulthood, as the child grows, they become maladaptive. These coping styles are considered maladaptive further down the road since, in adulthood, the individual is provided with more promising options than childhood conditions to respond to the threats. Nevertheless, she tends to react to them in the same old ways, thus perpetuating the schemas. The making use of these maladaptive coping styles generally takes place outside of the individual's awareness, and he is not conscious of these operations.

When an individual is suddenly faced with a gray wolf, he might experience intense fear and flee from the scene in an instance (the flight response). He might get hold of a stone or a stick from the ground and throw it at that wolf (the fight response), or he might get so terrified and paralyzed that he momentarily loses the ability to move (the freeze response). Due to living and moving within natural terrains, our ancestors continuously encountered outside threats, especially wild animals, during the hunter-gatherer and agricultural era. Therefore, our ancestors gradually realized distinctive ways of fighting or escaping for each instance of threatening situations. It is important to note that the fight, flight, and freeze responses are physiological reactions of the organism to perceived threats. Hence, the organism might choose to fight, flee or freeze to save her life in threatening situations. These reactions have evolved over thousands of years and helped the organism to survive and surmount the threats. Walter Bradford Cannon coined the term "fight or flight response," also known as "the acute stress response," for the first time in 1920. He preferred to use the term "acute stress response" to describe these phenomena since the fight or flight response is part of the symptoms that organisms utilize to cope with stressful situations.

Now, according to Young, we can consider schemas as instances of threats. Schemas threaten the survival of emotional needs. Just like how the threats can endanger the individual's physical survival that means his life and livelihood (i.e., getting hunted by a wolf), schemas endanger the emotional survival of the person by frustrating the five core emotional needs. Please refer to the below table 1-1:

Table 1-1: The adaptation of physiological reactions with maladaptive coping styles

Factors	Reactions	Goal	Different Strategies		
Threats (such as facing a wolf)	Physiological reactions	Physical survival	Fight	Flight	Freeze
Schemas (like abandonment)	Coping styles	Emotional survival	Overcompensation	Avoidance	Surrender

Even though the physiological reactions of fight, flight, and freeze have contributed to our ancestors' survival throughout history, the maladaptive coping styles of overcompensation, avoidance, and surrender are not helpful in adulthood. These coping styles prevent the individuals from meeting their needs adequately, thus perpetuating the schemas. Therefore, the person who submits to her schema and presumes it to be accurate, in fact, "has surrendered to her schema." As an example, the individual with abandonment/instability schema might subscribe to the core belief which states: "It is only a matter of time before others abandon me." While searching for a potential romantic partner, this person would eventually choose someone who is either inaccessible, not committed, or, due to being already married, refuses to commit to a stable relationship. Thus, based on this person's frustrating choices, his schema perpetuation has turned the schema into a self-fulfilling prophecy. When his next beloved also leaves him, while whining with an intense emotional pain which stems from the sense of rejection would state: "I have been abandoned once again! No one is ever willing to stay with me forever."

"Schema avoidance" refers to the person who organizes her life in a way that prevents her schemas from being triggered. Even though this person has no prior knowledge of her schemas and coping styles, nevertheless, due to her past unfulfilling life experiences will not enter any romantic relationship. She refuses to do so since she does not want to experience the negative emotions and sorrows associated with the separation period of a relationship. Thus, this person does not want to risk being abandoned again. Since due to her abandonment/instability schema, she believes that "eventually everyone would abandon me one day," she would not even think about forming a casual relationship with someone, let alone falling in love with that person. In case someone expresses his interest in her or she starts to develop feelings for someone, she would quickly distract herself or try to prevent herself from thinking of the person who has won her affection.

In "schema overcompensation," the individual strives to exhibit a different behavior from his childhood as much as possible. For example, the person with an abandonment schema with its origin in his parent's divorce and failed attempts to prevent their separation from happening tries to overcontrol his partner in adulthood. By controlling different aspects of his partners' behaviors, coercion, or exhibiting excessive dependence, he attempts to extend their relationship's durability and make sure that separation is out of the question. All of this takes place even when the partner might seek a way out. Even though the core belief of this person's abandonment schema states that "Eventually, everyone would abandon me one day," yet he is constantly fighting in order not to be abandoned. Subsequently, he traps his partner by means of manipulation and annihilates the attempts of anyone who tries to get close to her.

When it comes to "schema surrender," the individual believes that her schema shows her the right way to undertake her life. Even Though the person experiences great deals of emotional pain due to adhering to schema-driven behaviors, she still refuses to make any modifications to those problematic ways of approaching her problems and difficulties. An example of this case would be an individual whose unrelenting standards schema has pushed him towards workaholism. Even Though he greatly feels the need for fun, spontaneity, and going on a trip, he still attends to his work even on holidays. He has surrendered to his unrelenting standards schema so intensely that even taking one day off from work would immensely stir up feelings of uselessness because of wasting time. Due to this belief, even if he becomes sick, he would take a day off to look after his health and well-being. In the case of surrendering to self-sacrifice schema, the individual assumes her moral and humanistic duty to help others out overtly. Even though over and over again, she has experienced significant levels of emotional pain due to her self-sacrifice schema, yet she is never willing to pay attention to her own needs. If she does so, she will view it as an act of selfishness and cruelty. Such an individual has surrendered to her self-sacrifice schema so severely that if she behaves in a way that is not in accordance with her schema, she will experience significant levels of guilt; thus, she has devoted her life to helping others and neglecting her own needs. Most often, cultural values also reinforce these behaviors. Consequently, the individual will not put any effort into modifying her schema.

Jeffery Young and colleagues (2003) have introduced examples for each coping style related to each specific schema presented in table 1-2. In the following table, besides the specific behaviors carried out in certain situations, the situations related to choosing romantic partners, friends, and working partners have also been mentioned.

Table 1-2, Examples for coping styles related to specific schemas

Schema	Surrender	Avoidance	Overcompensation
Abandonment/ Instability	Selects partners and significant others who are unavailable or unpredictable.	Avoids intimate relationships altogether out of fear of abandonment.	Pushes partners and significant others away with clinging, possessive, or controlling behaviors.
Mistrust/ Abuse	Chooses untrustworthy partners and significant others; is overvigilant and suspicious of others.	Avoids close involvement with others in personal and business life; does not confide or self-disclose.	Mistreats or exploits others; acts in an overly trusting manner.
Emotional Deprivation	Chooses cold, detached partners and significant others; discourages others from giving emotionally.	Withdraws and isolates; avoids close relationships.	Makes unrealistic demands that others meet all of his or her needs.

Defectiveness/ Shame	Chooses critical partners and significant others; puts him- or herself down.	Avoids sharing "shameful" thoughts and feelings with partners and significant others due to fear of rejection.	Behaves in a critical or superior way toward others; tries to come across as "perfect."
Social Isolation/ Alienation	Becomes part of a group but stays on the periphery; does not fully join in.	Avoids socializing; spends most of his or her time alone.	Puts on a false "persona" to join a group, but still feels different and alienated.
Dependence/ Incompetence	Asks for an excessive amount of help; checks decisions with others; chooses overprotective partners who do everything for him or her.	Procrastinates on decisions; avoids acting independently or taking on normal adult responsibilities.	Demonstrates excessive self-reliance, even when turning to others would be normal and healthy.
Vulnerability	Worries con-	Engages	Employs

to Harm or Illness	tinually that catastrophe will befall him or her; repeatedly asks others for reassurance.	in phobic avoidance of "dangerous" situations.	magical thinking and compulsive rituals; engages in reckless, dangerous behavior.
Enmeshment/ Undeveloped Self	Imitates behavior of significant other, keeps in close contact with "enmeshed other"; does not develop a separate identity with unique preferences.	Avoids relationships with people who stress individuality over enmeshment.	Engages in excessive autonomy.
Failure	Sabotages work efforts by working below level of ability; unfavorably compares his or her achievement with that of others in a biased manner.	Procrastinates on work tasks; avoids new or difficult tasks completely; avoids setting career goals that are appropriate to ability level.	Diminishes achievements of others; tries to meet perfectionistic standards to compensate for sense of failure.

Entitlement/ Grandiosity	Has unequal or uncaring relationships with partners and significant others; behaves selfishly; disregards needs and feelings of others; acts superior.	Avoids situations in which he or she cannot excel and stand out.	Gives extravagant gifts or charitable contributions to make up for selfish behavior.
Insufficient Self- Control/ Self- Discipline	Performs tasks that are boring or uncomfortable in a careless way; loses control of emotions; excessively eats, drinks, gambles, or uses drugs for pleasure.	Does not work or drops out of school; does not set long-term career goals.	Makes short-lived, intense efforts to complete a project or to exercise self-control.
Subjugation	Chooses dominant, controlling partners and significant others; complies with	Avoids relationships altogether; avoids situations in which his or her wishes	Acts in a passive–aggressive or rebellious manner.

	their wishes.	are different from those of others.	
Self-Sacrifice	Engages in self-denial; does too much for others and not enough for him- or herself.	Avoids close relation-ships.	Becomes angry at significant others for not recip-rocating or for not showing ap-preciation; decides to do nothing for others anymore.
Negativity/ Pessimism	Minimizes positive events, ex-aggerates negative ones; ex-pects and prepares for the worst.	Does not hope for too much; keeps expect-ations low.	Acts in an unrealistic-ally positive, optimistic, "Pollyan-naish" way (rare).
Emotional Inhibition	Emphasizes reason and order over emotion; acts in a very controlled, flat man-ner; does	Avoids activities involving emotional self-expres-sion (such as express-ing love or	Acts impul-sively and without inhibition (sometimes under the influence of disinhib-

	not show spontaneous emotions or behavior.	showing fear) or requiring uninhibited behavior (such as dancing).	iting substances such as alcohol).
Approval-Seeking/ Recognition-Seeking	Draws the attention of others to his or her accomplishments related to status.	Avoids relationships with admired individuals out of fear of not gaining their approval.	Acts flagrantly to gain the disapproval of admired individuals.
Punitiveness	Acts in an overly punishing or harsh way with significant others.	Avoids situations involving evaluation to escape the fear of punishment.	Acts in an overly forgiving manner while being inwardly angry and punitive.
Unrelenting Standards/ Hypercriticalness	Attempts to perform perfectly; sets high standards for self and others.	Avoids taking on work tasks; procrastinates.	Throws out high standards altogether and settles for below-average performance.

The History and Concept of Coping Modes

In this chapter, we focus our attention on the maladaptive coping modes related to the coping styles of surrender, avoidance, and overcompensation. However, it is vital to first briefly review the formation and development of the concept of the modes in schema therapy during the past years. Jeffery Young and his colleagues first introduced schema modes in the first edition of the "schema therapy, a practitioner's guide" book (2003). This was a decade after that the "reinventing your life" book outlined maladaptive schemas in 1993, also by Young and his colleagues. In the beginning, only ten modes were introduced, which were categorized into the three groups of the child, parent, and coping modes. The child modes included (vulnerable child, angry child, impulsive/undisciplined child, and happy child modes), the Dysfunctional parent modes included (Punitive/Critical Parent and demanding parent modes), and the maladaptive coping modes included (Compliant Surrenderer, Detached Protector, Overcompensator modes). The happy child mode and the healthy adult mode were considered the adaptive schema modes. Following this, Arnoud Arntz and David Bernstein expanded the mode model further and transformed it extensively to the extent that today, more than twenty modes and their educational card sets have been developed and introduced. For example, the iModes cards set was developed by David Bernstein (Maastricht University of Netherlands), which includes 25 cards to address different modes, with each card designed twice to represent different gender types. Paul Kasyanik and Elena Romanova (Schema Therapy Institute St. Petersburg, Russia) have also developed specialized card sets to work with schema modes. In schema therapy with children and adolescents, these mode card sets have been developed as well. Peter Graf (in Germany) and

Mariya Glimzyanova, with her colleagues (in Russia), have each separately developed card sets to address working with schema modes in children and adolescents as well, the latter being named "the journey to the modes valley."

Modes Related to the Maladaptive Coping Styles

Since the aim is to further expand on the concept of maladaptive coping modes in the following chapters of this book, the history, and concepts behind this group of schema modes shall be reviewed.

Initially, Jeffery Young introduced the three classifications of coping modes: the Compliant Surrenderer, the Detached Protector, and the Overcompensator. These three modes were associated with the three coping styles of surrender, avoidance, and overcompensation, respectively. Thus far, the coping modes have gradually changed and evolved.

Surrender

The only coping mode related to the process of surrendering is the compliant surrender mode introduced by Jeffery Young. The compliant surrenderer appears as passive and submissive when dealing with other people. Individuals in this mode adhere to self-deprecating, subservient, and reassurance-seeking behaviors, obeying others without questioning them. They experience themselves as weak, dependant, and helpless while faced with a powerful and self-confident figure. While in this mode, individuals do their best to avoid any discord, conflict, and trouble with others. They are afraid of being rejected hence will not display an appropriate reaction to the abusive behaviors of others. Individuals in this mode are terrified of any revenge or retaliation coming from others, and in case they get threatened, they would quickly back down and quit their claims. While in this mode, individuals would make room for any abuse, neglect, control, or devaluation coming from others and would allow them to move forward with any harm they are willing to do to them to preserve the connection.

When it comes to the compliant surrender mode, one of the parties in the relationship gives in to the other party's demands. Usually, people tend to subjugate themselves in order to prevent others from getting angry at them. This usually occurs as the internalized responses are usually accompanied by the basic emotions of fear, covert panic, or sadness (Stevens and Roediger, 2016). Here three other new modes are being suggested alongside the compliant surrender mode (Young and colleagues, 2003):

✓ **Compliant Surrender Mode**: behaves passively and compliant to prevent threats, any retaliation, or the other person from getting angry.

1. **Adherent Surrender Mode**: Completely follows through the other person's orders to get rewarded despite feeling against it inwardly yet putting up the act of agreeing with them outwardly. While being in the adherent surrender mode, if the individual does not receive any rewards after a while or upon receiving it, might get out of this mode.

2. **Determined Surrender Mode**: Even though initially the person did not believe in the task he was being forced to do by the other person, he has become very much determined and consistent in following through it. Now he appears to believe firmly in what he has been put up to do even more than the other person. The determined surrender mode might occur after the individual spends long periods in compliant surrender and adherent surrender modes. This phenomenon occurs since we usually start believing in the things that we have followed or defended or have come to accept after some time.

3. Attendant Surrender Mode: out of obligation, does things as others do them. Gets influenced by others' actions and ways of doing things and tries to imitate them in order to be in accordance with society. The individual changes her true thoughts and behaviors despite her inner desire to not be perceived as different, not being discriminated against, not being made fun of, and in general managing to get accepted.

Most patients tend to believe that what they do is in line with their own free will and choice of action. Nevertheless, the clinical results reveal that patients have surrendered to others on many occasions without being aware of it themselves. The following section points out socio/cultural examples related to each one of the modes mentioned above (compliant, adherent, determined, and attendant):

- **Compliant Surrender Mode:** The individual easily allows her husband to carry on with his aggressive and humiliating behaviors. She further responds amiably and with flattery to the ignorant behaviors coming from her husband's family.
- **Adherent Surrender Mode:** The individual is not happy with the dress code at her workplace. However, she forces herself to adhere to the dress code as long as she works there to preserve her high income and salary.
- **Determined Surrender Mode:** The individual initially had no faith in marriage, yet due to family and social pressures finally has married. Despite not being satisfied with his own marital life, he starts to state the importance and values of marriage and shared life repeatedly whenever he comes across a single person without considering the individual's psychological, economic, and other conditions.
- **Attendant Surrender Mode:** According to his friends, he is a decent friend who would go out of his way to help them.

He never gives no as an answer, even to the unrealistic demands of his friends. He is even willing to give his life away when it comes to his friends and takes pride in having such manners and possessing a heart of gold.

It is interesting to note that while working with patients in clinical settings, we came across some who believed that they have never used the surrender coping style and that they cannot find any signs of this style in their behavior. Upon further thorough and detailed examinations, a more deep-rooted basis and contributing factors leading to surrender were revealed. Most of these patients had chosen a pleasant attribute for describing their surrender coping style, which carried with itself a positive feeling for them. Thus they did not experience any adverse effect as a result of their surrender. Further, they had managed to change the negative emotions associated with surrender coping style into a positive emotion for themselves. This all took place while the central act of surrendering was still going on. Please pay attention to the following table.

Table 1-3: Modes, The Basis for Surrender and The Pleasant Attributes

Modes	Basis for Surrender	Pleasant Attribute	Behavior
Compliant Surrender	Gives in to the wishes of stronger individuals or figures of higher status.	I am a loyal person.	By flattery and putting oneself down, constantly expresses loyalty towards perceived stronger or individuals of higher status.
Adherent Surrender	Surrenders to the task which has been assigned to and has accepted responsibility for.	I am a committed individual.	Follows through assigned tasks with consistency and perseverance, thus strives for staying

	Follows through the commands without questioning them even if causing harm to others.		committed to carrying out the task which has accepted responsibility for.
Determined Surrender	Gives into a valuable concept. also surrenders to credible individuals.	I am a value-oriented person.	Moves toward gaining credit and reputation by encouraging others toward accepting values and spreading value-oriented concepts
Attendant Surrender	Gives in to the demands of the loved one or friends with him has formed attachments.	I am in love / I have a heart of gold.	Gives all he/she has when it comes to romantic partners or friends by being overly companioning, approving and supportive.

Putting pressure on others to force them to give in is a behavior of domineering and authoritarian individuals. Therefore domineering individuals easily make the compliant surrender mode to give in by being forceful and threatening, adherent surrender mode by financial bribery and promises, determined surrender mode by indoctrination and brainwashing, and attendant surrender mode by forming friendships and intimacy.

Many domineering men utilize different approaches to force their spouses to surrender. Even though these approaches might temporarily reduce the tensions, they are not going to be as effective in the long run. Domineering men force their spouses into "compliant surrender mode" by being threatening, physically aggressive, displaying violent behaviors, and inducing fear. Others provide financial prosperity for their wives. They lavish their spouses with luxurious gifts and throw around money, forcing their spouse into "adherent surrender mode." Therefore they politely pay hush money to their wives to put up with their inconsiderate and abnormal acts. Another group of men induces their deviant or wrong values into their spouse, thus putting them in the position of changing their beliefs. They shape their spouse into someone else. Someone whom they like them to be (Determined Surrender Mode). Another group forces their wives into being in "attendant surrender mode" by pressuring them through the presence of children, families, or society. Sometimes domineering men have all these approaches at their disposal and utilize them to force women into surrender. They benefit from physical strength and loud tone of voice, immense wealth, high intelligence quotient (IQ), strong persuasive manners of speech, vast general knowledge, high emotional intelligence (EQ), and lots of experience.

When it comes to the basis for surrender coping style, what is essential is the lack of cohesion between the individual's actions and personal values. Simply put, while being in any one of the surrender coping style modes, what the individual does (the function) is not in accordance with her beliefs, worthiness, and competencies (the value). Therefore the individual is forced to think of a "reason" for persuading herself and the ones around for this lack of cohesion between her held values and inconsistent actions. Finally, the individual manages to develop an unaware way to introduce herself by figuring out that reason.

Table 1-4, Surrender Modes (compliant, adherent, determined and attendant) and function-value

Modes	Reason	Approach	Issue (Function - Value)
Compliant Surrender	Preventing others from	Introduces him/ herself as con-	His/her functions are not con-

	being angry at or retaliate against him/her	flict, dispute and tension free when it comes to interpersonal relationships	sistent with his/her values yet follows through due to being afraid.
Adherent Surrender	In order to be rewarded or gain a benefit	Thinks of him/herself as an intelligent person with clever maneuvers.	His/her functions are not consistent with his/her values, yet "temporarily" follows through them to gain some sort of benefit.
Determined Surrender	Self-Inducibility and others-inductionism	Acts as if has reached the ultimate truth. Encourages others to follow it as well.	The functions are in contrast with previously held values yet in accordance with the new ones.
Attendant Surrender	Preventing from being discriminated against, made fun of etc.	Introduces him/herself as an easy-going and flexible person.	His/her functions are different from his/her values yet acts out of obligation in order to please the group.

When the patient fails to resist the demands of the domineering person, she surrenders and experiences negative emotions. These negative emotions, especially anger and disgust, do not have any outward appearances since the patient does not dare to express them. In clinical settings, most therapists are surprised with their patients' satisfaction for being in a surrender coping style. The reason for this satisfaction and unwillingness for stepping out of surrender modes and into healthy adult mode is not solely due to habituation or being accustomed to acting in accordance with the modes of this coping style. Patients who utilize the surrender coping style for a prolonged period have no other choice but to move toward satisfaction. Since they find themselves with no options but to follow through the orders of the domineering person, they tend only to consider the positive aspects of those commands. Taking only the positive aspects of the given orders into consideration ultimately results in reaching a state of satisfaction over time. If the individual were to decide out of her free will, she would consider both the positive and negative aspects of the given issue.

Avoidance

When it comes to the coping style of avoidance, the first related mode that we observe among the ten initially introduced modes is the detached protector mode. In this mode, the person withdraws from the pain of schema activations by emotionally detaching. Also, Jeffery Young identified the detached self-soother mode while working with narcissistic personality disorder (NPD) patients. According to Young, if the narcissistic patients are alone or cut off from the admiration they derive from interacting with others, they usually flip into the Detached Self-Soother mode. In this mode, narcissistic patients engage in activities that will somehow distract them from unpleasant feelings, thus soothing themselves to an extent. Additionally, there is the avoidant protector mode which is related to this coping style.

- Detached protector mode: According to Young (2003), shutting down emotions and disconnecting from others are among the most important signs of this mode. Depersonalization, emptiness, boredom, self-injury, and "blankness" are other symptoms of this mode. Young believes that patients with borderline personality disorder spend most of their time in the detached protector mode. When in this mode, patients with BPD often appear normal. If the patient attends the sessions and no progress and breakthrough happens during his therapy, it can indicate that the patient has been in the Detached Protector mode nearly the entire time. Arntz and van Genderen (2009) describe patients in this mode as relatively mature and calm. Therefore, they believe that while patients are in this mode, therapists might mistakenly believe that the patient is doing well, while in fact, the patient is utilizing this mode to avoid experiencing her negative emotions. In that way, the patient has cut off her connection with her inner needs, emotions, and thoughts, thus feeling empty.

- Detached self-soother: According to Arntz and Jacob (2013), individuals in this mode shut off their emotions by engaging in activities that will somehow soothe, stimulate, or distract them from feeling altogether. These activities can include workaholism, gambling, drug abuse, promiscuous sex, overeating, or excessive television watching.
- Avoidant protector mode: In this mode, behavioral avoidance is in the foreground. Individuals in this mode tend to avoid social situations, particularly of a challenging nature, and conflicts (Arntz and Jacob 2013). Other symptoms of this mode include pushing others away, breaking connections, emotional withdrawal, and isolation (Farrell, Reiss, and Shaw 2014).

Overcompensation

Jeffery Young suggested an overcompensation in which the person usually puts in an intensive and excessive effort to counterattack or control others or situations. According to Farrell, Reiss, and Shaw (2014), the immediate need for this mode is connection and empathic confrontation. The long-term need is to learn healthy coping that fits better with adult life. Today, other coping modes which belong to the overcompensation coping style and are being taught to the patients include:

- Self-aggrandizer mode: While in this mode, the person behaves in a competitive, grandiose, denigrating, or abusive way to get and maintain whatever they want. Almost completely self-absorbed and shows little empathy for the needs or feelings of others. Demonstrate superiority, Craves admiration, and frequently brag or behave in a self-aggrandizing manner to inflate their sense of self (Arntz 2012).
- Bully and attack mode: The person directly harms other people in a controlled and strategic way emotionally, physically, sexually, verbally, or through antisocial or criminal acts. His motivation may be to overcompensate for or prevent abuse or humiliation. He has sadistic properties (Simeone-DiFrancesco, Roediger and Stevens 2015). He uses threats, intimidation, aggression, and coercion to get what he wants and prevents real or perceived abuse.

- Attention-seeker mode: While in this mode, the individual tries to get other people's attention and approval by extravagant, inappropriate, and exaggerated behavior. She usually compensates for underlying loneliness or lack of recognition (Arntz and Jacob 2013). She tries to obtain the approval and attention of others by exaggerated behavior, erotomania, or grandiosity (van Vreeswijk and colleagues 2014).

- Conning and manipulative mode: Cons, lies, or manipulates. This mode is often seen in criminal offenders but is also seen in some narcissistic individuals who try to get what they want. In this mode, the person uses deceit or manipulation in order to either victimize others or escape punishment.

- Predator mode: The person focuses on eliminating a threat, rival, obstacle, or enemy in a cold, ruthless, and calculating manner. In contrast to the bully and attack mode, which involves "hot" aggression, the predator mode involves cold, ruthless aggression. This mode is almost exclusively seen in individuals who are psychopathic.
- Over-Controller mode: Attempt to protect themselves from a perceived or real threat by focusing attention, ruminating, and exercising extreme control. Two subforms can be distinguished:
    - Perfectionistic over-controller: Focus on perfectionism to attain control and prevent misfortune and criticism.
    - Paranoid over-controller: Focus on vigilance, scanning other people for signs of malevolence, and controls others' behavior out of suspicion (Arntz and Jacob 2013).

The Difference between Coping Styles and Coping Responses

Usually, differentiating coping responses from coping styles is a matter of complexity for a majority of students. According to Jeffery Young, a coping style is a trait, whereas a coping response is a state. To illustrate this point further, consider a lover who has subjugation as one of her schemas. Her coping response to her subjugation schema in situations involving her beloved one is "surrender." Therefore, surrendering is a trait of this lover. To put it more precisely, she is "a surrendered lover in the face of the beloved." After a while, the beloved would find out about this trait of the lover (surrender coping style) and can identify the lover's states (coping response) one after the other. Thus, the beloved would eventually find it easy to predict the behaviors of her. As an example, when the beloved asks the "surrendered lover" about the time and place of their next date, she would grant all the choices to the beloved. After a while, this incident happens so often that the beloved will not even ask about the time and whereabouts of their date from her and starts to plan for it on his own. He does so since he has identified the usual coping response (state) of the lover and knows from experience that she would grant him the choice like the previous times. According to him, the lover's trait is surrender, and her state is to give all the choices to him. The great Saadi Shirazi, in his Divan, states: I surrender my control to love, just like the rein of the camel in the hands of the cameleer.

Therefore there are some statements that couples might exchange while in a romantic relationship. These are statements such as I know you like the back of my hand, I know you more than you know yourself, or I can guess what you will do. If we were to rephrase these statements in schema therapy terms, they would be: Since you incorporate certain coping styles (traits) for your schemas and always tend to express particular coping responses (states) habitually, it is pretty much straightforward for me to predict your behavior. That is the reason why I claim that I know you very well. While in the beginning stages of a romantic relationship, couples are not familiar with each other's traits and states, yet after a while, they can figure out each other's traits and states without necessarily having any knowledge of schema therapy concepts.

The Two-phase Coping Cycle Patterns

Getting ourselves familiarized with each schema's different coping styles helps us recognize the behaviors of ourselves and others better. The coping style which each person incorporates might change in response to different triggering situations. Hence, when it comes to the function of coping responses related to each specific schema, the lack of knowledge in this area would cause confusion and misunderstanding for both ourselves and others. As an example, before marriage, a woman with a coping style of surrender to her subjugation schema would appear seemingly attractive to her controlling, manipulative and suspicious (mistrust/abuse schema) husband-to-be. Hence, the woman's traits such as being a follower, compliant and obsequious earn the man's trust and motivate him to propose. As a short time passes after their marriage, the woman changes her coping style of surrender to overcompensation for her subjugation schema. Thus she begins to engage in acts of disobedience, stubbornness, opposition, aggression, or passive-aggressive behaviors. Consequently, the man would hear the voice of his mistrust/abuse schema, which states: This woman is an evil person and a liar. She entered this relationship while having prior plans in mind in order to abuse me, and now she tries to ruin my life. So I have to stand up to her domineeringly. What we witness here is the coping cycle of surrender (woman) - overcompensation (man) in the couple prior to their marriage which has changed to the coping cycle of overcompensation (woman) - overcompensation (man) after a short period that they got married.

Atkinson (2012) and Simeone-DiFrancesco, Roediger, Stevens (2015) have pointed out five main two-phase coping cycle patterns based on the modes related to the coping styles. These styles of interaction are as follow:

1. Overcompensator—Overcompensator cycle: the marital life is the battleground of the husband and wife. They enter arguments and disputes over different issues. Their martial life is highly unstable.
2. Overcompensator—Compliant Surrender cycle: One of the partners is domineering, and the other one is submissive. As long as this cycle is in play, the relationship is stable. If the compliant surrender partner stops being obedient and obsequious (a return to the overcompensator—overcompensator cycle), the relationship would become unstable. On the other hand, some people tend to surrender to the degree that they would become dull and lack any excitement for their partner. Ultimately the overcompensator partner would leave the relationship.
3. Overcompensator—Detached Self-soother cycle: One of the partners attacks the other in different ways over different issues, criticizes and complains while the other partner occupies himself with abusing alcohol, workaholism, watching movies, etc., and not caring about these behaviors of his partner. The relationship is moderately unstable.
4. Overcompensator—Detached Protector cycle: When one of the partners enters an argument, the other ignores what is being said, hence avoiding experiencing negative emotions. Therefore by not hearing out the other partner's criticisms, she cuts off her connection with negative feelings and intrusive thoughts and appears as aloof and withdrawn regarding the topics brought up during the argument. Even though this is not a satisfying situation for them, since one of the partners always avoids conflicts, the relationship is relatively stable.
5. Detached—Detached cycle: Each partner engages in his or her own activities without caring about what the

> other partner is up to or having any plans for mutual activities. Usually, no exchange of either positive or negative emotions takes place between the couple. They lead a relatively stable life by living parallel lives under the same roof or, as Atkinson (2012) put it, living together apart.

Clinical experiences show that many of the couples have lived through different cycles. They present the therapist with many memories and instances of each of these cycles. The main issue is that none of these cycles have been able to satisfy their emotional needs in the relationship. Some couples state that they have tried out all the methods (cycles) to resolve their conflicts, but none have worked out for them. This indicates that even though utilizing schema modes of the maladaptive coping styles might help shape a long-term stable relationship since the emotional needs are not being met while these modes are in play, the satisfaction with the relationship is relatively low.

The Necessity of Examining the Childhood Origins in the Process of Treatment (Evolution and Time)

Many patients find it difficult to recall their childhood years due to the avoidance coping style. Some others believe that nothing unfortunate has happened to them due to their over loyalty to their parents. There are also a group of patients who even manage to recall bitter memories, yet they believe that going back to childhood memories is fruitless and a waste of time during the course of therapy. Precise, thorough, categorized, and case-by-case examination of unpleasant childhood events is one of the significant features of schema therapy. If there was an approach intended to ignore the unpleasant events of childhood years, this approach has denied the opportunity to heal the primary traumas from its patients. Even if the patient had spent her childhood years with good enough parents who were knowledgeable regarding parenting issues, there is still a probability that she might have gone through traumatic events concerning her surrounding environment and coming from other figures rather than her parents. This is because the childhood period for humans is much longer compared to other living beings, and many events take place during this period, which leads and contributes to the formation of schemas.

Humans spend more than 87 thousand hours next to their parents, either being awake or asleep from the moment of their birth to the end of the first decade of their life. These 87 thousand hours are the most significant period regarding the formation of schemas, whereas when it comes to many other living beings, the childhood period is limited to a single hour up to a single day, and in some mammals, this period is no longer than a year. Therefore from the evolution point of view, the childhood period for human beings is too long, slow, and sensitive compared to other spices. On the other hand, the details of the events taking place in childhood are very difficult to recall once the individual has gone through this period. It takes at least a year before the child is ready to say goodbye to her mother's breasts. It takes another year for her to take her first clumsy steps with her tiny feet. It takes at least two years to express complete and comprehensible sentences. Three years is required for her to express her need for using the toilet and six or seven years before she is ready for going to school. Last but not least, it takes her two decades to be regarded as an adult by her family and the ones around, and that is if she has that luck on her side!

The child is entirely dependent on the parents for nutrition, clothing, transportation, health, play, etc., for long years. This long-term neediness paves the way for vulnerability. If, like most other species, human beings had to rely on their parents just for the first year of their lives, indeed, they would not have ended up this vulnerable. They would have started living their life the way they liked them much sooner and began meeting their needs. Thus, the childhood period is a period of physical and emotional vulnerability regarding its long duration regardless of whether it is growing up with good enough parents. The focus of schema therapy is on the patients who have the experience of growing up with parents who were not good enough during the childhood years, and naturally, many of the child's emotional needs were frustrated. However, the issue of the long period of childhood years has nothing to do with the behavior of the parents, yet it is a matter of evolution and the developmental process in human beings. This long developmental process has faced humans with three significant issues which require more contemplation. These three issues, which are the consequences of the "evolution and time," are relation, internalization, and immutability:

A: Relation: The longer a living being spends time with others, the more familiarities, ties, and relations are formed among them. Family ties, ties with relatives, friendship ties are all among the relations which take place for human beings due to time. If an infant was to be separated from her parents and being brought up by her godparents, the familiarities and interest that she would take in them are higher compared to her biological parents, whom she has met in her twenties for the first time. Therefore, the passage of time forms ties for the individual with those around her, which lasts a lifetime. This phenomenon can be observed among other species such as dogs, cats, and even elephants. Nevertheless, when it comes to the starry sturgeon (Acipenser stellatus), a precious fish economically speaking due to producing Caviar, it easily ovulates millions of its eggs into the depths of the Caspian sea without having any familiarities or interest in them. The relations can not be observed in any form here for the fish which easily leaves her eggs. These relations being formed over time are a harmful issue where the patient cannot distance himself even slightly due to the associations he has formed during the long period, despite suffering and getting severely harmed by the parents, relatives, and friends. This holds even for the sexually abused individuals who are not able to cut all relations with the predator forever. The great Saadi Shirazi in his Divan states:

To the friend's meets are used the eyes *** It is a pity for them to get used to someone else's

B: Internalization: Since early childhood years, everything is being taught by the parents and later on by the teachers for an extended period of time. With the developments made in universities and advancements made in different sciences, the duration of education is being increased every year. Today some individuals are still involved with learning and education in some fields of study even until they have turned 35 years old or older. Living beings who spend a short childhood span with their parents tend to start gaining experience from their surroundings rather quickly, yet human beings get accustomed to consuming from other's experiences for an extended period. The child is not able to free her mind in the first decade of her life. Her mind is filled with all the things that the parents, teachers, and media have intended to be filled with. Gradually, the child becomes accustomed to systematically learning everything from others, leaving less space for personal investigation and exploration of different matters. Focusing on solemnly learning from others leads to the individual forgetting his sense of self-support and empiricism. The habit of learning leaves the individual to seek learning and be less eager to produce something of his own. Human beings gradually get addicted to learning and grow fond of it, thus forgetting to produce something of their own sooner, expand upon it and teach it to others. Attar of Nishapur (1145 – 1221), Persian poet, Theoretician of Sufism and Hagiographer in (Asrār-Nāma - section 19), states:
Based on camaraderie is the disposition of the man *** From everyone gets habits the man.

C: Immutability: It only suffices to plant a sapling somewhere with appropriate conditions for its growth and wait for twenty years. Indeed, one will not be able to pull it up after this long period since that small sapling has made its roots deeply in the soil, turning itself into a thick tree. Therefore the only way to do so is cutting down the tree from the lowest parts of its body. It takes two decades in the West and three decades in the East for the child to be accounted as an adult by the parents. This long time forms such an Immutability which many families prefer their children living with them before marriage or choose their place of living close to them after getting married. This phenomenon occurs since, like cutting down the tree, separation from the parents is such a painful act for both the parents and the children. Immutability which has its evolutionary roots in the scale of time has long played a role as a sub-culture, especially among the traditional families. Eastern and Islamic countries have always been proud of this immutability and all that comes with it. Immutability takes place with the family or the friends and the ethnicity, the city, and the country the individual has a sense of belonging to as well. We observe severe prejudices in many patients stemming from living in a particular district, city, or country for an extended period of time, generation after generation. Prejudices stemming from immutability will not leave room for the unbiased thinking of the individual nor prevent him from unwise insistences. The Prejudices stemming from immutability is the root cause of many interpersonal/marital problems and the cause of many racial conflicts and international wars. Hafez Shirazi in (Ghazals - Ghazal 37) states: Come! For most unstable is the foundation of the Palace of Hope *** Bring the cup; for the foundation of life is on the wind.

Beneath the azure vault, I am that slave of resolution who *** Is free from whatever taketh color of the attachment.

The examination of the association, habit, and immutability

concepts in the childhood origins and childhood years of the patients can help while considering the issues of evolution and time in the child's developmental process. It requires more investigation before we are able to find a connection between the formation of some of the schemas based on evolution and time.

Many patients live in a world where the changes tend to take place around them at a staggering pace. Thus the psychological world of the patients is dependent on the context and rapid conditions of their environment. Nevertheless, schema therapy has managed to address personal, family, and social changes very well to comprehend all of these changes that are taking place rapidly and accelerate the compilation of the knowledge in accordance with these changes. Human beings often or always grow anxious due to the haste of their daily lives, which is not compatible with their human nature. I call this type of anxiety which results from the new technological way of living, "Modern Anxiety." The efforts put in for telling the future regarding emotional, economic, social, political, and military issues related to their destiny are among the apparent characteristics of this type of anxiety. Thus individuals tend to turn to psychics, fortune tellers, and soothsayers in an effort to find out about their destinies in the future. Most of them lack the resilience for experiencing and facing life taking place at its relatively rapid pace. Schema therapy has the potential to predict some of the adverse events in the patient's life, which is different from fortune-telling. Prediction is the identification of the wrong path that the patient has taken repeatedly and most often has been harmful to her, yet fortune-telling emphasizes that a specific event will definitely take place in the future. If the prediction is not capable of changing anything, then what is the benefit of it? Just the same way Gynecologists are expected to identify the gender of the babies before birth or Geneticists to verify whether a potential child of a couple is going to be born free from any genetics problems based on the tests taken from the couple, schema therapists are expected to predict the future of a marriage. How successful is the given marriage going to be in the future? Is their sexual relationship going to be satisfying forever? Or whether their partner is going to be a good parent for their children or not?

Final Words

In this chapter, the aim was set to describe the maladaptive coping modes and their schema modes rather briefly. Given that the main literature of schema therapy has already elaborated and expanded upon the core concepts of schema therapy such as maladaptive schemas and other topics such as the innate child modes or dysfunctional parent modes, therefore restating what has been stated before has been avoided in order to save the time of the readers. That being the case, the first chapter is solely focused on reviewing the maladaptive coping styles so that the new maladaptive coping styles get introduced in the following chapters of this book.

CHAPTER TWO

GETTING TO KNOW THE "NEW" MALADAPTIVE COPING STYLES

In this chapter:

- The adaptation of the sextet physiological reactions in accordance with the maladaptive coping styles
- Getting to knowing the new coping styles (indolence, mockery, gaucherie)
- The necessity and importance of the new coping styles
- The story of the chimney and coping thieves
- Introducing the new maladaptive coping styles related to schemas
- Getting to know the behavioral, cognitive, and emotional components of coping styles
- The climax in coping styles
- The Octet Substitution Model
- Introducing the nine new schema modes
- Behavioral strategies and the murk heritage

Does schema therapy require innovation? Yes! Taking into account the incredibly dynamic and yet unknown mind of humankind, the existence of more responses and new maladaptive coping styles in order to adapt to schemas is not that far-fetched. Years of clinical experience in working with patients, especially patients with personality disorders, indicated that it is impossible to categorize some of their coping responses into just the three groups of the coping styles of surrender, avoidance, and overcompensation. In fact, some patients display different styles of behavior from surrender, avoidance, and overcompensation in distinct situations to cope with their schemas. Moreover, these styles of behavior are unknown and ambiguous for therapists. This complexity suffices in order to focus on the behavior of the clients with more precision.

So far, schema therapy has categorized many of the behaviors of humans into the three coping styles of "surrender, avoidance, and overcompensation." Nevertheless, as we examine the behaviors of the patients with more precision and seriousness, we come to realize that it is a rather difficult task to classify all these behaviors into this triad. Since "classification" is one of the core methods humans have invented to grasp the meaning of different subjects more efficiently, the more this classification is done with precision and extensiveness, the more meaningful the patients' responses would get for the therapists. This holds, especially if we accept that the three coping styles tend to repeatedly change over time or upon gaining new experiences for a given individual. Therefore not only the coping styles of a person will not stay fixed over time, but also he would behave with more intelligence and cleverness. As an example, an individual might choose avoidance when it comes to romantic relationships and refuses to enter any relationship of this nature. However, one day without anyone finding out why, she might stop her avoidance and begin a new romantic relationship to overcompensate by constantly dominating, over-controlling, and interrogating her new partner.

Therefore, coping styles usually tend to have a covert nature, especially when it comes the time that they shift or change to each other. Furthermore, most patients utilize a range of coping styles that vastly differ and sometimes contradict each other. It is even possible that an individual might utilize separate coping styles in different circumstances facing people with different statuses during the same period of her life. As an example, a person with an abandonment/instability schema might overcompensate his schema in his romantic relationship yet uses avoidance as a coping style when it comes to his other intimate relationships in his life. For instance, he might choose to see his friends less often and not get that intimate with them.

Indeed, it is highly beneficial to reveal the coping styles to the patients and give them an awareness of how incorporating these styles have adverse effects on their lives. In some patients, clinical interviews and reviewing their filled out questionnaires and inventories related to the coping styles (i.e., the Young-Rygh Avoidance Inventory) in addition to an extensive assessment of their behaviors as part of the coping responses indicates that it is not possible to classify all the schema driven behaviors into just three coping styles (surrender, avoidance, overcompensation). Due to the fact that coping styles render themselves not only in the form of behavioral responses but also in the form of cognitive or emotional aspects, there was a need for a more extensive structure in order to comprehend patients more than before.

On the other hand, Eckhard Roediger and his colleagues (2018), in their book Contextual Schema Therapy state that: "We relate submissive behavior with surrender, not with freezing. A "frozen" rabbit (or a dissociative person) is trying to avoid harm through withdrawal. The message of the frozen rabbit to the fox is, "I am not interesting for you, so do not take notice of me" (detachment). Freezing is thus an example of coping through passive flight and not surrendering. The triad of freeze, flight, and fight does not represent the full spectrum of coping options."

At the present period, there are "four main theoretical concepts" in schema therapy which every therapist is required to teach to her patients in a simple, understandable manner in order to educate them about schema therapy. These concepts include: A) early maladaptive schemas, B) coping styles, C) schema modes, and D) core emotional needs. Afterward, the patients can gain tremendous benefits from this extraordinary knowledge in order to develop and accelerate in their personal, family, work, and social aspects of their lives. Last but not least, harnessing the therapy relationship, especially through limited reparenting and utilizing experiential, cognitive, and behavioral interventions, are the winning vital components in controlling schemas. In order for schema therapy to continue its path of growth as firm and strong as it has been so far, there is a need for presenting and expanding upon new concepts, more research being carried out on other disorders, and comparative studies being conducted on patients coming from differing cultural backgrounds. For this reason, the aim of this book has been set to exclusively focus on the second concept of the four main theoretical concepts of schema therapy, which is "B) coping styles." Furthermore, adding three new coping styles (indolence, mockery, and gaucherie) to the existing coping styles (surrender, avoidance, and overcompensation) has been tried to help therapists assess human behaviors in a more precise and profound manner.

By introducing three new physiological reactions to the 3F set (fight, flight, and freeze), this new set is being introduced by the name of 6F (fight, flight, freeze, faint, farce, and fumble). Therefore, in the following sections, we will focus on introducing the three new physiological reactions of faint, farce, and fumble, which are compatible with the "new" maladaptive coping styles. These "new" maladaptive coping styles are indolence (faint), mockery (farce), and gaucherie (fumble), just like the coping styles of overcompensation (fight), avoidance (flight), and surrender (freeze), have many physiological resemblances among other living organisms. Please refer to table 2-1.

Table 2-1: Comparison of the sextet of physiological reactions with maladaptive coping styles

Physiological Reactions	1.Fight	2.Flight	3.Freeze	4.Faint	5.Farce	6.Fumble
Maladaptive Coping styles	Overcompensation	Avoidance	Surrender	Indolence	Mockery	Gaucherie

In the following section, we are going to attend to a few examples from animal behavior (Ethology) in order to get acquainted with the reactions of faint, farce, and fumble in the animal's world.

Faint: Mice are among the creatures which pretend to be dead while faced with threatening situations. Mice usually incorporate the "faint reaction" when they have run out of options for escaping from the situation (the "flight reaction"). Hence the enemy might refuse to take the mouse while faced with its dead body. Since the reason for the death of the mouse is not clear for the hunter, it would not risk its well-being and gives up on taking the mouse. It is interesting to note that besides mice, other creatures such as snakes, cats, dogs, pigeons, goats, and gazelles also tend to utilize the "faint reaction" heavily in threatening situations. In human beings, the "faint reaction" can take place in the same fashion. As an example, an individual with abandonment/instability schema, while faced with a situation in which her partner needs to be away on a trip or work mission for a while (the triggering factor for the schema), might try to pretend to be sick (faint reaction/ indolence coping style), therefore changing her partner's travel schedule. As soon as the partner cancels his trip in order to stay with her and take care of her and upon she feels that the threat is no longer relevant (the partner is not going away), she starts to feel well again. This pretentious behavior can not be associated with any coping styles of surrender, avoidance, or overcompensation except for the coping style of indolence. Even though malingering is accounted as one of the simplest manifestations of faint reaction/indolence coping style, more complex instances will be examined for other schemas in the forthcoming sections of this book.

Nonetheless, we are a long way from associating all the instances of malingering, Conversion Disorder, and Factitious Disorder to the faint reaction/indolence coping style. Consider a soccer player who is an expert in throwing himself to the ground when he is in the 18-yard box in order to obtain a penalty kick for his team. After a while, although he has managed to obtain several penalty kicks in different matches, the referees gradually start to become aware of this trick of his and would not take him seriously even when there is a real foul being happened involving him.

Farce: There have been many cases reported regarding the pet dogs making strange noises and engaging in clownish behaviors. These incidents take place when these dogs have ruined or damaged something and have witnessed their owner's disapproval afterward. Nevertheless, "farce reaction" can be observed more frequently among the animals which are biologically speaking closer to human beings. This includes the primates such as chimpanzees, gorillas, orangutans, and bonobos. Researches of Marina Davila-Ross and her colleagues (2011) at the University of Portsmouth indicate that chimpanzees utilize laughing as a social lubricant. Also, the chimps that have formed a new colony tend to laugh twice more than those who have already formed their colony for a while. Primates usually laugh when they wrestle, play chase, and tickle. When in the zoo, they also usually mess with their keepers. For example, they tend to hide their food and water plates to make jokes with their keepers. Furthermore, sometimes they suddenly pat others on the back in order to shock them or make some noises which are intended to be used when there is a danger threatening the group while in reality there is no danger concerning the group and they only do so in order to mess with other group members and challenge them. In human beings, behaviors such as ridiculing others, mockery, making fun of others in the group, clowning, and superficial laughter can be categorized as manifestations of "the farce reaction/ mockery coping style."

Fumble: When it comes to "fumble reaction," too, there have been many cases reported in the wildlife, pets, and also among the animals inhabiting the zoo. To the degree which an animal lacks lived experience, the chances of exhibiting a fumble reaction would increase. Even though the fumble reaction sometimes leads to the animal's injury or even death, in general, it helps it to gain more support from its mother or other members of the group. For instance, one of the fumble reactions in the wildlife, which is common among the lion cubs and baby elephants, is that they separate themselves or detach from other group members. Although this fumble might be dangerous, it makes other group members, especially the mother, pay more attention to its cub or child. Among mature animals, too, the fumbling behavior might take place when choosing a place for rest, ambush for hunting, and choosing their subject of hunting. It has been witnessed many times when a female lion takes off on her own for hunting buffalos; she has got attacked by their group, leaving her severely injured. Therefore this is the reason which attributes to the group cooperation among the female lions. However, the reason that makes a lion female go on hunting on its own (fumble reaction) might lie wherein in case she succeeds in her individual endeavors for hunting, she would end up with more food resources. Thus she is not required to share that food with others. This can be an exemplification of haste makes waste. In fact, fumble might occur due to excessive greed, haste, or penchant, bringing about harm and damage. To illustrate this point further, consider a wolf was attacking a herd of sheep. When this happens, killing one sheep will not stop the wolf from proceeding further to suffocate other sheep of the herd, one by one. This results in the wolf spending much of its time struggling with the flock, giving the shepherd and his dogs time to take him down. Certainly, the mass murder of sheep by the wolf and not being eaten by it is not accounted as an act of amusement or doing sports, but it is accounted as part of an effort for survival called surplus killing. As Saadi Shirazi the great put it: The clever keeps the avarice in his eyes to himself *** greed locks the hen and fish in the trap.

The fumbling behavior is also witnessed in flocks of the sheep when the leader or bellwether tries to jump over a cliff but falls in the valley and the rest of the sheep follow it down the way. Even though unnecessary following and blind full imitation sometimes cause trouble for sheep's flock, their survival depends heavily on the group. According to Rumi:" Blind imitation of people has brought them to ruin: two hundred curses be on that imitation!"

Sometimes hunter animals such as cheetahs might choose other animals as their food which are either stronger or are equipped with more functional defense methods. The attack of a cheetah on wild boar is one of these instances where the cheetah's attempt is usually not successful. Hence the chances of the cheetah getting injured during this attempt are relatively high. Additionally, the attack of cheetahs on hedgehogs is also shown to be resulting in an injury of the cheetah. Here, the saying: bite off more than one can chew is a clear indication of the fumble reaction. However, the simplest form of fumbling can be observed when it comes to making "the wrong estimation." Many cats, despite having the ability to land on their feet while jumping from a height, sometimes due to an error in their estimations, tend to fall and pass away. When it comes to human relationships, the "fumble reaction/Gaucherie coping style" can be observed abundantly in many instances. Some people are always controversial. They experience different sorts of problems, and not having fully dealt with them, they face yet another horrible event that overshadows their peace or health. They choose the wrong paths in their life and drag others down with themselves. Their plans will not go ahead as planned, and they make a mess of situations.

The question that might arise in this case is how can gaucherie be considered a coping style? What can an individual achieve by gaucherie? For instance, when it comes to the avoidance coping style, the individual plans her life to prevent her schemas from being activated; thus, she gains the advantage of experiencing painful emotions less frequently on her own account. Since a human is a social being and lives in the family and society, gaucherie behaviors not only affect the individual but also damage the family and society. In case someone starts to drill a hole at the bottom of the boat instead of rowing, certainly, others will not keep silent, and they would show reactions to this behavior. By taking a simple look around yourself, you can witness individuals in your family, relatives, and workplace whom others are almost always putting lots of time and effort into cleaning up their mess. These efforts can take the shape of paying money in the form of a fine or compensation and risking one's reputation and credit in order to atone for the wrongdoings of the troublemaker. Therefore, the individual who tends to use the gaucherie coping style puts his individual and social responsibility on others' shoulders, thus relieving himself from psychological/social pressures and feeling at ease.

The aim of introducing instances of faint, farce, and fumble in the above examples was not meant to give a sense of Anthropomorphism since humans themselves, due to their schemas, poses an extraordinary capability in rejecting awareness and refusing to experience their negative and unpleasant emotions through the coping styles of faint, farce and fumble in their own unique ways.

The Necessity and Importance of The New Coping Styles

As we know, early maladaptive schemas resist change and treatment since the surrender, avoidance, and overcompensation coping styles are in action in order to perpetuate the schemas. The patient's schemas perceive schema therapy techniques as dangerous and threatening for themselves; thus, the patient might choose to escape from the "treatment room" as attending to it might result in reducing the power of her schemas (avoidance coping style). Also, after being in search of a desirable therapist for some time, some individuals finally settle for the one who would validate their schema-driven behaviors. Take a therapist with a severe self-sacrifice schema as an example. This therapist, who is either not aware of this schema in herself or has chosen to surrender to it, would encourage the patient to stay in her long term marriage at any cost for the sake of her children despite living with an abusive husband for years and repeatedly being subject to domestic violence. Therefore a therapist who has surrendered to her self-sacrifice schema would eventually lead her patient in the same direction of surrendering to the self-sacrifice schema. Thus maladaptive schemas usually tend to survive since the patient in his life or even while getting help from a therapist would incorporate the three coping styles of surrender, avoidance, and overcompensation. This is due to the reason that these coping styles provide the patient with temporary relief in the short run.

Patient's schemas tend to give automatic responses in the form of surrender, avoidance, and overcompensation styles in order to continue their survival. This usually happens outside of the patient's awareness, and he would behave under the influence of his schemas and without having made an informed choice to do so. Accordingly, schemas do not set the stage in a way to perpetuate themselves only through the three coping styles of surrender, avoidance, and overcompensation, but they also utilize the other three coping styles of indolence, mockery, and gaucherie. This makes it a necessity to become familiar with these new coping styles. If we are to empower schema therapy to fight the schemas and schema modes, we should equip it with the results we gain from exploring and assessing the new coping styles. This is because each of the indolence, mockery, and gaucherie coping styles plays a unique and significant role in schema perpetuation. In clinical settings, too, the unaware use of these new coping styles has been witnessed in patient's behavior, thoughts, and feelings.

In fact, in case we solely focus on the surrender, avoidance, and overcompensation styles that help schema perpetuation while treating patients and neglect the indolence, mockery, and gaucherie styles, schemas would continue to perpetuate themselves through the use of these new coping styles. Therefore by identifying the new coping styles and their related schema modes, the process of schemas modification and healing can be facilitated, accelerated, and enhanced with more precision. A process that is rather a timely and challenging procedure right now. When the patient is being educated about the new coping styles among other concepts in schema therapy, and the therapist acquires more information from her patient's behaviors, thoughts, and feelings related to the coping styles, the patient and therapist can discuss the cognitive, behavioral, and emotional components in more details in their therapeutic relationship.

The Chimney and The Coping Thieves

Six coping thieves led by "overcompensation" are about to enter a rich man's house through the chimney. They are listening to the overcompensation while standing on the rooftop: "There is only one way for us in order to enter this house, and that is through this chimney, I know it is a difficult route, but we are going to enter it one by one. Now, who is going to be the first?" Everyone stared at the overcompensation and overcompensation said: "Hey "surrender," you go first!" Surrender shook his head in disapproval, sat on the edge of the chimney, and eventually entered it. After surrender hit the ground, overcompensation turned to the others and asked:" who is going to be the second one?" Avoidance took a look around herself and said: "No! I am not in!" and without saying much, slowly started to walk backward and left the group in no rush. Overcompensation started to look at the remaining members. Suddenly "Indolence," said: "Oh! I do not know what is wrong with my belly. I've got cramps; maybe it's diarrhea. Oh my god! It hurts!" She got some distance from the group and tried to think of a way in order to deal with her cramp. "Mockery," witnessing indolence's physical difficulties, burst into laughter. Overcompensation, not being happy with the situation, turned to mockery and said: "Shut up! Stop laughing! The landlord is going to hear you. You are going to jeopardize our plan". Mockery, having put one hand in front of his mouth and another one on his belly fell on the ground and rolled side to side while struggling with himself to stop his laughter.

Meanwhile, overcompensation turned to "gaucherie" and said: "Hey! You go in!" Gaucherie hesitated for a while, brought up some excuses but none of them was accepted. Forced by overcompensation, she sat on the edge of the chimney and was getting prepared to enter it that she lost her balance and fell into the chimney while screaming. It was an unpleasant situation since she got stuck in the middle of the way through the chimney, hanging between earth and sky, and on the other hand, surrender was hiding in one of the corners of the house, waiting for others to join him. Overcompensation was filled with rage, but there was nothing that he could do. The coping thieve's plan of rubbery had failed.

After the police officers managed to arrest all the coping thieves, they were sent to court. In the courthouse, all of the six coping thieves were there, standing in front of the judge. The judge asked them: Do you agree that you have made a mistake? I am going to sentence each one of you to five years of prison. "Surrender" burst into tears and started to repeatedly beg for forgiveness by saying, "Sir! I did wrong, I'm sorry!" However, "overcompensation" started cursing the judge, the jury, and the crowd present in the courthouse with a loud voice. The crowd got disturbed; the court officers went for the "overcompensation" in order to calm him down. Meanwhile, "avoidance" took advantage of the situation and ran toward the exit door. Even Though the "avoidancc" attempt for escape was almost successful yet in the final moments, the officers managed to catch her and return her to her seat. After the conditions in the courthouse were restored to normal, the trial continued.

"Indolence" took the stand and addressed the judge and the crowd: "I am a poor and miserable citizen of this city. I had no money, and I had to pass days starving, being in misery at its worst. I had nothing to do with rubbery business before, but what could I do? There was no other way I could think of!" "Mockery" while laughing, said:" I hope we get to eat and rest well during these five years of our sentence in jail." He then turned to the jury and told them while smirking: "I couldn't ask for more, we are going to make lots of cool friends while being in jail, hahaha!" Finally it was the "gaucherie's" turn which was the last one. She stated: "I didn't want to enter into that chimney, they forced me to! I have got to tell you that this was not our only rubbery. We together have rubbed many houses before this one. If I'm being sent to jail unfairly, I am going to reveal everything I know." With the gaucherie's new confession and the trouble that she caused, each of the thieves' sentence was increased from five years to ten years of prison. In the end, the judge announced the verdict:

1. Surrender, due to expressing remorse and regret, was sentenced to seven years in prison.
2. Overcompensation due to the cursing and picking up a fight with the courthouse officers had three more years on his

prison sentence. His prison sentence increased to thirteen years in total.

3. Avoidance because she attempted escaping from the court had to take two more years on her prison sentence. Her prison time was increased to twelve years in total.
4. Indolence got a reduced sentence of one year with the judge's approval due to getting involved in the robbery for reasons having to do with her poverty and agony. She was sentenced to nine years of prison.
5. Mockery had one year increase in his sentence since he was rude to the court and made fun of the jury. He was sentenced to eleven years of prison in total.
6. Gaucherie got a reduced sentence of five years due to her cooperation with the law enforcement, but upon entering the prison got murdered suspiciously.

Considering the above story, the utilization of maladaptive coping styles by individuals under different circumstances bears distinct consequences. As we witnessed in the story of the courthouse, not all the coping thieves shared the same destiny. We would be making a mistake if we were to suppose that given each situation, individuals try to act in a way that is in their best interest and would reduce the harm in any form coming their way. What decides the coping style of a given individual in each situation has nothing to do with thinking of minimizing the negative consequences, yet it has to do with collecting thoughts, emotions, experiences, and the conditions of the environment. Here four important issues get arise regarding the maladaptive coping styles:

The First Issue: Ambiguity and doubtfulness in choosing the maladaptive coping style

When individuals are faced with frustrations, they doubt their coping style of choice by reviewing their past behaviors. As an example, a recently divorced woman in therapy session stated: "I have no idea why I surrendered (compliant surrender mode) this much to that dominant man throughout our whole years together. If I knew back then what I know and have experienced now, I would have certainly put up fights with him (overcompensation)." Here in this instance, the patient is filled with uncertainty since the style of her choice for her life had no result but a divorce. On the other hand, putting up fights with the tyrannical husband would not bear any positive outcomes as well.

The Second Issue: The fixation of maladaptive coping styles under certain circumstances

The coping styles in humans have pretty much gotten into a fixed shape under certain circumstances. For instance, when it comes to certain cultures, the children are asked to always surrender to their parents and never overcompensate. Hence, despite being psychologically damaged by their parent's behaviors in the past and these harmful behaviors still going on today, many adults see no other option but surrender while dealing with them.

The Third Issue: Modeling others maladaptive coping styles

Individuals tend to adhere to the maladaptive coping styles of others. This adherence is highly observed when it comes to social relationships. For example, a young girl who used to have normal relationships with men, upon making friends with one of her avoidant classmates, would start to avoid men just like her newly found friend and classmate.

The Fourth Issue: The reinforced maladaptive coping style

What motivate individuals to utilize a particular coping style in most situations, in other words remaining in that style over a long period of time, are the preferred outcomes that they gain after using that style. As an example, an associate of an organization gets to hold his position after twenty years because of being in surrender style while dealing with all the principles. Many principles came and left their managerial position one by one, yet he was still holding his associate position.

Introducing the New Maladaptive Coping Styles Related to Schemas

In the first chapter, you were presented with the maladaptive coping styles table developed by Jeffery Young and his colleagues (2003). In the following segment, we are going to introduce the new maladaptive coping styles (indolence, mockery, and gaucherie) associated with each maladaptive schema. By examining table 2.2, the reader would understand the new dysfunctional behavioral patterns associated with each of the schemas.

Table 2-2: examples of new coping styles associated with maladaptive schemas (The defenitions of schemas are taken from Schema Therapy, a Practitioner's Guide, Young and colleagues, 2003).

1- ABANDONMENT/ INSTABILITY:
The perceived instability or unreliability of those available for support and connection. Involves the sense that significant others will not be able to continue providing emotional support, connection, strength, or practical protection because they are emotionally unstable and unpredictable (e.g., have angry outbursts), unreliable, or present only erratically; because they will die imminently; or because they will abandon the individual in favor of someone better.

New Coping Styles	**Examples of each New Coping Styles**
Indolence	***(Intimate Relationships)*** Fussing and intentionally giving the partner too many short term silent treatments, which in

	turn leads to the partner's burnout; ***(Partner's mission trip)*** fakes illness in order to change partner's schedule for going away on a mission trip; ***(Workplace)*** Pretends to be tired because of his or her heavy workload in order to prevent from getting fired; ***(During breakup)*** Make the partner return to the relationship by appearing as miserable, helpless, and victim.
Mockery	***(Intimate Relationships)*** Exhibits excessive coquettish and flirtatious behavior with partners or significant others in order to avoid rejection; ***(Workplace)*** Appears as the "office clown" in order to prevent from getting fired or seeking promotion and raise; ***(Social Relationships)*** Drives others away by making fun of them. ***(Gatherings)*** tries hard to make others laugh in order to get invited again
Gaucherie	***(Intimate Relationships)*** Despite partner's repeated warnings and notices, continues to engage in annoying and irritating behaviors, which leads to the partner's leaving the relationship; ***(Love)*** Excessive patience and long term anticipation in the hope of one day, winning over the person they are in love with which this hesitation ultimately leads to the loss of the beloved.

2- MISTRUST/ ABUSE:
The expectation that others will hurt, abuse, humiliate, cheat, lie, manipulate, or take advantage. Usually involves the perception that the harm is intentional or the result of unjustified and extreme negligence. May include the sense

that one always ends up being cheated relative to others or "getting the short end of the stick."

New Coping Styles	Examples of each New Coping Styles
Indolence	***(Interpersonal Relationships)*** When gets threatened, abused, or is aggressively treated by others, might physically display symptoms of a heart attack or fainting while psychologically might display signs of being victimized and hurt; ***(Intimate Relationships)*** Plays the role of a depressed person so that others won't abuse him or her.
Mockery	***(Interpersonal Relationships)*** Reveals details of his or her personal life in a funny manner to others who are not that close; ***(Workplace)*** Constantly smiles at others, tries to be humorous, and performs physical and sexual jokes on them in order to get close to them, thus gaining their trust and preventing possible harm coming from them.
Gaucherie	***(Workplace)*** Doesn't keep company's classified documents and letters in a safe place which ultimately leads to them getting leaked; ***(Interpersonal Relationships)*** Divides people into two groups of good people and bad people without sufficient evidence while fumbles in dealing with them by constantly replacing them in their group; ***(Intimate Relationships)*** publishes images of his or her private life on social media, leading to abusers taking advan-

	tage of him or her, recording romantic and sexual memories in a diary, and keeping it in an inappropriate easy-to-access place.

3- EMOTIONAL DEPRIVATION:
The expectation that one's desire for a normal degree of emotional support will not be adequately met by others. The three major forms of deprivation are:

A. Deprivation of Nurturance: Absence of attention, affection, warmth, or companionship.
B. Deprivation of Empathy: Absence of understanding, listening, self-disclosure, or mutual sharing of feelings from others.
C. Deprivation of Protection: Absence of strength, direction, or guidance from others.

New Coping Styles	**Examples of each New Coping Styles**
Indolence	***(Intimate Relationships)*** Pretends to have physical weakness and repeatedly expresses his or her physical and psychological difficulties in order to gain partner's attention, physical affection, and support, giving the partner silent treatment to receive more attention and affection; ***(Workplace and interpersonal relationships)*** talks about emotional difficulties of his or her intimate relationship with friends and colleagues while victim-playing and pretending to be hurt.
Mockery	***(Intimate Relationships)*** Gets funny and tries hard to make his or her partner laugh in order to gain attention and affection from the partner.

Gaucherie	***(Intimate Relationships)*** doesn't answer to the partner's affection and attention since he or she doesn't find them desirable and pleasant; ***(Interpersonal Relationships)*** Doesn't answer back other's love and support since he or she finds it strange and unacceptable; ***(Love)*** excessive patience and long-term anticipation, hoping that one day the person he or she loves might love him or her back.

4- DEFECTIVNESS/ SHAME:
The feeling that one is defective, bad, unwanted, inferior, or invalid in important respects or that one would be unlovable to significant others if exposed. May involve hypersensitivity to criticism, rejection, and blame; self-consciousness, comparisons, and insecurity around others; or a sense of shame regarding one's perceived flaws. These flaws may be private (e.g., selfishness, angry impulses, unacceptable sexual desires) or public (e.g., undesirable physical appearance, social awkwardness).

New Coping Styles	Examples of each New Coping Styles
Indolence	***(Acting)*** Always accepts the roles of miserable and poor characters. ***(Dialogue)*** Mutters when wants to express something. ***(Exams)*** Makes excuses for his or her failure and tries to convince the teacher by telling statements such as "I knew it all, but I forgot the answers" or "I couldn't tackle the question," this way tries to make excuses for not passing the exam.
Mockery	***(Interpersonal Relationships)*** When is being

	made fun of in a group, accompanies them by making fun of himself or herself and makes faces and gestures.
Gaucherie	***(Making Decisions)*** Does things without considering all the aspects of it, which leads to making mistakes. ***(Interpersonal Relationships)*** does inappropriate behaviors or uses wrong words which cause repeated apologies and disgrace; ***(Having Conversations)*** Changes his or her voice and imitates radio or TV hosts' voice to appear attractive.

5- SOCIAL ISOLATION/ALIENATION:
The feeling that one is isolated from the rest of the world, different from other people, and/or not part of any group or community.

New Coping Styles	**Examples of each New Coping Styles**
Indolence	***(Interpersonal Relationships)*** Pretends to be fatigued and weary while in a group; ***(Taking Trips)*** Refuses to take trips with close friends and family members by Making excuses such as not having sufficient funds or having run out of leave days; ***(Parties and Gatherings)*** Pretends to be busy with work in order to avoid attending parties and gatherings.
Mockery	***(Interpersonal Relationships)*** By smiling at others and having silent quiet laughter, tries to conform with the group.
Gaucherie	***(Interpersonal Relationships)*** Fumbles and gets in a flap especially over meeting someone for the first time.

6- DEPENDENCE/INCOMPETENCE:
Belief that one is unable to handle one's everyday responsibilities in a competent manner, without considerable help from others (e.g., take care of oneself, solve daily problems, exercise good judgment, tackle new tasks, make good decisions). Often presents as helplessness.

New Coping Styles	Examples of each New Coping Styles
Indolence	***(Interpersonal Relationships)*** Pretends to be confused and baffled while being asked to do something; ***(Workplace)*** Daydreams or, in order to avoid new responsibilities, pretends to be tired.
Mockery	***(Activities)*** dreams big about the future and, in the end, makes fun of him or herself for having such imaginations.
Gaucherie	***(Fixing)*** Aimlessly plays around with a device; ***(Housework)*** does household work too slowly; ***(Trip)*** Moves slowly and falls behind the group; ***(Game)*** Loses the ball or is unable to hold the racket properly.

7- VULNERABILITY TO HARM OR ILLNESS:
Exaggerated fear that imminent catastrophe will strike at any time and that one will be unable to prevent it. Fears focus on one or more of the following: (A) Medical catastrophes (e.g., heart attacks, AIDS); (B) Emotional catastrophes (e.g., going crazy); (C) External catastrophes (e.g., elevators

collapsing, victimization by criminals, airplane crashes, earthquakes).

New Coping Styles	Examples of each New Coping Styles
Indolence	***(Finance)*** Despite having sufficient funds, pretends to be broke while shopping and spending money; ***(Having arguments)*** Faints, gets paralyzed, grows weak, has seizures, and gets headaches; ***(In relatively dangerous situations)*** faints upon seeing blood at the car crash scene, trembles and faints while hears news of an earthquake, storm, or a terrorist attack from television or radio; ***(At hospital settings)*** Exaggerates symptoms in order to get the doctor to have a more precise examination, prescribe medicine, conduct specialized tests, get hospitalized or undergo surgery.
Mockery	***(In relatively dangerous situations)*** Reads or tells funny poems or makes fun out of the situation.
Gaucherie	***(purchasing a house or vehicle)*** Searches excessively while being worried and ends up with an inappropriate choice of a house or vehicle; ***(Medical)*** Prescribes medicine for him or herself and also for others on his or her own, without professional consultation, which leads to more problems; Despite being aware of the dangers, touches electronic or heat-generating devices which gets him or her burned or electronic shocked; ***(Financial Decisions)*** Sells assets and properties to the lowest price and purchases stocks for the sake of higher profit which mostly re-

	sults in financial loss. ***(Immigration)*** Leaves the country illegally by paying lots of money to human traffickers, which leads to getting drowned, caught, or forced to live in refugee camps.

8- ENMESHMENT / UNDEVELOPED SELF:
Excessive emotional involvement and closeness with one or more significant others (often parents) at the expense of full individuation or normal social development. Often involves the belief that at least one of the enmeshed individuals cannot survive or be happy without the constant support of the other. May also include feelings of being smothered by or fused with others or insufficient individual identity. Often experienced as a feeling of emptiness and foundering, having no direction, or in extreme cases questioning one's existence.

New Coping Styles	**Examples of each New Coping Styles**
Indolence	***(Responding)*** When being asked a question, gazes helplessly at his or her parent or partner so that they would answer on his or her behalf. ***(Marriage)*** Constantly complains to him/her parent about slightest misfortunes of his/her marital relationship and the parent accompanies him/her in all the complaints, pampering him/her and becoming sorrowful.
Mockery	***(Relationship with parent)*** Tells unfunny or lame jokes which only his or her parent laughs at; Plays imaginary games along with chasing and running with the parent; On some occasions is willing to play different

	roles such as little mama's boy, little mama's girl, yellow chicken, or little rabbit for the parent.
Gaucherie	***(Dressing)*** Chooses unsuitable clothes for the occasion since there wasn't the partner or parent available to give him or her proper consultation; ***(Speech)*** Speaks nonsense in the absence of the parents or partner, continuously requests for providing him or her with correct words; ***(Career)*** Lacks necessary skills for finding a job and does not follow through to acquire the required skill(s).

9- FAILURE:
The belief that one has failed, will inevitably fail, or is fundamentally inadequate relative to one's peers in areas of achievement (school, career, sports, etc.). Often involves beliefs that one is stupid, inept, untalented, lower in status, less successful than others, and so forth.

New Coping Styles	Examples of each New Coping Styles
Indolence	***(Competition)*** Complains about lack of facilities; ***(Exams)*** Tells others how the questions were difficult and the time being allocated was not sufficient. ***(Financial)*** Repeatedly talks about bad economic situations. ***(Plans)*** States being unfortunate and having bad luck in his or her activities.
Mockery	***(Finance)*** Tells memories of financial losses while laughing; ***(Intimate Relationships)*** Makes jokes about his or her unsuccessful marriage or divorce.

Gaucherie	***(Success)*** Amateurishly Copies the thoughts and methods of successful people without considering his or her circumstances and the given situation; ***(Career)*** Doesn't make use of his or her creativity and constantly follows successful people or corporations; ***(Plans)*** Blindly models plans and activities after others and follows through them without considering his or her potential and talents.

10- INSUFFICIENT SELF-CONTROL / SELF-DISCIPLINE:

Pervasive difficulty or refusal to exercise sufficient self-control and frustration tolerance to achieve one's personal goals or to restrain the excessive expression of one's emotions and impulses. In its milder form, the patient presents with an exaggerated emphasis on discomfort avoidance: avoiding pain, conflict, confrontation, responsibility, or overexertion at the expense of personal fulfillment, commitment, or integrity.

New Coping Styles	**Examples of each New Coping Styles**
Indolence	***(Belongings)*** Loses others belongings and refuses to accept the responsibility for it by self-victimization; damages others property and, when being questioned about it, pretends not to know what has happened; damages others belongings and assets while refusing to pay for it by pretending to not having sufficient funds; ***(Interpersonal Relationships)*** Forgets about an appointment and makes excuses such as being sick or having an accident, ***(Educational)*** Doesn't properly plan and prepare for the exams and doesn't

	go to the exam session by pretending to be sick or stating that a close relative has passed away; ***(Social Manners)*** Constantly and easily flatulates or belches by pretending to have digestion problems.
Mockery	***(Workplace)*** Uses foul language and makes sexual/physical jokes, thus disturbing the work environment's safety; ***(Social behavior)*** By constant use of dirty words doesn't adhere to social manners.
Gaucherie	***(Doing things)*** Does things that is not competent enough in tackling, thus leads to a mess up; ***(Projects)*** Progresses projects without prior planning, which causes the project to stop or fail; ***(Driving)*** Drives carelessly and ineptly. Ignores the driving signs and lights. ***(Speech)*** Talks about whatever comes to mind and doesn't stick with the subjects he or she was talking about, which makes the audience confused. ***(Decisions)*** Is unsure about setting time for tasks, postpones, and loses the time.

11- ENTITLEMENT / GRANDIOSITY:

The belief that one is superior to other people; entitled to special rights and privileges; or not bound by the rules of reciprocity that guide normal social interaction. Often involves insistence that one should be able to do or have whatever one wants, regardless of what is realistic, what others consider reasonable, or the cost to others; or an exaggerated focus on superiority (e.g., being among the most successful, famous, wealthy) in order to achieve power or control (not primarily for attention or approval). Sometimes includes excessive competitiveness toward or domination of others: asserting one's power, forcing one's point of view, or controlling the behavior of others in line with one's own desires without empathy or concern for others' needs or feelings.

New Coping Styles	Examples of each New Coping Styles
Indolence	***(Interpersonal Relationships)*** Express what he or she wants and gets his or her needs met by fakely admiring others and telling them affectionate statements without really meaning them. ***(Intimate Relationships)*** Acts as if tired or incapable so that the partner steps up to take care of his or her daily needs. ***(Workplace)*** shifts his or her responsibilities onto colleagues' shoulders by announcing to be exhausted.
Mockery	***(Classroom)*** teases the teacher or makes fun of the studious classmates to feel superior ***(Interpersonal relationships)*** Calls others names. ***(Intimate Relationship)*** Ridicules his or her partner in front of others in order to express power and exercise control.
Gaucherie	***(Career)*** Decides to kickstart a prominent economic activity without having sufficient experience. ***(Competition)*** Trash talks to the stronger team's fans. ***(Interpersonal Relationships)*** Gives strange opinions and expects others to accept them.

12- SUBJUGATION:

Excessive surrendering of control to others because one feels coerced—submitting in order to avoid anger, retaliation, or abandonment. The two major forms of subjugation are:

A. Subjugation of needs: Suppression of one's preferences, decisions, and desires.
B. Subjugation of emotions: Suppression of emotions, especially anger.

Usually involves the perception that one's own desires, opinions, and feelings are not valid or important to others. Frequently presents as excessive compliance, combined with hypersensitivity to feeling trapped. Generally, leads to a buildup of anger, manifested in maladaptive symptoms (e.g., passive–aggressive behavior, uncontrolled outbursts of temper, psychosomatic symptoms, withdrawal of affection, "acting out," substance abuse).

New Coping Styles	Examples of each New Coping Styles
Indolence	***(Interpersonal Relationships)*** Continuously apologizes by making up excuses or constantly expresses his or her regret and remorse in order to prevent retaliation. ***(Workplace)*** Plays the victim card after getting reprimanded. ***(Driving)*** playing the poor me after being fined.
Mockery	***(Workplace)*** Appears in front of authority figures or clients by wearing a fake smile "smile mask". ***(Dealing with Boss/Superiors)*** laughs Pretentiously at unfunny and unpleasant statements. ***(Intimate Relationships)*** Tries to calm down the yelling partner by making jokes.
Gaucherie	***(Oral Exams/ Defense Presentation)*** Mumbles after being asked a question by professors and students. ***(In dealing with the boss or customers)*** Is not able to give a direct and clear re-

	sponse. ***(Asking for a pay raise or days off)*** Mumbles and doesn't state clearly what he or she wants.

13- SELF-SACRIFICE:

Excessive focus on voluntarily meeting the needs of others in daily situations at the expense of one's own gratification. The most common reasons are: to prevent causing pain to others; to avoid guilt from feeling selfish; or to maintain the connection with others perceived as needy. Often results from an acute sensitivity to the pain of others. Sometimes leads to a sense that one's own needs are not being adequately met and to resentment of those who are taken care of. (Overlaps with concept of codependency.)

New Coping Styles	**Examples of each New Coping Styles**
Indolence	***(Interpersonal Relationships)*** By constantly telling statements such as "I was only trying to help" or "no good deed goes unpunished," rejects or changes the facts that he or she had failed to consider. ***(Intimate Relationship)*** demonstrates marital conflicts with his or her partner or problems with the kids in the form of physical pain.
Mockery	***(Interpersonal Relationships)*** Gets humorous while doing grueling and overwhelming tasks which are beyond his or her capacity.
Gaucherie	***(Games)*** Loses on purpose by making mistakes in order to make the other person happy, which the other person usually finds out about, and it leads to annoyance. ***(Competition)*** hesitates and reacts slowly so that the

	opponent can get ahead in the game. ***(Marriage/Making an offer of marriage)*** Doesn't go forward and doesn't make a proposal in order to prevent the love rival from getting defeated.

14- APPROVAL-SEEKING/RECOGNITION-SEEKING:
Excessive emphasis on gaining approval, recognition, or attention from other people or on fitting in at the expense of developing a secure and true sense of self. One's sense of esteem is dependent primarily on the reactions of others rather than on one's own natural inclinations. Sometimes includes an overemphasis on status, appearance, social acceptance, money, or achievement as means of gaining approval, admiration, or attention (not primarily for power or control). Frequently results in major life decisions that are inauthentic or unsatisfying or in hypersensitivity to rejection.

New Coping Styles	**Examples of each New Coping Styles**
Indolence	***(Interpersonal Relationships)*** Moans excessively in order to grab others attention and time, calls him or herself names, diagnosis him or herself with mental disorders such as depression or borderline personality disorder. ***(Classroom)*** continuously asks questions and challenges the teacher by pretending not to understand him or her and appears dissatisfied with the answers given. ***(Illness)*** Exaggerates the symptoms of his or her illness in order to grab others' attention.
Mockery	***(Interpersonal Relationships)*** Tells sexual and dirty jokes, mocks others, memorizes satires, and tells them to others by heart. ***(Party)***

	grabs everyone's attention by talking too much without being sensible and even sometimes being nasty. ***(Classroom)*** asks irrelevant questions to make others laugh.
Gaucherie	***(Interpersonal Relationships)*** Engages in seductive behaviors which might cause him or her problems. ***(Workplace)*** Continues his or her Hypocritical behavior even though others have found out about his or her hypocrisy. ***(Party)*** Wears inappropriate clothes and unusual makeup. ***(Driving)*** Drives while playing a loud music in the vehicle or drives aggressively which might get pulled over by the police. ***(Soccer)*** Takes off his or her clothes after scoring or performs inappropriate gestures even though he or she is aware of getting a yellow card or fined by the referee.

15- NEGATIVITY/PESSIMISM:

A pervasive, lifelong focus on the negative aspects of life (pain, death, loss, disappointment, conflict, guilt, resentment, unsolved problems, potential mistakes, betrayal, things that could go wrong, etc.) while minimizing or neglecting the positive or optimistic aspects. Usually includes an exaggerated expectation—in a wide range of work, financial, or interpersonal situations—that things will eventually go seriously wrong or that aspects of one's life that seem to be going well will ultimately fall apart. Usually involves an inordinate fear of making mistakes that might lead to financial collapse, loss, humiliation, or being trapped in a bad situation. Because they exaggerate potential negative outcomes, these individuals are frequently characterized by chronic worry, vigilance, complaining, or indecision.

New Coping Styles	Examples of each New Coping Styles
Indolence	***(Interpersonal Relationship)*** Complains about living conditions and moans constantly about family and friends in order to receive attention and sympathy. ***(Intimate Relationship)*** continuously nags and complains to his or her partner in order to receive affection and support. ***(Career and Financial Issues)*** constantly expresses dissatisfaction and uncertainty about his or her job without any solid decisions for resigning.
Mockery	***(Interpersonal Relationships)*** Gets sarcastic, ridicules hopeful others with positive beliefs about the future, and discourages them from being hopeful. ***(Career and Financial Issues)*** Makes fun of future plans and goals, feeds others his or her chronic anxiety and tensions.
Gaucherie	***(Interpersonal Relationships)*** Causes others troubles by constantly discouraging and frustrating them and being a wet blanket in a way. ***(Career and Financial Issues)*** Prevents others from excelling in different areas by negative interference and unintentional obstruction.

16- EMOTIONAL INHIBITION:

The excessive inhibition of spontaneous action, feeling, or communication, usually to avoid disapproval by others, feelings of shame, or losing control of one's impulses. The most common areas of inhibition involve: (a) inhibition of anger and aggression; (b) inhibition of positive impulses (e.g., joy, affection, sexual excitement, play); (c) difficulty expressing vulnerability or communicating freely about one's feelings, needs, and so forth; or (d) excessive emphasis on rationality while disregarding emotions.

New Coping Styles	Examples of each New Coping Styles
Indolence	***(Activities)*** Announces that despite his or her wish, due to some difficulties or illness cannot do certain things such as ***(Singing a Song)*** Pretends that he or she has caught a cold therefore can't sing, ***(Party)*** tells everyone that his or her legs hurts and refuses to dance, ***(Speech)*** announces that he or she doesn't have enough time now.
Mockery	***(Interpersonal Relationships)*** Makes up harsh physical pranks and jokes and does them on significant others. ***(Intimate Relationship)*** constantly uses dirty language with sexual content while talking with the partner and close friends. ***(Workplace)*** pulls pranks on his or her colleagues at work without anyone noticing. ***(Dialogue)*** speaks in a way that most of the time, the audience can't distinguish whether he or she is serious or is making a joke
Gaucherie	***(Party)*** Seriously tries to perform dance moves in the correct form but fumbles in the process. ***(Singing)*** Sings the song with a harsh, loud, and out-of-tone voice. ***(Formal Speech/Speaking)*** expresses certain Phonemes strangely and unfamiliar to some extent. ***(Ro-***

	mantic Relationship) Missing the chances to step forward and telling the other person that he/she has feelings for them. ***(In general)*** asking others to carry out the activities which require an expression of emotions on his/her behalf. e.g., asks someone close to reveal his/her feelings to his/her crush.

17- UNRELENTING STANDARDS/ HYPER-CRITICALNESS:
The underlying belief that one must strive to meet very high internalized standards of behavior and performance, usually to avoid criticism. Typically results in feelings of pressure or difficulty slowing down and in hyper-criticalness toward oneself and others. Must involve significant impairment in pleasure, relaxation, health, self-esteem, sense of accomplishment, or satisfying relationships. Unrelenting standards typically present as (a) perfectionism, inordinate attention to detail, or an underestimate of how good one's own performance is relative to the norm; (b) rigid rules and "shoulds" in many areas of life, including unrealistically high moral, ethical, cultural, or religious precepts; or (c) preoccupation with time and efficiency, the need to accomplish more.

New Coping Styles	Examples of each New Coping Styles
Indolence	***(Career wise issues)*** When he or she hasn't finished the project on time and faces his or her business partner or the other party involved in the agreement, pretends that it was sickness or some other unexpected emergency which caused the project to delay. He or she won't admit to taking on multiple projects at once and not being able to finish all of them

	on time. ***(Intimate Relationships)*** Gets so busy that fails to meet his or her partner's emotional and sexual needs and, when being confronted, plays the victim card by saying statements such as I only try this hard to provide for our family and that this has nothing to do with me and my personal success.
Mockery	***(Educational or Career wise issues)*** When talks about an educational subject or entering a career area which doesn't have sufficient prior knowledge about, starts joking and makes others laugh, therefore wastes their time. ***(Politics/Management)*** As an official or person in charge, when being asked a serious and important question, replies with a sense of humor and telling jokes.
Gaucherie	***(Broken device)*** Insists on fixing a broken device without having the necessary tools and sufficient knowledge about fixing it. ***(Arguments)*** Insists too much on his or her point of view while arguing, hence tries to force his or her opinion on others. ***(Competition)*** puts too much effort into winning the stronger opponent despite having continuous losses.

18- PUNITIVENESS:

The belief that people should be harshly punished for making mistakes. Involves the tendency to be angry, intolerant, punitive, and impatient with those people (including oneself) who do not meet one's expectations or standards. Usually includes difficulty forgiving mistakes in oneself or others because of a reluctance to consider extenuating circumstances, allow for human imperfection, or empathize with feelings.

New Coping Styles	Examples of each New Coping Styles
Indolence	***(Activities)*** Severely punishes others while expresses his or her regret for doing so and that it's against his or her best wishes. Examples include: ***(School)*** School principal to the guilty student:" I don't like to expel you at all but I do it for your own good", ***(Parents)*** Father tells his son or daughter: "Dear, I don't like to punish you at all but unfortunately you force me into doing so"
Mockery	***(Physical Contact)*** While joking, bites, or pinches others that might even leave bruises on them. ***(Intimate Relationships)*** After a long argument with his or her partner, states that they have been fighting over nothing and makes fun of their problem in order to go on the partner's nerves. ***(Children upbringing)*** When faced with his or her children being lazy, makes sarcastic remarks about "how well their living conditions are."
Gaucherie	***(Interpersonal Relationships)*** By making silly mistakes puts her or himself into the position of getting punished or fined. ***(Workplace, sport's competition or courtroom)*** plays a lose/lose game strategy, therefore by losing intentionally, obviously causes him or herself and others to get punished.

Behaviors that stem from indolence, mockery, and gaucherie would result in schema perpetuation. This is how behaviors that come from surrender, avoidance, and overcompensation would contribute to this effect. Therefore, therapists should educate their patients about new coping styles so that their incorporation of indolence, mockery, and gaucherie comes to an end; hence, schema modification occurs. By modifying these new coping styles and the old ones, the patients' needs start to get met gradually, and as a result, they become more motivated and] eager in the treatment process.

As a matter of fact, behavioral pattern-breaking usually takes place as the last stage of the treatment plan. That is, after forming the therapeutic relationship and going through the cognitive and experiential techniques and interventions, the therapist brings the focus of attention to the behavioral patterns. Indeed, the focus of behavioral pattern-breaking is also on the coping styles. It is important to note that the therapists should first bring their focus of attention to the behaviors of their patients, which stem from surrender, avoidance, and overcompensation to their maladaptive schemas. Only then should they go after assessment of the indolence, mockery, and gaucherie behaviors. If none of the behaviors that the patient exhibits can be categorized as surrender, avoidance, or overcompensation, the therapist can directly put the new coping styles as the central axis of modification and treatment.

There exist two highly critical reasons for familiarizing schema therapists with the coping styles of indolence, mockery, and gaucherie. The first reason is that some of the patients might, upon being educated about the coping styles of surrender, avoidance, and overcompensation, sensibly yet unconsciously stop relying on them but replace them with the new coping styles. The second reason is that even if the patient is well aware of her schemas and the cognitive and experiential techniques and interventions have been conducted on her by an experienced therapist, without undergoing a complete behavioral pattern-breaking phase, there is a high chance for the relapse of the existing disorder. This makes the behavioral pattern-breaking phase the most critical, challenging, and prolonged phase in the course of schema therapy. Being highly critical, this stage of treatment requires higher levels of deliberate observation and intervention from the therapist. Thus, the more delicate and exhaustive the behaviors of the patients are categorized, the higher are the chances for successful completion of this challenging phase for the therapists. Thus far, by targeting 54 maladaptive coping styles, we used to put our effort into replacing the schema-driven behavioral patterns with healthy responses. Hereafter, by having 54 new coping styles at our disposal, thus 108 in total, we will help the patients overcome their schema's dominance.

Patients start to get into a more observer stance after becoming familiar with the new coping styles. They assess the behaviors of themselves and others and gain an awareness of the instances of indolence, mockery, and gaucherie, which are schema-driven and harmful to the self or the ones around. As we know, the broader aim of schema therapy is to modify the maladaptive schema-driven behaviors and ultimately replace them with the ones of the healthy adult mode. Therefore, fundamental modifications should be made before indolence, mockery, and gaucherie can cause more intense difficulties.

Even though coping styles attribute a significant part of the individual's behaviors to themselves, yet these styles contain cognitive and emotional components as well. In fact, while in different coping styles, not only do individuals tend to think in certain ways specific to that style, but also their emotions get involved in distinctive manners. Even when an individual is in an avoidance coping style and seems not to be able to recall the memories of his childhood, he repeatedly questions the therapist about the reasons for this inability. He asks, why can't I recall any memories from my childhood? Of course, many of these patients are not yet aware of their avoidance; hence, they mistakenly worry about the gradual loss of their memory or being diagnosed with Alzheimer's disease in the the future! Therefore, even a patient in an avoidance coping style tends to think of the present or past issues, but it is only natural not to recall anything. While assessing the emotional component of this style, we arrive at a relatively identical situation as well. When a patient with an avoidant coping style faces a situation in which her emotions are activated to a degree, she tends to flee from the scene quickly, either physically or mentally. That being the case, most people experience a small part of their emotions when being in an avoidant coping style. For instance, upon hearing some sad news and incorporating this style, the individual might get some wet eyes for a brief moment and move on. Table 2.3 presents the dissimilarities of the behavioral, cognitive, and emotional components of each of the six maladaptive coping styles.

Table 2-3: behavioral, cognitive, and emotional components of the six maladaptive coping styles.

Coping styles	Behavior	Cognition	Emotion
Surrender	Recurrence of the childhood patterns and looking for people or situations which resemble the past.	Accepting the information which is aligned with the schemas perspective, schemas validate and approve of along with selective abstraction in different contexts.	Directly and wholly experiencing the emotional pain.
Avoidance	Active or passive escape of the triggering situations of the schema	Denial of unpleasant past events and incidents; inability to recollect painful childhood memories.	Not experiencing any emotional pain or experiencing them to a small degree.
Over-compensation	Engaging in excessive behaviors which are in contrast with schemas	Thoughts are contrasted with the childhood learned experiences and the contents of the mind.	Covering up unpleasant feelings with the opposite ones.
Indolence	Preventing schema activation by exhibiting incompetency and poor per-	Choosing the weak position in order to gain benefit.	Exaggerating with the aim of reducing unpleasant feelings

	formance.		
Mockery	A temporary and despicable act to cover up the activated schema.	A seemingly convenient navigation through tense situations by not taking matters seriously.	Replacing pseudo-pleasant feelings with unpleasant feelings.
Gaucherie	Not taking responsibility while the schemas get activated, thus transferring consequences to others.	Deriving pleasure from and believing in mistakes and repeating them; not learning from mistakes intentionally.	Creating a new unpleasant feeling as a means to replacing it with the old unpleasant feeling for the purpose of feeling relieved.

The Climax in Coping Styles

Undoubtedly, most of the patients can only incorporate a single coping style at once. In other words, it is not a usual observation to witness two distinct coping styles present at the same time by the same individual. However, the incorporation of a given coping style certainly is not a permanent stance, and it would change over the course of time, but the length of this duration through which this change occurs is varied. What is it that can replace a specific coping style with another? When a patient reaches the climax of a particular style, she would eventually substitute it for another one. The climax takes place when the incorporation of the current coping style has reached its maximum possible degree, and the incorporation of that style is no longer considered functional or helpful. A given patient might stay in a single style for years, while another one might tend to substitute it over a much shorter period of time. It is clear that the coping styles change, and no one incorporates only a single one of them throughout their whole life. The substitution of styles takes place in both humans and animals. This incorporation makes situations trustworthy for a period of time. As an example, consider an animal abuser who has found a cat that has taken shelter in the corner of a wall and is completely rolled up (freeze/ surrender). In case this person continues his abuse and passes the surrender climax of the cat, the cat, in turn, might jump at the abuser and scratch him (fight/ overcompensation). At the time when the cat has already scratched its sharp nails on the face of the abuser, its overcompensation climax has reached; thus, it flees from the scene (flight/ avoidance). In case the cat does not find an opportunity for escape, after lots of struggles, it would eventually pass the avoidance climax and exhibit behavior which is closely a resemblance of the one we have observed in the comedy animation Shrek by the Puss in Boots which is playing the innocent (faint/ indolence). In both human and animal worlds, the passage from surrender and overcompensation climax is an entrance into the avoidance coping style.

The Octet Substitution Model

When being reached the surrender climax, the patient states:" I'm at the end of my patience." When being reached the overcompensation climax, the patient states: "I lost my temper," and when it comes to the climax of avoidance, she would state: "I don't want to go on like this anymore." Considering the significant role that climax plays out in coping styles, we can point out the eight substitution models. For further details, please refer to figure 2-1. In the preceding section, the octet substitution model has been explained for the case of domestic violence among couples. It is important to note that besides domestic violence, this octet model can be used in other instances as well.

1. *Surrender to overcompensation*: The patient that has greatly grown tired of absolute submission herself starts to engage in dominance and hurtful behavior.
2. *Surrender to avoidance*: the patient who is done with being

submissive ultimately comes up with an Escape Plan in order to save her life.

3. *Overcompensation to avoidance*: Being in the dominant role for an extended period of time has left the patient both frustrated and burnt out; thus, she leaves the relationship.
4. *Avoidance to indolence*: This occurs when the patient is unable to find a way to escape from the dominant partner; therefore,, he ends up with depression and other difficulties that present themselves through physical symptoms.
5. *Indolence to overcompensation*: even though the patient tends to play the innocent for an extended period of time, yet he will eventually take revenge as the good opportunities reveal themselves.
6. *Indolence to avoidance*: The patient is desperate to find an escape route to get away from the dominant person by displaying weakness and powerlessness.
7. *Indolence to Gaucherie*: Even though the patient is in a state of helplessness, yet she continues to make trouble for the dominant partner.
8. *Gaucherie to mockery*: after the dominant partner confronts the patient about her mess ups and sabotages, the partner who had previously made the troubles attempts to make fun of the situation and try to be funny.

Figure 2-1: The substitution of coping styles after reaching climax

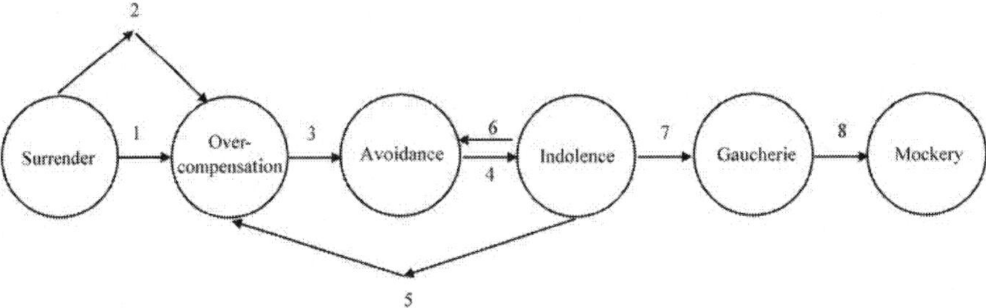

In case you tend to live close to seashore, you have gradually grown your expertise in distinguishing different breeds of fish from each other. You will eventually find out about the breeding, spawning, and fishing seasons and precisely at which date each of these starts and at which date they end. Yet the most critical issue is that based on the physical characteristics of each breed, you're able to distinguish between the wild-caught fish and the farm-raised ones. Consequently, human beings gradually learn to incorporate different coping styles while dealing with different people in distinctive situations. Moreover, over time, they grow their ability to distinguish and recognize the coping styles from each other. Back to the fish metaphor, we realize that the three styles of surrender, avoidance, and overcompensation are entirely natural (wild-caught), and on the other hand, the three styles of indolence, mockery, and gaucherie are somewhat human-made (farm-raised). As most of the products in a given fish market are farm-raised, so does the octet model. Except for the first three items, which involve the surrender, avoidance, and overcompensation coping styles, the remaining five items are based on the indolence, mockery, and gaucherie coping styles. This is due to the complex structure of the human psyche compared to the other related species. Most of the Species possess items 1 to 3, and as we make our way up in the continuum towards the more evolved species, we witness a growth in the presence of these items. Last but not least, it's the human beings at the end of this continuum that might incorporate all of the eight models.

In the Shrek animated comedy, we have witnessed over and

over during the movie that the puss in boots fights till the last breath and never welcomes the idea of surrender (item one); he escapes before being caught (item two). Sometimes he might become weak due to the intensity of the fight; hence he flees from the scene (item three). When an escape is not possible, he plays the innocent, especially with the help of his eyes (item four). As soon as the predator starts to think about his innocence and hesitates, he draws his sword and surprises the predator (item five) or takes advantage of the predator's compassion and escapes from the scene (item six). Sometimes he breaks and destroys all the valuable equipment (item seven), and when he is being caught in the end, he starts to be funny or tell funny things (item eight). It is interesting to note that most of these coping style substitutions not only take place in the behaviors of the puss in boots but also in the behaviors of many of the different popular movie characters.

Clinical Case

Sairus is a 52 years old CEO of a big government organization who, despite lacking academic education and relative experience in this field, is being assigned to this role. He has two children with his former wife, whom he got divorced from 4 years ago. Both of their children are now university students. Soon after his divorce, he married another woman who was 27 years old. From early on, he stated that he never really believed in psychotherapy and that he has been forced to attend the sessions. The reason for his attendance was his wife's threats of getting a divorce after four years of marriage. Sairus told us: "my wife has grown tired of the jokes that I make about her family and others. She believes they are bitter and way out of line. She also thinks that I am lazy, sponger, and a hanger-on". After the therapist identified the entitlement/grandiosity schema of Sairus during the first weeks of therapy, she started to educate him and provide him with proper information regarding this schema. Sairus could identify the origins of the schema within his childhood life experiences. These included receiving excessive freedom from his parents, being pampered and spoiled, and forcing his parents to get him everything he asked for. However, he wouldn't accept any of the behaviors associated with the coping styles of surrender, avoidance, and overcompensation about himself. He told us: "Im very much in love with my young wife, and I treat her with love and respect. However, I admit that I was cold and unfair with my ex-wife. It is true that with my ex-wife, I used to surrender to my entitlement/grandiosity schema. However, with my current wife, it is not the case at all." Also, regarding avoidance and overcompensation, he stated:" In most occasions, where there are going to be a group of people over whom I know that I am not accounted as superior or anything, I tend to show up and don't avoid these situations. However, as I arrive there, I tend to make fun of the ones I perceive as superior to me in my unique ways. Also, I am not used to giving away lavish gifts or making considerable donations to charities or organizations (overcompensation coping style).

In contrast, I always tell everybody that the main problem with our organizations is the lack of budget and credits (indolence coping style). I am well aware that I'm not educated or experienced enough in order to handle day to day tasks of a CEO, yet I love to be the one in charge, and when my name was brought up as a possible choice for being the CEO, I totally welcomed it (gaucherie coping style)." Sairus's marital life was coming to its end due to him constantly making fun of his wife and her family, and his professional life was in crisis because of his lack of required knowledge and experience. The associates and other employees had found out about his incompetencies as a CEO and his ways of transferring the primary responsibilities to others by making excuses such as being tired due to work overload, having a backache, or simply being busy (indolence coping style). When confronted by one of his friends who told him that it is better if he resigns before any serious troubles are caused for the organization and that as a CEO, he has no room for trial and error, he thoughtfully told his friend: "I am gradually starting to learn my responsibilities" (gaucherie coping style).

Schema Modes Related to the New Coping Styles

When young and his colleagues tried to utilize schema therapy for treating patients with more severe disorders (borderline and narcissistic personality disorders), they gradually started to develop the concept of modes. According to Young (2003), a mode is "those schemas or schema operations—adaptive or maladaptive—that are currently active for an individual." Also, Arntz and Jacob (2013) describe schema mode as an emotional state of an individual related to a specific schema. Schema modes can constantly flip to each other, or they can be fixed and stable. While treating patients with personality disorders, educating them about the concept of modes and doing mode work is of great importance.

As during the past decade, schema therapy has moved towards a treatment model which emphasizes the mode model alongside its traditional schema model, and many modes have been introduced during this time, introducing the modes related to the coping styles of indolence, mockery, and gaucherie can play a complementary role in the process of treatment. Lobbestael and colleagues (2007) have demonstrated that more modes are involved in the development of the borderline disorder. Also, van Genderen, Rijkeboer, and Arntz (2012) have stated that the schema modes will not stay in the same numbers as they are now. Since the patients can identify the modes much easier than the schemas while they attend to their feelings, identifying and distinguishing the new dysfunctional coping modes adds to the patient's self-awareness and makes a positive impact on their performance.

The most important mode in schema therapy is the vulnerable child mode. Therefore the main aim of therapy has been set to making the most healing and progress taking place regarding this mode. This is the mode that expresses the most intensive emotions and compared to it; there are the coping modes that experience the least amount of emotions. In order to understand the reasons and significance of using coping modes by the patients, we should review the role that they play and their advantages and disadvantages in the patient's life.

Most of the patients, either consciously or unconsciously, are aware of the benefits of using these modes in their daily lives. If they did not get their almost desired outcomes out of using coping modes, they would have stopped incorporating them a long time ago. Hereon, nine new dysfunctional coping modes, which are based on the three coping styles of indolence, mockery, and gaucherie, are going to be pointed out. These three new coping styles are most used during the Adolescent years. Even though they play an adaptive (useful, compatible, functional) role during childhood years, just like surrender, avoidance, and overcompensation coping styles, they begin to exhibit their dysfunctional role as the individual reaches the adult years. In short, the use of these new coping styles during adulthood causes interpersonal problems for the individuals regarding their partner, families, and colleagues.

Table 2-4: Classification of new coping modes along with their schema modes

Indolence Coping Style	**Mockery Coping Style**	**Gaucherie Coping Style**
Hesitant Imagined Mode (HIM)	Automatic Laughter Mode (ALM)	Obstructionist/ Saboteur Mode (OSM)
Distressed/Helpless Mode (DHM)	Self-mockery Mode (SMM)	Misguide/Misdirect Mode (MMM)
Moral Preacher Mode (MPM)	Others-mockery Mode (OMM)	Controversial/ Troublemaker Mode (CTM)

According to Young, modes tend to change constantly, and they appear momentary and instantaneous. Unlike schemas which are fairy stable, modes lack any stability and tend to have only a short-term condition. Despite all this, modes possess high potential in causing troubles for the patient. It is important to note that being an exception; some modes may be present for an extended period of time and be reasonably stable. It is a faulty conclusion to draw that modes only belong to individuals with personality disorders. In fact, they can be observed plentifully among normal populations. The two main differences of the modes in individuals with personality disorders and normal populations consist of the intensity and independence of the mode. The modes in people with personality disorders are highly powerful and do not act independently from each other. Thus the individual with a personality disorder is presented with less independence and freedom of taking action while dealing with her modes. In this situation, a single schema mode is in the foreground while the rest are present in the background. Hence we will examine the new schema modes and personality disorders in more detail in the following chapters of this book. It is known that schema therapy has shown significant results in treating patients with personality disorders, and its applications and effectiveness have been profoundly examined. Now, with new modes in place, they can also get observed and identified while working with patients with personality disorders. Each of these new modes is going to be clearly explained and further illustrated with accompanying examples in the following chapters in this book. It is important to consider that Young's approach to schema therapy has been undergoing changes and developments since the early years, and the introduction of these new modes to the list of the already existing ones not only does not change the structure of schema therapy concepts but also helps to develop them even further.

Behavioral Strategies and the Murk Heritage

Many patients complain about the inappropriate and harmful behaviors of the ones around them to the therapist. A lady once stated: "Every time after an argument, my 45 years old husband gives me silent treatment just like a five years old boy. He goes on like this until he gets me forced into stepping forward and asking for an apology." The husband also stated: "My wife tends to lie to me without any apparent reason. She lies to me even about the simplest matters. She is also highly secretive and this habit of hers, I'm telling you, it has affected all the financial, family and social aspects of our life. I have no idea about what's going on around my life anymore."

Sulking, lying, and secrecy each are a "Murk Heritage" that might have been utilized since our childhood years until now as a behavioral strategy. Many adults still find themselves trapped in their childhood strategies. In order to meet their needs, they behave in accordance with their "primary strategies." Besides the three murk heritages mentioned so far, there are other prevalent ones, including hypocrisy, threat, flattery, snitching, sneaking away, cliquism, foul mouthedness, cheating, and forging.

Individuals take their murk heritages from childhood to adulthood and still tend to incorporate them in their interpersonal relationships. These murk heritages were proved to be effective in the past as they helped the child meet her needs and get to what she wanted. Thus the fulfillment of the child's needs has reinforced these behavioral strategies through the course of time, and now when it comes to adulthood years, the individual tends to still utilize the same old strategies as in childhood years in order to get what she wants. For instance, a child who, upon sulking, was used to quickly receiving what she looked for from her parents now tends to give her husband the silent treatment in order to get to what she wants. What this individual is not aware of is the fact that during her childhood years, her parents did not want to upset their child and drive her away from themselves due to their self-sacrifice and, of course, abandonment/instability schemas, whereas now the husband does not care at all about her sulking even if they go on for days or even weeks. Here the husband's indifference is immensely strange for the wife since she expects her husband to quickly step forward and ask for an apology just like her parents used to do so.

To easier comprehend this issue, we ought to see the first days of school through the lenses of children. The child has been told to be prepared for attending school long time before the academic year has even begun (The distress prior to the event), Then the child joins the crowd in the school (the crowd and fear of the new environment), the mother leaves him there (separation anxiety), he is forced to form a line with others (inability in controlling the environment), he is being pushed around (feeling weakness), he is being sent to the back of the line (the pressure of the new circumstances accompanied by fatigue and tension), he gets jostled and his clothes are being pulled (confusion and unreliability), gets into conflict with his classmate when choosing their seat (other's display of power and being forced to be dominated), another classmate takes his pencil and refuses to give it back (getting bullied by others and inability in defending himself), his snack gets taken from his bag (the feeling of lack of safety), The teacher yells at one of the students and pulls his ear (forced politeness and respect accompanied by fear). If we were to take into consideration the cultural issues as well, then the matter would become even more complicated. The child might experience all the instances mentioned above in his first week of attendance at school. The behavioral strategies he was used to utilizing at home while dealing with his parents are no longer of use while facing his peers.

Therefore, from the early school days, the child is forced to develop "new behavioral strategies to rescue himself from the troubles" and put them to use. These new behavioral strategies have to stop others from harming him, prevent punishment from teachers, take care of his tools and snacks, and not feel isolated and accepted by the classmates. The child comes up with some of these strategies and learns some of them from others. These strategies are designed in order to rescue the individual from a harmful situation; thus, they are accounted as survival mechanisms, and besides, humans are clearly observed among other species as well.

In the following section, five "behavioral strategies" common among humans and other species, transferred from childhood years to adulthood as "murk heritage," are pointed out.

The First Strategy - Camouflage

The message = "I am not here."

According to Ethology, camouflage is a passive message. *Camouflage* is a reaction given by organisms in order to keep themselves safe by staying out of the sight of predators by remaining indistinguishable from the surrounding environment. Camouflage takes place in two forms in nature—a camouflage for attacking purposes and a camouflage utilized for defense. The case of a cheetah silently making his way through the grasses of a meadow while crawling in order not to be seen by his prey is a case for attacking camouflage. Whenever a chameleon changes its color to match its surrounding environment, it usually does it for defense purposes. Many other insects, too, such as cockroaches, mantises, grasshoppers, and butterflies, utilize the camouflage method to survive very well. "The teacher enters the classroom, according to their last session, today is the day where the teacher is going to ask questions from the students. Some of the students have failed to study; the teacher looks around the classroom looking for a potential student to bring forward. Some of the students try to hide completely behind the person sitting in front of them." The child is trying to convey the message that I am not here! A couple of students are asked questions about the subject they had to study, the time for class is up, and the camouflage method proved to be a success. Thus the child gets positive reinforcement. These continued reinforcements result in the perseverance of camouflage reaction in the future and during adulthood years. Hiding from tax officers and escaping from paying taxes, refusing to wear a safety helmet by motorcyclists and camouflaging themselves among the cars in order not to get fined by police officers, Hiding at home, and not going to military service during war times are all instances of reinforced childhood behavioral strategies. Many of the secrecies taking place among couples are rooted in camouflage strategy as well. Even Though camouflage is a natural reaction for animal survival, just like fight or flight response, yet it can not be categorized as any of the six coping styles.

The Second Strategy - Rotation and Throw

The message = "I am harmful."

As a millipede is on the move, finding its way around, many dangers might threaten him from his surrounding environment. Many millipedes get crushed under the wheels of the passing vehicles, and many others get hunted by predators. Millipedes tend to move very slowly, which leaves them with almost no chance to escape from their predators. The "curling up" response is the most important strategy of millipedes. This interesting strategy has been proven to be effective on many occasions, leaving the millipedes safe by making the predator either letting go of the attack or making it scared, thus leaving the scene. Millipedes are entirely helpless when it comes to the abilities like stinging and biting, yet when they utilize their "curl up" response as a defense method, they tend to throw a stinky yellow liquid substance around themselves. The millipedes can spread this liquid based on hydrogen cyanide up to 25 centimeters of distance. Experienced toads have learned well not to do anything with the millipedes since eating the millipedes has left them with a bitter taste of acid and hours of dizziness, nausea, and vomiting. At school, "The teacher is going over the new lesson that she suddenly hears a loud voice from the back of the classroom cursing. The teacher goes over to the student who was cursing only to find him bending over his belongings and the student sitting next to him surprised and slightly scared." The foul-mouthed student has been told at home that when it comes to students' belongings, he is not to share them with anyone and also not to use anyone else's. The student sitting next to him wanted to use his rubber, yet he refused to do so, and after a short struggle, he decided to throw himself over his belongings and started to curse. Gaining success from utilizing the rotation and throw strategy yields in the reinforcement of this behavior in adulthood years presenting itself as a murk heritage such as foul mouthedness. Most people are well aware that they should not run into conflicts or mess with a foul-mouthed person since, from experience, they are afraid that she might say something harmful to them in the presence of others. Individuals with the foul-mouthedness murk heritage have protected themselves over the years utilizing this strategy. "Presenting one's face filled with a combination of dissatisfaction, anger, and irritation along with cursing the driver of a close by car, the habit of spitting while being angry and rolling eyes at others in order to intimidate them" are among other instances of rotation and throw strategy in adulthood. Furthermore, the accumulation of task forces together taking a ball-shaped form during the time of political and social protests carrying massive riot shields to keep the protestors at bay and using water cannons to disperse them is among instances of rotation and throw strategy in militarism.

The Third Strategy - Replication

The message = "I am someone else."

When different species change their color to match their surrounding environment, they have utilized the camouflage method, but when they make themselves look like another species, they have thus incorporated the replication strategy. This method of action has been frequently observed among the butterflies inhabiting the Amazon area, which tend to make themselves look like lizards or frogs. Instances of "healthy replication" can be observed among children while they are playing. When children wear the masks of different cartoon characters and imitate their behaviors and ways of speaking, they have used the healthy replication in a way. On the other hand, instances of "unhealthy replication" can be observed frequently in the behaviors presented by children as well. Examples of these cases include: After the exam, the teacher finds out that the student has intentionally miswritten her real name at the top of her answer sheet. Another experienced teacher finds out the letter of consent has been signed by the student himself instead of his parents. Another student copies the answers to the math problems given as homework from his classmate. If these behaviors are not being corrected during school years, they usually tend to accompany the individual into adulthood and take a more severe form. The murk heritage of cheating and forgery includes behaviors such as forging documents and records, plagiarism and copying from others articles and theses, data tampering, and falsifying statistics and numbers. These instances are samples stemming from childhood behaviors that were left free to go on and were not corrected.

The Fourth Strategy - Warning and Alarm

The message = "I am very dangerous."

Some children gradually learn that the best defense is "inducing fear into others." There are many instances to this strategy: Even Though the child appears calm at home, he tends to threaten others at school. When the child's parents are called to school due to their child threatening someone else, they get surprised since this is something very strange to them coming from their child, who always appears calm. They regard their child as very polite, kind, and without any expressions of aggression whatsoever. Nevertheless, the reality is that their child has threatened other children repeatedly while being at school. As we are well aware, incorporating some authoritarian parenting methods and inappropriate use of punishing and rewarding the child at home results in aggressive behavior of the child being displayed outside of the home. As a matter of fact, the child does not dare to misbehave while being at home, and this does not mean that the child is necessarily calm.

Furthermore, there is a possibility that the child might model after one of the parents threatening behaviors and exhibit such manners while being at school. In the animal kingdom, in case you have witnessed poisonous snakes, you have undoubtedly noticed how they constantly take out their fang, inducing fear in others intentionally or unintentionally. Monkeys, too, tend to open their mouth and display their sharp teeth when they feel threatened. Furthermore, they might even make a slight jump toward the predator after displaying their teeth. Tomcats also tend to threaten each other with rather loud noise lasting for minutes when it comes to competition over mating. Indeed, with respect to animals, the act of threat takes place as a means of prevention of physical aggression, since in case a fight breaks out between the parties, either one might end up hurt or killed. The child, too, utilizes this strategy as a means of self-defense without having any intentions of physically getting into a fight with anyone else. The threat is a murk heritage and a factor working against the individual's safety which can take any of the verbal, emotional, and physical forms. Wherever there is a threat present, the person's need for safety is getting challenged. Just like other murk heritages, threats too can be reinforced during childhood years and play themselves out in social relationships, couple's relationship, relationship with the one's child, and also at the workplace during adulthood. It is interesting to note that many politicians and military leaders have utilized the warning and alarm strategy throughout history to threaten other countries. Different military parades and maneuvers all carry the same unmistakable message within themselves: "Do not get close to our borders; we are very dangerous!" When it comes to the individualistic domain, too, many individuals tend to increase their body mass and muscle strength several times more than the average amount using different kinds of supplements and engaging in heavy body-building exercises. This behavior, along with putting on different tattoos on the body, sends a message to others besides seeking attention. The message is: "Be afraid of me and do not get close," which is a covert threat.

The Fifth Strategy: Group Defense

The message = "We are a united circle."

Termites always work as a group when it comes to defending themselves or taking on an attack. If you have the experience of breaking up a hive and making honey out of it, you have undoubtedly witnessed an organized attack by the bees on yourself. Buffaloes, too, tend to stick together and fight as a single unit when it comes to pushing away the troublesome predators. Group defense is basically a good survival reaction among animals. Group defense bears in itself an active message for others: "We are a united circle; thus we are invincible." For instance, young boys playing soccer at the schoolyard might enter a conflict as one of the players intentionally fouls on the opposition player causing him injury. The opposition team players might attack the player at fault together and start pushing him around, thus displaying their alliance. Even Though some of the players are not used to disputes and putting up fights, they enter into the group defense strategy in order to support their team. The message which is being sent to the opposition team and their fans under these circumstances is: "We are a united team, and hurting one of us is the same as hurting all of us." It has been witnessed many times over and over again that in these situations, even the players on the bench tend to join the group defense as well. Often, children carry out group defense successfully; thus, their fear of group fights gradually wears off. They gradually come to accept group fights as an effective solution for addressing problems. This is the starting point for the cliquism murk heritage. Individuals who belong to the same circle tend to favor each other and conspire together in order to reach their common goals in different situations. They tend to do each other favors under different circumstances and keep track of them. With respect to political affairs, factionalism yields to work in favor of the members of a single Cabal. Therefore, factionalism is not just limited to animals, school years, or the workplace, yet many countries have formed different political, military, and economic alliances together. Cliquism is a dangerous murk heritage since it most often results in corruption, favoritism, economic rent, and lack of transparency.

The more the species are developed and evolved, the more complex "behavioral strategies" they tend to incorporate for their survival. Even though these strategies carry within themselves positive aspects for the individual or the given species, yet they are irritating and negative for others. These strategies usually become reinforced as their utilization proves to be successful in particular situations, resulting in them taking place repeatedly in the future. It is important to note that even though insects and other species tend to utilize these strategies as a means for their survival when it comes to human adults, these strategies taking the form of murk heritages and stemming from childhood years are severely harmful. Human beings are social creatures, and adhering to individualistic, self-centered behaviors results in the break of social norms and disarray in the society's order. Murk heritages result in the incompatibility of the individuals with their surrounding environment. As an example, it has been many years since our efforts in many countries to promote the culture of driving vehicles correctly on the streets have been fruitless. We have failed to resolve the issue of traffic to an acceptable degree by encouraging enough people to use public transportation more frequently or to learn the culture of the appropriate use of natural resources, to fight the environmental pollution and put in the effort to have a city with clean air. Children during school years are best prepared for accepting and respecting the rules. It is in this phase where the effects of behavioral strategies should get neutralized. Thus the parents, teachers, and other professionals working with children are the most appropriate figures who can step in to prevent the reinforcement of murk heritages from getting passed on from the previous generation to the next ones and stop this intergenerational transfer.

Taking into account the definitions and examples brought up thus far both from the animal kingdom and human's life, we find out that the 1) Camouflage, 2) Rotation and Throw, 3) Replication, 4) Warning and Alarm, and 5) Group Defense strategies are all physiological reactions being used for the survival of the organism just like the fight, flight, freeze, faint, farce and fumble reactions. Nevertheless, these strategies do not have the potential to be transformed into a maladaptive coping style yet. However, they can be formed as a murk heritage during childhood years and play themselves out in adulthood. Here the physiological reactions of faint (Indolence Coping Style), farce (Mockery Coping Style), and fumble (Gaucherie Coping Style) had the potential to function as a maladaptive coping style for each one of the maladaptive schemas.

Final Words

Considering the popularity which the "schema mode model" has gained so far and its practicality not only in treating the patients with borderline and narcissistic personality disorders but also in addressing the difficulties of patients with other personality disorders, the new schema modes can also be examined among the patients with personality disorders. Clinical reports from the Iranian Institute of Schema Therapy (IIST) therapists who have attended recent research have indicated the presence and identification of the new schema modes. Furthermore, educating the patients about the new coping styles lead the patients to identify their behaviors based on each of these styles conveniently. Indeed, besides clinical work, there is a need for in-depth studies and researches regarding the three new coping styles and the nine introduced modes. This practical development can be applied not only to personality disorders but to a wide range of other disorders as well. Askari, Madgaonkar and Rowell (2011) have stated that anxiety patients reported more frequent use of worry and social control strategies, and less frequent use of punishment and re-appraisal. Patients with depression reported more frequent use of Punishment, re-appraisal and distraction and less frequent use of worry and social control. Further, all of the strategies were positively associated with MAD. In another research, Askari and Hakami (2012) have indicated that when it comes to couples, both the adaptive and maladaptive coping strategies for reducing anxiety can affect both partners. They shape each other's coping styles thus the overall quality of the relationship is affected by this issue.

CHAPTER THREE

THE INDOLENCE COPING STYLE

In this chapter:

- Indolence Coping Style Explained
- Behavioral Components in Detail (playing the martyr, playing the poor me, playing the victim)
- Cognitive Components in Indolence Coping Style
- Emotional Components in Indolence Coping Style
- The Hesitant Imagined Mode (HIM)
- The Distressed/Helpless Mode (DHM)
- The Moral Preacher Mode (MPM)
- Personality Disorders and The Coping Modes In Indolence Style

When it comes to this coping style, the individual tends to exhibit behaviors of the person who is drained, sick, tired, and has physical weaknesses during distressing situations. Therefore the person either fakes these states or plays the role of a poor, broke, and miserable person who is in need in order to make some gains and take advantage of the current circumstances. Also, the individual utilizing this coping style might act as being confused, dazed, or spaced-out while under lots of pressure. Therefore individuals might present themselves as weak, inept, and helpless in order to meet their emotional needs or gain some financial advantage or prevent the real or perceived threat. If indolence becomes the dominant coping style for most of the patient's schemas, playing the martyr or playing the victim would be the evidence signs in his behavior to the degree that others regard him as someone oppressed, inept, and irresponsible.

Nizami Ganjavi (1141-1209), a romantic epic poet in Persian literature, points out in his book of poems, Khamsah (Section 55 - Khosrow finding out about the Farhad's love) that all thoughts and solution-seeking are weak and immature while being in indolence coping style.

Cannot find a way to solve his problems *** The ideas of an ill man are ill-judged
Words are well fitted while being spoken in well being *** As, in indolence, all measures are weakening

Nizami Ganjavi also in another section of his book, Khamsah (section 58 - Farhad digging the mountain and mourning), stresses the point that indolence is a form of a person's nature (part of the individual's temperament or disposition) and the person who possess an indolent nature has no interest in facing and dealing with healthy individuals.

As there exists not a single moment where I am free of sorrow *** I shall not want anyone else happy in the world
O' heart! You know what the wise men said *** The ones who are at the depths of the minds ocean
The one who is in indolent nature *** Does not want well-being for anyone

Moreover, in other verses (section 82 - Nakisa singing on behalf of Shirin), Nizami Ganjavi points out the advantages and the benefits that people gain with this coping style by being indolent in order to get help from others. Even though sometimes individuals attain their goals in an unhealthy manner using the indolence coping style, they would face difficulties in the long run since indolence is a maladaptive coping style. This has been emphasized in the second verse of the following poem by Nizami Ganjavi:

Thought if I welcomed Indolence *** You would hold my hands in that hardship

Now that I have fallen being indolent and intoxicated *** You held my hands, yet you tied my legs

Suppose the patient constantly complains about being ill-treated and tyrannized or facing difficulties in day-to-day activities. In that case, the therapist is better off examining traces of indolence coping style in the coping responses the patient utilizes for her schemas. When it comes to this style, the individuals might easily meet some of their needs, but this takes place at the expense of one of their emotional needs going unmet. Thus during treatment sessions with these groups of patients, they usually complain about the need that has been frustrated, yet they will not bring up the gain or benefit they easily got or regard that gain as ordinary and insignificant. In the following sections, more in-depth definitions and examples regarding behavioral, cognitive, and emotional components of this coping style are brought up for further understanding.

Behavioral Components in Indolence

The patient tends to display signs of weakness, incompetence, and lack of proper performance in order to prevent her schemas from activating and providing herself with a safe zone. The behavior of "playing the martyr" for gaining lots of attention from others, "playing the poor me" as a means of justification for abusing others, and "playing the victim" in order to change others view of them to their own benefit takes place in this coping style. Examples below further illustrate these behavioral instances:

1. ***Playing The Martyr***: A patient with enmeshment/undeveloped-self after finally getting the parent's approval he is enmeshed with for his marriage steps forward and proposes. After the marriage, the patient would constantly complain about the abuses and mis-

treatments of his wife to his parent. The parent would, in return, accompany him in his complaints and caresses him. Usually, the parent is also upset about the bad luck and misfortune of the son in his marriage.

2. ***Playing The Poor Me***: A patient with vulnerability to harm and illness schema despite having sufficient funds for going on a trip and paying her share would present herself as lacking enough money and being so poor that her companion would step up for paying her shares of expenses. In justification of her behavior, she states: "You know, my friend, she is rich, and making her do these payments won't bother her at all!"

3. ***Playing The Victim***: A patient with unrelenting standards/hyper-criticalness does not have time for meeting his spouse's emotional and sexual needs due to spending long hours working and being constantly occupied with work issues. While faced with his spouse's complaints, he says:" I put all these efforts for you and the kids. So that you can live an easy life, it has nothing to do with my own personal success. I work hard and suffer so that you and the children are at ease!"

Studying the behavior of patients while being in indolence coping styles reveals that based on their schemas, they play the martyr; poor me, or the victim in order to gain excessive attention from others, abuse them or influence their views on different events. Even though there are other behaviors when it comes to this coping style, yet most of the patient's behaviors can be classified among these three groups.

Cognitive Components in Indolence

Choosing the position of weakness in order to gain some benefit is the most significant issue in cognitive components in indolence coping style. These benefits can take the form of gaining excessive attention from others, abusing others, and changing other views. Some patients have learned through their life experiences to get what they want by taking advantage of the indolence style. Therefore some therapists who are at the beginning stages of their professional work and have little experience might mistake the utilization of indolence coping style by the patient with the needs of the patient's vulnerable child mode. Thus, if the therapist fails to distinguish between the vulnerable child mode and indolence style clearly, he would unintentionally reinforce the incorporation of indolence coping style despite wanting to help the patient. For making a clear assessment, one can consider these points:

1. Schema therapy emphasizes caring for the patient's vulnerable child mode, attending to this mode above all others, and providing it with the love, warmth, and support which it needs. This also means that the therapist's amount of attention and love provides the patient's vulnerable child mode with should be balanced. In case the patient receives excessive attention from the therapist by constantly playing the martyr, the course of therapy might not progress successfully. This happens since, during most of the sessions, the patient learns to get excessive and overt attention from the therapist by playing the martyr (excessive crying, constant complaining, and extravagant moaning). In the indolence coping style, the patient learns to avoid taking responsibility for his life through playing the martyr. After long hours of therapy, the therapist finally

realizes that all the sessions have been dedicated to the patient's complaints while being in that role. This role takes up so much of the sessions that even when it comes to the opportunities in the patient's life where he has the chance to take another role in order to bring change into his own life, he refuses to take the most minor steps in that direction. Therefore while being in this style, the patient wants to have the therapist's full support of his vulnerable child yet does not want his healthy adult mode to develop and actualize. Playing the martyr can be mainly observed among the patients with emotional deprivation, abandonment/ instability, dependence/ incompetence, failure, enmeshment/ undeveloped-self, and defectiveness/ shame schemas.

2. The behavior of playing the poor me quickly unravels itself at the early stages of the therapy by bringing up financial issues and payments for the therapy sessions. In countries such as Iran, where insurance policies do not cover psychotherapy expenses, this behavior is observed more frequently. Some patients would pay for the beginning sessions of therapy in full, and as the therapy progresses and the therapeutic relationship is formed would play the poor me and ask for discounts by getting into the indolence coping style. In fact, some of these patients abuse the therapeutic relationship and the attachment being formed with the therapist despite doing well financially. Playing the poor me is usually observed in patients with vulnerability to harm and illness, failure, mistrust/ abuse, and even entitlement/ grandiosity schemas. Also, patients with unrelenting standards/ hyper-criticalness are usually willing to have their therapy sessions with the most famous and experienced therapists. It is only natural that the therapy sessions with these therapists would bear more expenses compared to the other therapists.

Therefore, the patient seeks therapy with famous and experienced therapists and, on the other hand, is not willing to pay in full for the sessions. Thus the patient bargains and claims doing very badly financially plays the poor me and gets into the indolence coping style.

3. Naturally, most humans are affected by other's physical and emotional sufferings. Indeed, therapists are no exception to this issue. However, the more experienced the therapist has become, the less she would get affected by her patient's behavior while playing the victim. For instance, while working with couples, some patients try to change the therapist's view of their spouses or their surrounding environment by playing the victim. While taking the role of someone who has been victimized by the other spouse, not only they hide the ongoing realities of their lives, but also they try their best to present themselves as vulnerable and the target of the cruelty of the other spouse by exaggerating the harms that have come their way by the other spouse. The utilization of the indolence coping style accompanied by behaviors of playing the victim takes place, intending to convince the therapist to get on board with bringing up changes in the behaviors of the other spouse. Therefore, given this situation, they attempt to put the therapist against the spouse. Indeed, the therapist's task in these situations would be to stand by the couple, not standing up to one of them in return for saving the other one.

Stephen Karpman (2014) divides the roles that people take into three general categories in his famous triangle. According to him, oppressor, victim, and rescuer are the roles individuals unconsciously get themselves involved with, thus putting themselves in a vicious cycle. A victim is a person who psychologically regards himself as a loser. He feels that he has lost in the relationship or the collaboration, thus plays the role of the victim. Therefore the role of the victim in Karpman's triangle is the person who, while being in the indolence coping style, plays the victim. Usually, the individuals with the self-sacrifice schema tend to take the role of the rescuer and step up to solve the problems of the ones who play the role of the victim. Since self-sacrifice as a conditional schema is overcompensation to several core schemas, the rescuer role is a cover for the person's own personality shortcomings. Therefore if the victim decides to put aside the indolence coping style, the rescuer might take the role of the oppressor. Individuals take the role of the victim (indolence coping style) since others are willing to take the role of the rescuer (self-sacrifice schema) and others who look forward to taking the role of the oppressor (overcompensation coping style - for instance, bully/attack and self-aggrandizer modes).

Emotional Components in Indolence

While being in the indolence coping style, the patient tries to make others understand her feelings. Thus she might turn to methods of exaggeration while talking about her problems so that others understand her unpleasant feelings better. If the therapist or others understand the unpleasant feelings of the patient, the severity of the negative emotions will decrease in the patient. Thus this style makes the patient exaggerate her unpleasant feelings most of the time. She wants others to be willing to listen to her complaints, troubles, sufferings, and moans all the time. Hence most of the time, she would start talking about her miseries and troubles while being bent, weepy, and wretched. She would do so as if there is no end to her problems and negative feelings. Eventually, others would regard her as someone who is constantly objecting and is never satisfied.

Even though there are some similarities between the signs

of the vulnerable child mode and the emotional components of the indolence coping style, yet they differ from each other in two main points. The first point is that the vulnerable child mode does not exaggerate the feelings being experienced and expresses what is really being felt. The second point is that the vulnerable child mode does not express negative emotions to benefit or get some gains out of the situation. Nevertheless, when it comes to the indolence coping style, the patient adheres to total exaggeration in expressing unpleasant feelings and negative emotions to an unnatural degree. Never forget that underneath most of the patient's helpless whining lies a motivation for gaining some benefit.

Clinical Case

Sina is 37 years old, teaches at a primary school, and was born in a village. After years of hard work and putting lots of effort into his career, he managed to purchase a small apartment in the southern parts of the capital city. Even though he was regarded as a successful, kind, and supportive teacher in his line of work and even had received several certificates of appreciation for the efforts, he had put in, yet he was always left disappointed when it came to romantic relationships in his life. Due to his emotional deprivation schema, Sina was usually attracted to cold people who were either unkind to him or showed no interest in him. He was highly interested in reading romantic novels and poems and had already read a great many of them. So it was part of his routine to leave some time for going to the nearby library every week and try to find a novel which he had not come across already. During these visits to the library, he met the young lady who worked there as a librarian, gradually got to know her, and after six months proposed to her. Tara was seven years younger than Sina and had lost her father in childhood due to the drug abuse problems. Tara was the only child and lived with her mother and grandmother. Even though her family was not doing well financially, since she was the only child who had lost her father, her mother and grandmother met her needs excessively, thus contributing to forming the entitlement schema in her. Therefore Tara had a dependent entitlement schema as one of her schemas.

Sina and Tara's engagement period was relatively short, and they soon were getting themselves ready for having their marriage ceremony. Their families also supported this decision of theirs. Sina was pleased about his marriage and was gradually getting himself accustomed to the idea that with Tara, he no longer is going to face another bitter romantic loss in his life ever again. He spent his days happy with these thoughts only two weeks prior to their marriage ceremony; Tara told him that she would only accept his marriage proposal if he is willing to officially transfer the ownership rights of his house into Tara's name. Sina's whole life working and savings financially summed up in a single asset: That small apartment in southern parts of Tehran. It was only natural that transferring the ownership of his house into his future wife's name was a very difficult thing for Sina to do, even though he had spent lovely days with Tara so far and was looking forward to spending more happy days with her in future.

When Tara was faced with Sina's resistance, she initially flipped into her distressed/helpless mode and, being about bursting into tears and with some degree of doubtfulness, told Sina: "You know, I grew up without having a father. I never had a supportive figure like a father in my life. I thought you were going to support me, but no! You are not supportive of me at all. If after we get married something happens to you and you are not going to be around, your family will come from the village, and they will throw me out of that house! Do you have any idea what will happen to me then? I will become an alone and homeless woman with no place to live in..."

Sina was utterly shocked about hearing what Tara had to

say. In the beginning, he tried to soothe her and told her how he loves her and that he will always do his best to look after her and provide her with the peace and welfare she is looking after. However, Sina's loving words were in vain and did not ring with Tara until she flipped into the moral preacher mode and told him: "Real men are the ones who sacrifice themselves for their wife and children. Unfortunately, I haven't come across one single real man all these years. Even though you are an honorable and hard-working man, you gotta know that a woman needs the full support of her husband." Tara continued her words by giving Sina examples of her university classmates who got married and how their husband has showered them with houses, villas, and high-end cars. She ended her words by advising Sina that it does not matter whom he decides to get married to; in the end, he should prove his love in action and not just by words.

Tara's advice made Sina deeply sad and broken-hearted. He felt that Tara had doubted his pure love for her. He was in his deep thoughts that he suddenly realized a voice in his head telling him:" Tara doesn't love you because you are not lovable. She wants to get married to you because of the house." This was the sound of his emotional deprivation schema that he was hearing. At that moment, Sina's vulnerable child mode got activated, and he burst into tears.

Sina got a couple of days off work, spent his days in his detached self-soother mode, and watched the titanic movie over and over again. He further got himself occupied with reading novels for long hours as well. Finally, he gave in, picked up the phone, called Tara, and helplessly told her: "I accept your request. Let us go to the office, and I will transfer the apartment into your name today." It was only to Sina's amazement when Tara told him while being in her hesitant imagined mode:" I don't want to make you do something you are not comfortable with! I know even if you do so, deep down, you disapprove of it. You know this makes me doubt our love. Maybe it was my mistakes that I thought you were different from other men, but I noticed no difference between you and others."

Sina did everything he knew to convince Tara to reconsider her decision, but Tara, who had an entitlement schema of the dependent type, had made her life's philosophy revolving around getting total support and care from others. She told Sina while being in her moral preacher mode:" I am sorry, People just don't value the chances coming their way, and they easily lose on them. I want a man in my life who is generous and brave so that I can be able to count on him. There are many unworthy and incapable men around me who look forward to marrying me, but the man I like is the one who is responsible and is able to take care of my family and me financially without wanting anything in return."

Sina became severely desperate and broken-hearted. He spent difficult days with his schemas and modes. This time, his abandonment schema was activated more severely compared to his others schemas due to being abandoned by Tara. His emotional deprivation schema was singing:" You are not lovable." His mistrust/abuse schema still emphasized: "Tara wants to take all that you have, just a single small apartment for herself." Among the schemas, the vulnerability to harm (poverty) strongly welcomed Tara's leaving Sina's life: "We are better off without her! We were about to lose our house and become homeless wandering the streets!"

Bearing those conditions was so difficult that Sina had to seek therapy despite his wish. During the first couple of sessions, the therapist attended to him and actively listened to what he had to say about his recent romantic relationship and those he experienced prior to that. The therapist empathized with him. During one of the sessions, he asked the therapist:" Was Tara really after my house? If so, then why didn't she didn't accept it when I was about to transfer the ownership into her name?" The therapist replied: "From what you have told me about Tara, I haven't recognized the conning/manipulative and predator modes in her. So she didn't want to rob you. It's probably your mistrust/abuse schema that has been triggered. The thing about Tara is that due to her dependent entitlement schema, she has used to present herself as weak and inept with her distressed/helpless mode since childhood in order to make others take the responsibilities in her life instead of herself. When at first you didn't give in to her unrealistic demand, she initially started to moan with her distressed/helpless protector mode and then nagged as much as she could. After a while, she presented the belief of her dependent entitlement schema, "Others should help me," with her moral preacher mode through giving you advice. By the time you finally came around and told her that you accepted that you made a mistake and you are willing to give her the apartment, Tara was in her hesitant imagined mode. She didn't even know what she wanted for herself and was confused between what she wanted and what she needed. She refused your offer of the apartment and ended the relationship."

Opening up a New Window

1. It is of utmost importance to distinguish between indolence coping style and Somatization as a defense mechanism. When it comes to Somatization, the patient is still worried about being sick despite the lack of medical symptoms. The patient tries to get reassurance by asking repetitive questions from the doctor. Therefore when it comes to Somatization, the patient does not find the tolerance needed for facing the psychological distress in himself. Thus, the body pays the price for it. On the other hand, when it comes to the indolence coping style, the person is faking physical pain and psychological difficulties most of the time (Factitious Disorder would be an example to this case). It is crucial to bear in mind that during the process of Somatization, the body becomes the patient's locus of attention so that the depression, loneliness, or marital

dissatisfaction stays outside of her awareness. However, on the other end, the patient tries to exaggerate her depression, loneliness, or marital dissatisfaction when being in the indolence coping style seeking some "gain."

2. The Horned Lizard is among the most equipped species when it comes to survival strategies since it has acquired different means for defending its survival throughout its evolutionary process. This lizard is capable of adjusting its color to its surrounding environment, thus camouflaging itself. Since it possesses a relatively fast pace for fleeing from the scene, its preferred strategy for most situations requiring a survival response is the "flight response." Nevertheless, in case of getting identified and caught by the predator, it tends to inflate itself, pretending to be bigger and stiffer than it really is so that the predator gives up on swallowing it. However, a mature snake would not easily get deceived by camouflaging, changing color, nor inflation. The most practical method for saving itself from the snake is the "faint response." With this method, the horned lizard inflates itself twice the size of its natural proportions; suddenly starts slowly getting overturned, open up its arms and legs, and displays its stomach to the snake. The gesture, which closely resembles an already dead animal, makes the snake lose its appetite and encourages it to leave the scene. What is interesting is that all of this takes place in front of the snake's eyes, and it is strange that the snake gets persuaded that the lizard is either dead or if alive; there must be something seriously wrong with it! Of course, it is worth mentioning that the horned lizard utilizes the "fight response" when faced with dogs, cats, and other animals except for birds. Squirting blood at the predator takes place with utmost ac-

curacy. It takes at least fifteen minutes for the predator to be ready to give a response after getting hit by the bloodstream since the volume, color, taste, and smell of the squirted blood are immensely horrible.

3. Immigration is among the most critical decisions that an individual makes in her lifetime. If the healthy adult is convinced that for her survival or personal/family growth and progress, it is wise to change her existing place of living, then she chooses to immigrate by making plans and providence in order to reach her set of goals. Of course, this all takes place by conforming to and following through with the set of rules set for immigration which varies by different countries. Even though some incidents such as a war breaking out might lead to mandatory immigration, yet during peace times, some individuals who have failed to gain and master any knowledge or skill and they even refuse to do so for future, tend to immigrate to countries that provide minimum support for them. They decide to immigrate to gain minimum support provided to them by the destination country. When they arrive at their destination country's migration agency, they present themselves as poor, socially harmed, politically tortured, or religiously or ethnically discriminated while being in the indolence coping style. Even though these unfortunate cases hold for a small group of applicants seeking asylum, these incidents have not taken place for most asylum seekers. Therefore, these majorities ask for minimum rights and privileges granted to them by the new country utilizing their indolence coping style. The utilization of this coping style has increased so much during recent years that the host countries have a tough time distinguishing between reality and indolence style. This has made the process of granting asylum difficult and slow. Since the indi-

viduals seeking asylum have no preference for returning to their home countries, they have lost the citizenship conditions of their own countries. Furthermore, it might take years before their asylum is granted to them or the new country refuses to take them in. Thus the individual might be in asylum-seeking conditions for years and live in refugee camps under difficult conditions. Therefore indolence coping style gradually pushes these individuals toward psychological difficulties such as depression or even committing suicide in refugee camps.

4. Passing out (faint) occurs when the brain is faced with the lowest blood supply levels. Under this condition, the patient initially starts to appear pale, loses consciousness, and subsequently falls on the ground. After one minute of lying down, the blood flow gets back to its normal conditions, and the person gains back consciousness. Thus, fainting in the medical sense has total physical symptoms and is different from the faint response in psychology. Some difficulties such as exhaustion, irregularities in the heart, hearing shocking, upsetting news, severe embarrassment, exposure to unpleasant scenes, and severe coughs can lead to a faint response in its physical sense.

The Hesitant Imagined Mode (HIM)

Emotional needs in childhood, especially the need for secure attachment (love, safety, attention, support, care, availability, stability, being accepted, etc.), the need for fun and spontaneity, and also the need for identity, competence, and autonomy to an extent, if not being appropriately met, might severely play themselves out through fantasizing at the beginning of adolescent and early youth years. Therefore if the child fails to meet his need for secure attachment from his parents in a healthy natural way, he seeks help from his imagination in order to get his needs met. This process of imagination is entirely natural and popular among the children who grow in orphanages. These children have many imaginary friends with whom they play and have fun and imaginary parents who buy them gifts, take them in their arms, and kiss them.

As we know, the power of imagination is of high significance and operates to an exceptional level since early childhood years. If this imagination gets utilized to meet the frustrated emotional needs, the individual has used the indolence coping style. The abandoned or deprived child, appearing as weary, groggy, and quiet being in the indolence coping style, sits in a corner imagining being hugged and cared for by the mother. The child meets his need for attachment with his imaginary mother (or a kind and supportive figure) and becomes too invested in meeting his need in the depths of his imagination as though it is taking place in reality. This fantasizing does not take place in "avoidance" of the unmet needs, yet it assists the individual in meeting them on a fantasy level.

Undoubtedly, meeting emotional needs in a healthy way is essential for humans to the degree that failure in meeting them pushes the individual to answer those needs in fantasy. This is entirely possible with the aid of the indolence coping style since coping styles, especially in childhood, try to protect the child from even more severe harm. Thus the proverb Speak of the angels, you hear the sound of their wings, can be functional for some time. This fantasizing takes place by the "hesitant imagined mode" with the aim of assistance in meeting the frustrated emotional needs. The person is under so much pressure in the vulnerable child mode that he seeks help from the indolence coping style and flips into the "hesitant imagined mode." This transformative flip takes off much of the pressure stemming from the frustrated emotional needs since the human brain is utilizing the imagination tool in order to get closer to reality.

There is no doubt that while being in a hesitant imagined mode, the individual is completely aware of her imagination and the process she is taking part in. This is due to the fact that while humans start to imagine a particular scene, the electronic signals in the brain take a completely opposite direction from the time that person is experiencing the scene in reality. In other words, while being engaged in imagination, the electronic signals move from the Parietal lobe towards the Occipital lobe, whereas while having a particular experience, in reality, the information flows from the Occipital lobe towards the Parietal lobe.

The function of hesitant imagined mode during childhood years bears a close resemblance to the imagery techniques. If the patient is carrying a memory with herself that is no longer helpful for her or is interfering with her day-to-day functioning, she can try to change that memory with the therapist's help by utilizing the rescripting imagery technique. When it comes to hesitant imagined mode, too, this time, the child attempts to bring about a change into meeting her emotional needs by using her deep imagination. The child strives to meet her emotional needs at all costs, even through imagination; otherwise, her survival might even be at stake. Thus the power of mind getting in action through the indolence coping style provides the child with the possibility of creating and receiving her desires through the hesitant imagined mode without having to do anything with the realities of the surrounding environment.

The hesitant imagined mode not only is not harmful to the child whose emotional needs is frustrated but also can prevent the child's psychological/emotional breakdown well through latent childhood years. The critical point to notice here is that in case the child starts to experience her needs being met adequately, the hesitant imagined mode will gradually wear off as the child comes out of the indolence coping style. Indeed, there stays the possibility of this mode's return if the emotional needs go unmet once again. Considering the fact that the brain (mind) continues with its function even during sleeping times, there is a possibility that the child visits and talks with her imaginary friend, animal, or thing. In case the child talks with others about her encounters with her imaginary friend, animal, or thing, this is an indicator of a deep connection between the child and that imaginary person or thing. Most individuals might get confused or worried upon hearing about this imaginary personality, but not only this phenomenon has nothing to be worried about, but also it bears a clear message for the child's caregivers on how to move forward with meeting their child's emotional needs.

In the movie "The Life Ahead" (2020), Sophia Loren stars as an old woman named Rosa. There is a young 12 years old orphan boy named Momo in the movie that tried to meet his financial needs through committing criminal acts (theft and selling drugs). We witness Momo in his hesitant imagined mode being cared for by and playing with a strong lioness during several scenes. Momo, who has no image of his mother, meets his need for secure attachment with the help of the beautiful, supportive, and kind lioness in his imaginations. As Momo's relationship with madam Rosa begins to take the shape of a secure attachment, the hesitant imagined mode weakens, and Momo no longer fantasizes about the lioness. Upon Madam Rosa passing away, we witness the presence of the lioness once more in Momo's imaginations.

The hesitant imagined mode does not help the adults the way it is helping the child with meeting emotional needs. In fact, the utilization of this mode in adults not only does not help them meet their emotional needs but also prevents them from meeting them. Furthermore, the more they utilize this mode, the further they get away from reaching the condition where their emotional needs are being met in reality. Like other coping modes, the hesitant imagined mode prevents the individuals from meeting their emotional needs as long as they stay in it.

Many adults who are stuck with "Limerence" might be in a hesitant imagined mode. The individual being in the hesitant imagined mode, finds himself in a constant mental struggle over entering a given romantic relationship or not. Since his emotional/sexual needs are not being met, the person fantasizes about the people who are in contact on a daily basis as well. In the following segment, four categories of romantic relationships in which the hesitant imagined mode is severely active are pointed out:

A. ***Having a fantasy love***: Having a relationship with a fantasy love results in the frustration of the emotional needs. Some individuals stay loyal to their fantasy love for years and regard having a relationship with someone in their real-life as a betrayal and having an affair. A patient with a hesitant imagined mode creates an imaginary loved one based on personality characteristics, appearances, and sexual orientations that she favors and adds more to it, eventually experiencing romantic, sexual, and leisure encounters and activities with the imagined figure. The patient might go on many trips with her imaginary lover, find the figure present during her academic and career success, and experience whatever she missed with a real person through fantasy love.

B. ***Having an unrequited love***: Having strong romantic feelings for someone without the other person being aware of them. This kind of love is entirely one-sided and exists only in the imaginations of the lover. There exists no objective actual romantic relationship between the lover and the loved one. This kind of love is usually called unrequited love, and it differs from the fantasy love in the fact that the beloved figure actually exists in reality. Even though in unrequited, the beloved might also consciously reject the admirer's affection, yet for the sake of clarity, this case will be examined in its own category, having a one-sided love (refer to item D). The patient might have been in contact with the loved one for an extended period, run up to her occasionally, talk with her and engage in some shared activities together, yet the loved one does not know the patient's feelings. In severe cases, the patient makes up different stories involving the loved one and sometimes believes in those stories as if they happened in real life.

C. ***Having consecutive loves***: Patient experiences constant mental/ emotional/ sexual struggles with the people with whom he is in contact on a daily basis. The patient interprets the slightest signs coming from others as indications of persistent shared feelings and emotions existing between them. He might consecutively and sequentially fall in love while being in this mode. Furthermore, the hesitant imagined mode in consecutive loves functions so that the patient can experience intense romantic feelings for several persons at the same time. He instantly falls in love with whomever he comes into contact with. Despite having romantic feelings for many, the patient does not form any relationship with any one of them in reality, and in case he decides to form a relationship with one of them, he still cherishes other loved ones in his mind.

D. ***Having a one-sided love***: Being stuck in a one-sided love where the loved one constantly rejects the troubled lover only goes on through the hesitant imagined mode. The loved one tries out every possible method to get rid of the lover, yet the patient being in the hesitant imagined mode, interprets every move of the lover as a sign of love and affection for herself. In a narrative by Jami (1414-1492), a Persian poet and writer of mystical Sufi literature, Majnoon, who is in love, dresses up as poor people and joins the crowd of the people in need

> who are after receiving charity food. When Majnoon's turn comes up, who steps forward, and Leyli (The one with whom Majnoon has a one-sided love) grabs his plate and breaks it into pieces by throwing it on the ground. Majnoon, only being in the hesitant imagined mode, can interpret this act of Leyli breaking his plate as a sign of her love for himself. Since being in this mode, Majnoon thinks Leyli has given him special attention. She gave food to everyone else, but when it was Majnoon's turn, not only did she not give him food, but also she broke his plate! If she had no feelings for me *** How come she broke my plate, this Leyli?

Some therapists might attempt to face the patient with reality as soon as possible, but hesitant imagined mode as one of the modes of the indolence coping style is taking care of the vulnerable child mode and will not accept the reality. The hesitant imagined mode constantly gives the message to the vulnerable child mode that you should not be worried or sad; your beloved will soon take you in. The hesitant imagined mode interprets every instance of beloved's "rejection" as opposite and as an indication of love for the vulnerable child mode. Even if the loved one goes on to get married to someone else, this coping mode would tell the vulnerable child:" Don't be upset! She doesn't like her husband, she belongs to you. Be sure, soon she will come to you". In fact, in this way, the hesitant imagined mode tries to take care of the vulnerable child and reduce the hurt feelings it is experiencing. Even Though this mode prevents the vulnerable child mode from a collapse for a period of time, yet it results in more frustrations in the long run. In the treatment process, as long as the lover thinks the loved one also loves him back or soon is going to take him in, we do not try to take the lover out of this mode. Sooner or later, as the healthy adult develops in the patient, the hesitant imagined mode gradually sets back, and the lover faces reality. It only suffices for the therapist to be next to the lover in the hesitant imagined mode as a good enough parent, listens to what he has to say, and expresses that he is aware of his need and understands his situation. If the patient receives the feelings of worthiness and being lovable from the therapist, his vulnerable child mode would gradually go to the therapist to meet its need for secure attachment instead of seeking help from the hesitant imagined mode.

Even though the hesitant imagined mode has been identified and observed abundantly among the individuals struggling with failed love stories, yet this mode has been reported in many other situations as well besides romantic relationships. As an example of this case, many patients have reported that their angry child mode rarely flips into the detached protector mode, but the anger they are experiencing decreases significantly by flipping into hesitant imagined mode. One patient stated:" As I disobeyed my boss's irrational orders, he started cursing me in front of everyone else! At that moment, I stared right into his eyes, remained silent, and was talking back to him, answering each one of his curses with the worst words I knew but only in my mind. As I left work while driving, watching tv, or doing whatever else, I was constantly reviewing the scene in my imaginations over and over again and tried to meet my needs in different ways. In my imaginations, I cursed him, yelled at him, and even hit him. Even Though this never takes place in reality, but I gotta tell you, I resolve most of my life's conflicts and arguments in my imaginations." It is interesting to note that this image is so powerful that after a while, even the patient himself believes that he has taught his boss a lesson.

What is important here is for the therapist to make a differential diagnosis between the hesitant imagined mode and Erotomania and visual hallucination. When it comes to Erotomania, the patient thinks that someone famous has fallen in love with her, yet in a hesitant imagined mode, it is the patient who is spending her days and nights with the fantasizes of her beloved. In contrast, this loved one is either incredibly inaccessible or unaware of the lover's feelings and has no interest in forming a romantic relationship with her. In the most severe cases of hesitant imagined mode, the beloved figure is entirely made up, and such a person does not exist in reality. Also, when it comes to hallucination, the patient experiences a smell of the loved one (olfactory hallucination), an image of him (visual hallucination), or the sound of the loved one (auditory hallucination), and is not aware of the full context of her conditions. However, these instances do not take place for the patient in hesitant imagined mode, and in case they hold true, the patient has total awareness of them existing only in her mind and not in reality. As an example, in the case of Lucy, a patient of Freud's who was displaying signs of olfactory hallucination, Freud attempted to review Lucy's past experiences and figured out that her olfactory hallucination has its roots in her past. Lucy had romantic feelings for someone in the past, and she had repressed those feelings.

The Distressed/Helpless Mode (DHM)

While in this mode, individuals tend to present themselves as more worried, afraid, in need, and helpless than they really are. They try to appear as someone poor, damaged, disheveled, struggling, and tied up by different means in order to gain others' pity and support. Most of these behaviors are being conducted to fulfill the wishes that are usually in contrast with the social rules and values.

Tina is a 28 years old master's degree student of Physical Education who is a member of her university Handball's team. Due to her insufficient self-control/self-discipline, she has difficulty adjusting her plans and routines to meet the demands in her daily life. Whenever she shows up late at her team's practice sessions, with a sad and anxious voice, she states:" I had an accident on the way here, I fell on the ground while climbing the stairs or my old mother was not feeling well, and I had to take her to the hospital." In order to convince her coach to let go of her and let herself off the hook, she used to present herself extremely worried. On the new year's holidays, while on her way to the airport, she got to the airport late as usual, but this time the gate was closed. At first, she tried to talk her way in, even by begging and attempting to persuade the airport staff to let her in. When her attempts were faced with the staff's resistance and their definite response: "We are sorry, but you arrived ten minutes late. The gate is closed, and all the passengers are already on the plane", she started to cry, threw herself on the ground and screamed so hard that she attracted the attention of a group of other staff and passengers, circling around her. This raised the pressure on the staff being in charge of that flight, and they had to open the gate, ultimately letting her in.

If we support a young lady who is on the ground crying in the face of the airport staff, we might gain "social approval." In case approval-seeking/recognition-seeking is among one of our schemas, this social approval can feed our schema, thus resulting in schema perpetuation. Furthermore, we can soothe the distress arising from our emotional deprivation schema by supporting Tina. On the other hand, while faced with someone who is upset and is in tears, our own vulnerable child mode might get activated, bringing tears into our own eyes. The activation of our vulnerable child mode puts us in distress; hence, to reduce this tension, we might attempt to provide aid with the issue or examine the situation with our obsessive-over controller mode. Therefore, the act of the crowd surrounding Tina can not easily be accounted as altruism which is one of the traits of the healthy adult mode.

Hormoz was a 77 years old single old man who used to spend most of his time at his small grocery store. Due to his entitlement/grandiosity schema, he had no interest in adhering to others' rights and respecting realistic limits. On some occasions, Hormoz intentionally tended to slightly bend his back, shake his hands and drag his right foot along while walking. This posture usually helped him escape the line while getting onto the bus, and by gaining the support of others, he never had to wait in the line. Also, while making a purchase at different shops, other customers would let him in front of the line so that he would be able to pay for his purchases to the cashier sooner than others. When it was the time for examining his tax payments, he used to dress up in an old suit and torn shoes, paying a visit to the revenue service organization appearing as a wretched and miserable shop owner who is on the verge of going bankrupt. He never paid his share of building charges, and the building manager had exempted him from the charges due to her unnecessary pitifulness. Hormoz always told the building manager that his business is at its worst, and sooner or later, he is going to be forced to close his shop. Even though the building manager was well aware that even during holidays, Hormoz's shop was open and running, yet she tried to get along with these behaviors of him.

No doubt, helping others increases the sense of self-worth in people. Also, in many cultures, helping and aiding the elderly is regarded as a value. Supporting the elderly or the people in need causes the individuals to feel good about themselves (an increase in their self-esteem). Therefore the most reinforcement for our constant help and looking out for the damaged people and the ones in need lies in finding a good feeling and satisfaction within ourselves. So as that being the case, helping others is inherently rewarding for us. However, unfortunately, some individuals like Hormoz tend to play the role of a poor, upset and distressed person with a distressed/helpless mode to activate the helping spirit in others and reach their own goals without paying for it either with their time, energy, or financial resources. On the other end, most people like the building manager tend to give in to Hormoze's behavior since they do not want to receive any messages from their guilt-inducing parent mode or are not looking forward to getting criticized by their own punitive parent mode. Individuals in indolence coping style have unconsciously experienced that while being in distressed/helpless mode, they can easily activate the self-sacrifice schema in others.

Since the feelings of guilt (guilty consciousness) are a severely painful emotion that can quickly get the person's life paralyzed, the three major religions of Judaism, Christianity and Islam have all suggested many ways to tackle this feeling of guilt throughout history. The diversity and the vast number of these suggested methods for relieving individuals from guilt feelings signify the importance of putting this feeling behind: giving away part of the assets and acquired wealth (paying Khums and Zakat), sacrificing animals (paying for keeping harm away), voluntary giving of alms or charity (paying Sadaqah), giving away wheat or rice (Zakat al-Fitr), Repentance (paying Al-Kaffarah) and confessing (giving away money for the sins to be forgiven). Despite all this, individuals tend to do anything in order to free themselves from the negative emotions stemming from the guilt-inducing parent mode and getting back to their happy child mode. Individuals with distressed/helpless mode exactly take advantage of these negative emotions of others stemming from their guilt-inducing parent mode to its fullest potential.

It is difficult for ordinary people to identify the utilization of indolence coping style in the behaviors of other individuals like Tina and Hormoz. Even when it comes to the therapists, conducting a differential diagnosis between the vulnerable child mode and distressed/helpless mode is a rather tricky task. There are two significant differences between the person who is really suffering and is in need of help and support (vulnerable child mode) and the person who plays the role of someone who is suffering and is in need (distressed/helpless mode). The first one is that the vulnerable child mode is sad and scared since his emotional needs are frustrated, whereas the distressed/helpless mode presents itself as someone who is in pain and not feeling well to meet her emotional, physiological, or financial needs easily. The second indicator is that by observing the sadness and fears emotions in the vulnerable child, we realize the purity, nobility, and realness of these emotions while the emotions in distressed/helpless mode are impure, fake, and false.

The distressed/helpless mode focuses on triggering the "social responsibility" behavior in others, which of course this behavior is part of the behavioral features of a healthy adult. You aim to provide aid for the ones who are really in need and are not able to pay you back with your healthy adult, yet the distressed/ helpless mode (who pretends to be in need) gets itself to you and plunders and receives parts of the resources you were giving away to help others with. After the 2012 earthquake in East Azerbaijan Province in Iran, many houses were damaged, and many people lost their homes. The Iran Red Crescent movement started to distribute tents among the damaged people. In the crowd seeking tents and other helping aids, a group of individuals presented themselves as miserable, wretched, and anguished with their distressed/helpless mode even though their houses were not damaged and were in perfect conditions for living. This group received the tents and other helping aids just like the rest of the crowd, yet they went on and sold them on the black market and made benefit from them (cunning/manipulative and predator modes). These were the tents given to them by the Red Crescent, and they received them while playing on Red Crescent staff's sympathy and whining.

The Moral Preacher Mode (MPM)

While in this mode, the individual tells others things that she herself does not believe in and does not follow through with them personally. When this mode gets activated, the patient starts to give advice to the other party or the ones around. The person actually tries to convince others by giving them advice while drawing from moralistic, humanistic, and religious issues. When it comes to conflicting interpersonal situations, the person in this mode starts swearing up and down instead of providing solutions or giving suggestions and expects others to trust in her swears. When the issue at hand remains unresolved, she gets frustrated and leaves the fate of others in the hands of god's judgment or the universe. If the patient gets stuck in a serious situation with no way out, being in this mode, she starts cursing and praying the worst things happening to the ones she holds responsible for her situation. She takes advantage of the situation by speaking about Karma, Dharma, and doomsday in her favor. The most critical issue regarding this mode is that the listeners and the ones to whom these bits of advice and preachers are directed rarely accept them since all of these literary statements are entirely meant to work in the preacher's favor. As the well-spoken Hafez puts it (Book of poems, Ghazal number 199):

The outward admonishers who, in the prayer - arch and the pulpit, grandeur of exhortation make *** When into their chamber they go, that work of another kind they make
A difficulty, I have. Ask the wise ones of the assembly, Those ordering penitence *** Why those ordering penitence, themselves penitence seldom make

Sometimes this mode gets activated in individuals upon hearing success stories of others and them making progress in life. In these situations, individuals in this mode state that those who have reached success owe it to following through with their advice. Thus it is a habit of them to give advice to others on issues regarding gaining success in their marital life, career, or academic area. The interesting issue to note here is that these individuals tend to give advice in the areas where they themselves have failed or have not done well. Of course, they do not preach from the point of view where others learn from the mistakes they have made, but they preach from the grounds of someone who is knowledgeable and has figured out the issue entirely for themselves. This mode makes others unwilling to have social interactions and encounters with the moral preachers, thus making it one of the modes that negatively affects interpersonal relationships, leaving the individual possessing it alone. Therefore, the social circle of the individuals who utilize this mode often consists of only those who are willing to listen to their advice, take them seriously, and follow through with them in their own lives.

A healthy adult does not see the need to give advice to others within herself. She keeps her advice to herself. The healthy adult does so since she is aware that advice given without being asked for is not practical and results in conflicting relationships. When someone asks for advice from a healthy adult, she would only give her personal remark if she has the necessary knowledge and information regarding the asked question; otherwise, the healthy adult would refer the question to someone who possesses the necessary expertise to answer that question. Advising others is an admired behavior in most religions, yet it has been stated there too the highly sensitive position of the person giving advice and that not everyone is suited to be in that position.

Usually, the parents who are anxious turn into the indolence coping style in order to reduce the distress stemming from their schemas, and they start preaching to their children in moral preacher mode. While being in indolence style, they state their own wants, which conflict with the wants of the child. They do so, taking the gesture that they want for their child what is best for them. As an example of this case, a mother with a mistrust/abuse schema feels in danger when she witnesses how her daughter has made many close friends. Thus getting into indolence coping style and while tries to display her distress in her face and behavior tells her daughter with her moral preacher mode: "You better socialize with good people not these inappropriate friends of yours, they are unworthy, your father and I tried really hard to raise you, we brought no money to this house but the money that was a direct result of our hard labor, every penny of it. That's why I'm telling you; these friends are not at our level. I have been through ups and downs of life, and I'm telling you, be careful, don't do something that would disgrace us and drag our name through the mud later..." Usually, these bits of advice, which have their roots in anxiety and are given while being in moral preacher mode, don't affect the listener much. As the great sheik, Saadi Shirazi (book of poems, Ghazals, Ghazal number 72) puts it:

It is difficult to keep your eyes from seeing the beautiful ones ***
Those who give us this advice it all goes in vain

Also, in the same book, he states:

Those being benevolent to me give me advice *** it goes in vain
just as putting adobe into the sea

Parents who constantly advise their children on different topics while being in moral preacher mode have a higher chance of dealing with their children being stubborn. Furthermore, the parents might bring up one of the child's peers as an example of someone to learn from or follow as a role model, but the child might feel that he has been unfavorably compared to someone else, thus resulting in him losing his self-confidence. Therefore individuals with moral preacher mode target others' self-concept and self-confidence and damage them with their words either intentionally or unintentionally. The person's self-concept contains all the understandings and feelings that the individual has for himself, and the moral preacher mode destroys it with its statements. As an example to illustrate this point further, we know the need for playfulness and spontaneity is among one of the core emotional needs. A person with unrelenting standards/hyper-criticalness might get into the moral preacher mode and start advising someone who is playing and having a good time. The person in moral preacher mode might refer to the ones having fun as bon vivant and pleasure-seeker. The label of pleasure-seeker in some cultures represents narcissism, irresponsibility, debauchery, and shamelessness. Albert Camus (1913 - 1960), the French philosopher in his book, the fall, states: "Then you'll see that true debauchery is liberating because it creates no obligations. In it you possess only yourself; hence it remains the favorite pastime of the great lovers of their own person." It is important to note that pleasure-seeking and having a good time can strengthen the happy child mode and make the person happy. In case pleasure-seeking gets the form of detached self-soother, then it has gone out of balance. Usually, individuals with unrelenting standards/hyper-criticalness, punitiveness, and negativity/pessimism even find it difficult to have fun and seek pleasure in a balanced way. Being in moral preacher mode, they start to refer to it as an unpleasant and unappealing thing to do. Hafez Shirazi, best known for composing poems of mystic content (in his book of Ghazals, Ghazal number 113), states:

O counsel utterer! Go, devise thy own remedy:
Loss to whom is it that wine and the sweet mistress gave.

While being in moral preacher mode, what is of utmost importance for the individual is his own needs, beliefs, and values, and he holds no regard for the other person's situation. Thus, even if being true, his sayings would not be as effective since they are not compatible with the conditions of the people they are directed at. Since moral preacher mode is part of the coping modes, it gets present with the activation of the schemas. Therefore it is of high importance for the therapists to uncover the underlying schemas for the moral preacher mode. If the therapist can help the patient discover the schema resulting in activation of this mode, the patient will gain awareness of her remarks while being in this mode. An example of this case is one of our female patients whose boyfriend has recently left her. Being in moral preacher mode, she tells the therapist: "He left me, but I'm not looking forward to him seeing the consequence of what he did to me from the universe. I want him to come back. Of course, he would only realize my worth by losing me. He thought he is so smart, but he doesn't know; it was just me being naive, not him being smart. Oh! I wish he knew what goes around comes around. You know what, good people get their hearts broken because of being too good with others. They are good with the ones who are not worthy of their kindness." The therapist emphatically explained that her boyfriend leaving her has severely triggered her abandonment/instability schema. Hence, being in an indolence coping style, she is saying these statements in her moral preacher mode to decrease her psychological pressure and separation anxiety. An experienced therapist is well aware that when a relationship ends, neither of the couples is the pure symbol of goodness and the other one complete badness and evil but knows that it was the schemas of the couples which caused them some troubles while initially made them attracted to each other and later throughout their shared life which ultimately resulted in their separation. Nevertheless, the moral preacher mode thinks of separation as the other partner being wrong, evil and ungrateful so that it can think of itself as good, thus soothing itself with the help of the indolence coping style.

Taking two points into consideration when it comes to making a distinction between "constructive recommendations" and "moral preacher's statements" is of importance. The first point is that "constructive recommendations" pay attention to the core emotional needs (such as the need for secure attachment) being met in their statements, and they give priority to them. In contrast, moral preacher mode does not pay any attention to meeting core emotional needs in its advice since it is an indolence maladaptive coping mode. As Saadi Shirazi puts it (Book of poems, Ghazals, Ghazal number 232):

Don't give me advice as love and piousness *** Are two features not going along with one and the other

The second point concerns the "frequency of the statements" being made. The advice of moral preacher mode gets repeated over and over again until the listener grows tired of hearing them. In the same source, Ghazal number 265 states:

To whom advising a lover one should state *** Go Khwaja! This pain has got no remedy

On the other hand, the "constructive recommendation" only

gets stated once by the healthy adult since stating it only once suffices to have an effective impact on its listener. This takes place since the recommendation in itself pays attention to meeting the emotional needs of its listener as a whole.

A patient with entitlement/grandiosity schema falsely considers himself as wiser and more knowledgeable compared to others. Hence when there is a problematic situation, he might not enter the conflict in just an overcompensation coping style like his bully/attack mode, yet he might get into a superior stance than overcompensation which is the indolence coping style, and start advising others in his moral preacher mode in order to resolve the issues at hand. Even though the patient might try to appear as a mystic and down-to-earth character (Since moral preacher mode is one of the modes of the indolence coping style), yet when examining the situation more thoroughly, he is positioning himself at a higher stance as someone giving advice. Therefore when narcissistic patience starts giving advice to another person, the person is experiencing nothing but unpleasant negative feelings. The reason for people showing resistance to taking these kinds of advice is the unpleasant negative feelings they experience while receiving them. Often this makes the receivers of these bits of advice prefer to move forward in the opposite direction even if they get hurt along the way rather than listening to the advice of a narcissist. When it comes to experiencing unpleasant negative feelings, too, most clients prefer having to deal with their sarcastic punitive parent mode's reproaches than hearing out the suggestions and recommendations of someone else's moral preacher mode. Same source, Ghazal number 341:

The stranger's advice is of no good for me *** As I prefer taking a slap on the neck from my own oppressor

Moral preacher mode annihilates healthy communications with others and results in the loss of effective relationships. The world we live in today has changed in many ways drastically compared to the past due to the advances made in science and technology. If being advised by the parents, teachers, and other elderly was of benefit for the previous generations, today with the rapid exchange of information and easy access to knowledge, the new generation is more oriented toward the self-learned approach to learning. Thus today, it is relatively rare to come across someone who displays a positive tendency to get advised by someone else.

Personality Disorders and the Modes of the Indolence, Mockery and Gaucherie Coping Styles

As we know, treating personality disorders comes with many complications. According to Arntz (2012), recent advancements in Schema Therapy in treating personality disorders have focused more on the modes model than the schema model. Thus this question is of utmost importance: Have we already identified all the modes within the context of personality disorders or not? Indeed, when it comes to treating personality disorders, a thorough and precise diagnosis of all the coping styles and modes is of great importance. If we were to accept that a personality disorder is a collection of psychological states of a patient that are behavioral methods rather than an illness, then we would be able to examine the new modes in the patients with a more thorough and precise approach. Therefore from the experience of working with disordered personality patients in clinical settings, the distinction of the rest of the new modes became apparent. Hence some of the modes which had not been identified in personality disorders previously are mentioned in the following table. Besides the table (3-1) below, table (4-1) examines the personality disorders and the modes of the Mockery coping style, and table (5-3) examines the personality disorders and the modes of the Gaucherie coping style in the following chapters of this book.

Right now, the mode's model in schema therapy makes the more complex and deeply rooted problems of the patients easier to understand and clearer for both the therapist and the patient. With the addition of the nine new modes to this model, the therapists can identify them as well while these modes are activated during treatment sessions. Thus this newly developed enhanced model has gained more efficacy when it comes to neutralizing the modes in the treatment process.

Personality Disorders and the Modes of the Indolence Coping Style

There is a close connection between personality disorders and the indolence coping style. The table below states the new modes which have been observed more frequently among the different personality disorders.

Table 3-1: Personality Disorders and the Modes of the Indolence Coping Style

Personality Disorders	**Modes of the Indolence Coping Style**	**The Expression of Emotions and Meeting the Needs in an Unhealthy Way**
Histrionic	Distressed/ Helpless	By presenting the self as poor and miserable, tries to gain other's "attention and love." Obvious exaggeration in agonizing the situations and poverty has been observed in order to get other's pity and compassion.
Narcissistic	Moral Preacher	By compassionately giving advice to others while taking the role of someone who knows everything meets

		the need for being "dominating and in control."
Avoidant	Distressed/ Helpless	When being in a group where perceived as not being welcomed or accepted, expresses concern about a close exam, backlogs, or an important meeting appointment, hence trying to conceal inner feelings.
Dependent	Distressed/ Helpless	While being alone or their primary caregiver being away for an extended period of time, asks help from others helplessly and being in tears due to "fear of not being able to take care of him/herself."
Schizoid	Hesitant Imagined	Due to being constantly occupied with individual activities and lack of intimate relationships, meets his/ her needs through "fantasies and hesitant thoughts." Forms strange attachment to pets and has deep conversations with them as if they really understand him/her. Also, there are fantasies of being intimate with unknown people or having imaginary friends.
Passive Aggressive	Distressed/ Helpless	Constantly complains about the behaviors of the one around and moans exaggeratedly about the difficulties and hardships of life in order to express "anger, disgust, and sadness."
Obsessive-Compulsive	Moral Preacher	In case this/her thinking principles and beliefs structure are crossed, lack "flexibility" and severely warns about "observance of values."
Antisocial	Moral Preacher	By bringing up moral and humanistic issues, changes the situation in "his/her favor" and "deceives" others with advice.
Borderline	A. Hesitant Imagined	A. By dreaming and fantasizing, tries to meet the "need for love and affec-

	B. Distressed/ Helpless	tion," which has been frustrated since childhood and remains unmet in adulthood. B. By the constant expression of being weak, lack of peace, worriedness and lack of assurance "neutralizes" others reactions to his/her abnormal behaviors.
Paranoid	Distressed/ Helpless	Presents him/herself as being dump and stupid so that the abusers get their chance to reveal their "true selves." Then goes on to identify them and collects evidence from their behaviors so that to be able to use the collected evidence against them when the right time comes.

Final Words

If patients were not to utilize the indolence coping style in the face of their schemas, what sort of people would they become? There is no doubt that this style's utilization sometimes helps people achieve their wants, but this style prevents individuals from achieving the actual heights of their goals based on their innate talents and capabilities. Most often, others tend to pity the person who is in the indolence coping style. This pity closely resembles giving away some money or something to a poor showing up on the street, constantly begging for help from people passing by. He sometimes gets a coin, and sometimes people pass him by indifferently. Maybe the reason for not liking the people who tend to be beggars lies in their obvious utilization of indolence style. It is relatively popular that we sometimes help the beggars we face in the city, but it rarely happens that we become friends with one of them and start paying visits to each other's houses every other day. In fact, as long as the utilization of the indolence coping style takes place, not that obvious, it is sort of acceptable for others, but when it takes place as evident as behavior like begging, it stirs up negative emotions such as fear, disgust, and even anger.

It has been observed in many charity organizations and communities where a healthy and mature individual is receiving different kinds of support for continuous years. She would never try to make a change in her life since she only needs to present herself as a poor and miserable being in the indolence coping style. While helping the poor is an important humanistic behavior, yet for the person who possesses suitable age, physical and psychological conditions being in indolence style pretending to be miserable, giving support only perpetuates this mode in them. The more the individual is able to distance himself from receiving social and even family support and move toward "self-support," the more developed healthy adult he poses.

Two issues are to be considered when it comes to committing suicide and its connection with the indolence coping style. First) When not, consider someone who has successfully committed suicide as being in the indolence coping style. Secondly) The case of a person who had Para-suicide (hurting oneself without the main intention being suicide) being in the indolence coping style should be examined more thoroughly. Even though most therapists find it difficult to be in contact with someone who has committed suicide, yet in case the therapist fails to form an appropriate connection with the patient, the chances of committing suicide once more increase. As an example, a patient with a severe emotional deprivation schema believes she is not lovable and, in the end, commits suicide to this belief of hers. In case during the therapy sessions, the therapist does not show much of an interest in her and seeks to finish the session earlier than usual, creates a great deal of anger in the patient, which this anger might get directed toward the patient increasing the possibility of committing suicide once again. Here just the same as the issue of beggary, the main issue is the obvious utilization of indolence coping style in individuals who have committed suicide. When an individual commits suicide, her parents, spouse, children, friends, colleagues, and even her therapist can no longer count on her as they used to do so. This holds since a suicide attempt is the last and final level of using the indolence coping style. On the emotional level, the individual is directing the hostility he feels towards others back at himself by committing suicide. The ones around also realize this hostility and blame him, thus losing their interest in him. However, what happens in the indolence coping style is that the individual tries to make others pay attention to his wants and achieve them by committing suicide.

By reviewing a case example, we reach the final section of this chapter. A 33 years old woman whose husband had left her attempted suicide by taking a considerable amount of Arplrozolam, which fortunately survived the incident with the aid of quick medical interventions. At the therapy session, she stated: "I no longer have any intentions for committing suicide again. I'm sure if I change my behavior just a little bit, my husband will come back to me for sure (hesitant imagined mode)." This all happened as her husband directly and assertively had told the therapist that even if there was a one percent chance of him returning to her, with the suicide she committed, he is never going to get back with her (lack of interest in the person who has done the final extent of indolence coping style). During another therapy session where both of them were present, the husband started to give her advice regarding her committed suicide in his moral preacher mode. The wife flipped into her distressed/helpless mode and presented herself as someone incapable of continuing her life and desperate toward the future without her husband being by her side. Since indolence coping style functions very cleverly, on some occasions but not always, individuals are forced to interact with each other only based on the modes of this mode, just like what we observed taking place between this couple.

CHAPTER FOUR

THE MOCKERY COPING STYLE

In this chapter:

- Mockery Coping Style Explained
- Behavioral Components (Leveling, Vulgarism and Legend Insulting)
- Cognitive Components in Mockery Coping Style
- Emotional Components in Mockery Coping Style
- The Automatic Laughter Mode (ALM)
- The Self-Mockery Mode (SMM)
- The Others-Mockery Mode (OMM)
- Personality Disorders and the Coping Modes in Mockery Style

When it comes to this coping style, the individual tends to play the clown, appear bantering, and play the fool in different situations. Furthermore, when the individual finds herself in emotionally difficult situations, she wears a smile, tells jokes, prefers to pick a topic to make fun of, and starts to fool around. In the mockery coping style, the individual has mastered making faces and imitating the voice and manners of others. She has mastered these skills so that she does not have to face her sadness, shortcomings, and fears. In case mockery has become a dominant coping style to most of the individual's schemas, talkativeness, exaggeration, and foul-mouthedness would be evident signs in his behavior to the degree that others regard him as frivolous, lame, and light-minded. These groups of people eventually master making fun of others. In the mockery coping style, the three modes of automatic laughter, self-mockery, and others-mockery operate in a maladaptive way. The operation of these modes is sometimes intentional but most often takes place outside of the individual's awareness.

Many philosophers and poets have emphasized the importance of incorporating the mockery coping style in Persian poetry since centuries ago. Thus, the historical roots of this behavioral response can be observed among Iranians, especially when it comes to social interactions. For instance, Ubayd Zakani (Persian poet & satirist 1300-1371) has emphasized the usage of mockery coping style many times in some of his poems. He states that the incorporation of this style brings ease, comfort, and success.

Make your career mockery and learn about minstrelsy *** If you seek your fate to be golden auspicious
If you seek all your prosperous Eids to become Nowruz *** If you seek your fortune to become night-illuminating
If you seek gifts and blessing coming your way every day *** Make your career mockery and learn about minstrelsy

Khwaju Kermani (Persian poet 1280-1352), also in his work (Ghazals, Ghazal number 894), describes the incorporation of mockery coping style as a practical yet unrecognized way of getting one's right from the youngsters and elderly in the society.

Despite all this, out of kindness, I shall share this point with you *** Even though I know, of this way you don't know
Make your career mockery and learn about minstrelsy *** If you seek to get you right from the insignificant ones and the mighty

Despite this, the main verse in the verses, as mentioned earlier, make your career mockery and learn about minstrelsy, most probably belongs to Anvari (Persian poet 1126-1189) wherein his book of poems (Book of poems, number 476 - In preaching) he states that he believes if people go after gaining knowledge, they have to struggle for earning their pension and rights every day. Thus, he proposes that they should go after getting their rights with the mockery coping style.

O Sir! Don't put all that you have in gaining knowledge *** If you do so, pension is what you have to run after every day
Make your career mockery and learn about minstrelsy *** If you seek to get you right from the insignificant ones and the mighty

The individual incorporates the mockery coping style when her schemas are triggered in order to alleviate and reduce the pain of the negative emotions. This mode can increase the tolerance for frustration and harshness in the given unpleasant situation to a great degree. Thus mockery might gradually become the maladaptive coping style for some of the schemas.
It is of great importance to distinguish between mockery coping style (farce) and humor. Here consider mockery as a maladaptive coping style where it displays itself in the patient's interactions with his partner, boss, friends, family, and even therapist. On the other hand, humor is a healthy trait of personality. Sometimes people might intentionally use exaggeration, irony, similar words but with differences in their meaning, grammatical inversion, and telling jokes during teaching, consulting, making love, or while being at parties in order to be entertaining. Therefore, humor helps bring out the happy child mode in the self and the ones around, while mockery coping style is an unconscious attempt to deal with the tense and conflicting situations.

While being in happy child mode, the person breaks the ice and makes others laugh by bringing up funny topics. She is sensible and sometimes makes up joyful jokes and stories with the help of her innate charm. She can also reduce the tension of a given situation by telling others funny things and entertaining the people around by playing entertaining intellectual games with them. A humorous person tells the stories of daily routine life in a funny way. Most of the time, she can positively affect the ones around her using her sense of humor.
Humorous people never put themselves in a position where they are only accounted as a means of entertainment for others. On the other hand, the people who use mockery coping style for

some of their schemas make fun of everything themselves and give others the chance to make fun of them. Humorous people are satisfied with this skill of theirs while people in mockery coping style do not feel well about their behavior and the ones of others and mostly complain about them.

Behavioral Components in Mockery

The mockery coping style based on the psychological-social functions, roles, and games consists of the reward and pleasure system elements in its structure. In other words, when the individual's schemas are triggered, he tries to make himself and others laugh with the use of the mockery coping style. These shared group waves of laughter are enjoyable for a while, thus reinforcing the usage of this style in the person. Therefore the transfer of pleasure takes place in the path of interpersonal relationships in a pervasive manner. This mode is a temporary and frustrating attempt to cover the triggered schemas. The individual tries as hard as he can to avoid the difficulties he is facing seriously or avoid dealing with those problems head-on. Thus the person consciously breaks sexual taboos, brings up topics involving genitals and different functions of the digestive system, makes fun of religious taboos, and sarcastically puts down social/political figures when his schemas are triggered instead of examining his thoughts.

As an example of this point, a man went grocery shopping when he was faced with the high price tag assigned for the cucumbers. Inside, he felt angry but being in the mockery coping style; he compared the size of the cucumbers to the genitals of small boys. This analogy caused himself, the shop owner, and other customers to laugh, and further, it might have temporarily helped with reducing the levels of anger he was experiencing, but ultimately it was of no use in making his basket full! Even though the man did not find the quality and the price of the cucumbers as reasonable, yet since he could not think of a solution to his problem and also not making the purchase only would have brought him disappointment, he chose to make himself and others laugh by the comments that he gave in his mockery coping style.

Leveling: Leveling is one of the Behavioral processes in the mockery coping style. Reviewing school years, many studious students used to get ridiculed by the majority who had no interest in studying. Since usually, the top students have the attention and praise of the teachers and other school's staff, other students tend to cause them pain by making fun of their appearances (for example, for wearing glasses) or assigning them ridiculing labels (such as geeky). In fact, other students attempt to level themselves with the top student and will not allow her to move up from their position much further. In the leveling process, the more attention and praise the top student receives from the teachers, the more suffering is going to be caused for her by her classmates. The same leveling process takes place for the obedient students by the majority of the students who tend not to follow the rules. The disobedient majority try to make the obedient student join their circle and prevent much difference from taking place regarding their positions by making fun of the obedient student.

Vulgarism: Vulgarism is another behavioral process in mockery coping style. Let us go back once more to the old school years. Many students were required to memorize different anthems and perform them in different ceremonies despite their contempt. This forceful act, accompanied by the student's contempt, made the students change some of the original words or the rhymes or add or omit some of the verses while being in the mockery coping style. Therefore these acts of students helped them relieve some of the pressure they were experiencing at those moments. They usually substituted original words with vulgar ones, and the more obscene the poems became, the more joy they used to take from it. The students learned that instead of making statements about forceful school activities, they would deal with those issues using the mockery coping style spiced up with a little bit of mocking creativity.

Legend Insulting: This behavioral process is rather way more complex compared to leveling and vulgarism. Up until now, it seems like legend insulting is the last behavioral process in the mockery coping style. It is important to note that more processes might be added to the current ones in the future. The essence of legend insulting lies in protest. In school, the opposing students try to break the solid and mighty picture of the teacher or the school principal by drawing funny pictures of them on the board in an attempt to make their voice of opposition being heard. On the social level, too, most of the jokes, caricatures, and humiliating stories are being made around the legends people believe are the primary source of their current difficulties. Therefore, they attempt to decrease the charisma of famous people while being in the mockery coping style to make the voice of their opposition being heard.

Cognitive components in Mockery

In this mode, an apparent easy passage of the stressful situations takes place by not giving serious attention to the critical issues. The mockery coping style forms the connecting axis between the painful reality and absolute farce. Since stressful situations take an important portion of our daily lives, mockery coping style ridicules the source of these events every appropriate chance it gets. The majority of the mockery coping style's usage takes place in stressful interpersonal situations among the couples. One of our clients reported: "In ten years of our marriage, whenever I brought up a serious issue to discuss it with my husband, he threw us off the topic by starting to be funny and fooling around, thus leaving that discussion with no certain conclusions." Another client also stated: "I have got this friend who is always fooling around and is making fun of everyone around. I haven't seen him once being serious in all the years I have been friends with him."

The mockery coping style also plays itself out in stressful social/political contexts. Usually, this style can be observed after certain events in the society, widespread incidents, or passing local/worldwide instances. For instance, Donald Trump, former United States of America's president, imposed strict sanctions on Iran during his presidency, which severely affected the livelihood of the Iranians and caused them serious economic difficulties. After Trump's loss in 2020's US elections, a series of jokes, manipulated images, comic videos, and short animations were created and published that constituted a collection meant to make fun of Trump. The mockery coping style adds a chain of items to the original set of material created during the stressful social/political situations, which go on for a long time after the initial incident has taken place. This goes on so long that after a while, only certain people who have been following these chains of created materials would only understand the meaning of the newly created ones.

When it comes to the couple's relationships, the dissatisfaction resulting from the incompatibility of needs and wants gradually gives a sense of frustration to the partners. These inconsistencies slowly increase, thereby making sense of frustration reaching its highest possible level. This sense of frustration resulting from the existing dissatisfaction in the relationships motivates the partners to take any action to change the given situation and try to meet their frustrated emotional needs. Nevertheless, when on the one hand, the objective conditions of the existing situation do not make any room for making improvements and taking constructive and regulatory actions. On the other hand, the couple finds themselves incapable of bringing any changes to their situation; there is a chance that an incorporation of the mockery coping style will take place.

Emotional Components in Mockery

While taking the emotional aspect of mockery coping style into account, this style results in a state where the person prefers to experience pseudo-pleasant feelings in favor of experiencing unpleasant feelings. Therefore in this style, the previous unpleasant feelings are replaced by pseudo-pleasant ones. As an example, we might have all experienced this where we have brought up a topic in the presence of someone else, and that topic had made the other person either angry or sad. In this situation, we might have experienced an unpleasant feeling in ourselves for making the other person angry or sad. Given this context, there is a possibility that we might want to use the mockery coping style in order to make both ourselves and the other person feel better. In this situation, we might opt for saying or doing something to make the other person laugh in order to change the current unpleasant atmosphere governing the relationship. This sometimes works, and if so (the reward and pleasure system), we have got the reinforcement for repeating the same behavior in similar situations in the future. Of course, it is important to note that on many occasions, the intensity of the negative feelings is so severe that our utilization of mockery coping style does not work out, and it only leaves us with the other person getting more upset or growing angrier.

Additionally, the opposite of this holds as well. As an example, consider a teacher who is growing frustrated and is experiencing unpleasant feelings because of the repeated or irrelevant questions of one of his students. He might make himself and other students laugh by giving a sarcastic remark to the student while being in the mockery coping style. Therefore in this instance, the teacher has used the mockery coping style to change unpleasant feelings (anger and frustration from repeated questions) Into pseudo-pleasant feelings (the relief from silencing the student). The student feels embarrassed in the presence of his peers, and he is quiet and upset. Precisely, this is what has caused the pseudo-pleasant feeling in the teacher. During this process, the teacher is not really feeling happy, he is keeping an eye on the student, but the fact that he has made the student back off by making him feel embarrassed gives him a sense of pseudo-pleasant feeling.

Opening up a New Window

The 1st Case: Laughter and Health

"Laughter is the best medicine" is one of the famous proverbs in Persian literature and is highly popular among Iranians. This proverb indicates the importance of living happily and laughing openly in this culture. Therefore, laughter not only results in happiness but brings well-being with itself as well. One of the engaging activities that have grown popular worldwide during recent years is laughter yoga and laughter therapy. Madan Kataria, the famous Indian physician who lives in Mumbai, opened the first center for laughter yoga in 1995 in that city, and soon many other centers started to appear in India and other places in the world. There is no doubt that lots of researches have been done into this activity, and the high effectiveness of laughter yoga on happiness and well-being has been proven.

One of the exciting researches conducted by the researchers in the University of Mannheim in Germany was done on "artificial laughter." During this research, the participants had no idea about the true intentions of the researchers, and they were told they are going to be researched about the difficulty of carrying out tasks without the use of "hands." The three groups of participants were required to hold a "pencil" with their mouth in one of the two following ways. The first group was told to hold the pencil with their lips which made them frown and their face look rather upset without them wanting to seem so. The second group had to hold the pencil with their teeth which made their face appear happy, again without them having the intention to appear as so. The third group members, the control group, were required to hold the pencil with their non-dominant hands. All three groups were required to fill in the questionnaire and rate the difficulty of the task they carried out afterward. The final task of the participants (which was the main objective of this research) was to rate the "degree of funniness" of a short cartoon while they were holding the pencil with their mouth or teeth, and their faces were unwillingly appearing as upset or happy. The research results indicated that the group members who had to hold the pencil with their teeth (the happy group) found the cartoon way funnier and amusing. They had no clue of the primary intention of this research. These findings indicate that artificial laughter can cause happiness. Furthermore, facial expressions can significantly affect our mood and feelings even with no intention behind them.

The 2nd Case: Jokes and the Right Hemisphere of the Brain

Neurologist scientists Shammi and Stuss (1999) believe that the brain's right hemisphere plays a critical role in understanding and comprehension of jokes. If the right hemisphere of the brain gets damaged, the person loses the ability to process a funny joke to a great extent. Jokes contain inconsistencies between different phenomena. On the other hand, the left hemisphere is more serious than that to approve of the surprise which stems from a joke or to get along with inconsistencies in a given phenomenon quickly. Furthermore, the left hemisphere has to get help from the right hemisphere while processing metaphors and non-verbal states. Therefore if the right hemisphere gets damaged, the brain faces severe difficulties in comprehending jokes.

Nevertheless, many people are incapable of a correct comprehension of inconsistencies in a given phenomenon, leading to making jokes and laughter without their right hemisphere having gone through any severe damages. If you tell them a joke, they cannot put together the phenomena and understand your humor. Thus they might ask you to expand further and elaborate upon your point. When you describe the elements of your joke to them, they smile and shake their head in order to convey their understanding of your point. This case might take place many times between you and the other person to the degree that you lose your interest in telling jokes to that person in the future, and sometimes you might even mistakenly doubt the other person's Intelligence quotient levels.

The 3rd Case: Laughing Animals

Aristotle believed that the main feature which distinguishes humans from animals is laughter. On the contrary, today, we know that chimpanzees and even other species such as mice express forms of laughter. For example, chimpanzees start to pant when they laugh, and mice make a rhythmic screaming sound from themselves. Dogs also sometimes panther in a way that closely resembles human's laughter. In an experiment, their laughter-like panting sound was recorded and played back to 120 other dogs. The dogs which heard the playback exhibited activation in their social behaviors, got ready for playing, their stress levels decreased, and their tail wagging increased (Simonet and colleagues, 2005). Also, a group of scientists studying dolphins in Sweden accidentally came across a group of specific sounds (resembling whistles) that they had not heard of before.

Further examinations revealed that these sounds are generated while the dolphins engage in play-fight. These sounds were never heard during real attacking clashes. According to scientists, these sounds are equivalent to the laughter in humans and are being made by dolphins in pleasurable and enjoying situations (Blomqvist and colleagues, 2004).

The 4th Case: The Difference between Humor as a Defense Mechanism and Mockery Coping Style

In psychoanalysis, humor, just like sublimation and altruism, is accounted as an adaptive mature defense mechanism (Gorge E. Vaillant, 1992). Erikson (1963) has stated regarding humor: "I can't imagine a wise old man who is not capable of laughing. The world is full of funny and ridiculous paradoxes." Erikson defines *humor* as the following: The ability in the person to play with the traditions of life and strange habits and their fearless examination, which occurs in rare instances leading to an increase in the individual's awareness of himself. Freud believed that humor's defense mechanism activates by incorporating two other defense mechanisms of condensation and displacement. When we save our energy with respect to our thoughts and speech, we use less amount of "psychological energy" and save up more of it. This is when condensation has taken place. Subsequently, displacement takes the saved-up psychological energy which has its roots in conflicts and turns it into a humorous story. During these two processes, the individual turns conflicts into humor to deal with them more conveniently.

In contrast, the mockery coping style is a temporary solution for reducing the emotional pain resulting from schema activation and furthers a minimum access to emotional needs being met. Just as Webster (2003) states: "Just as not every experience adds to wisdom, not every kind of humor is wise. Sarcastic remarks, messing with others and bugging them are not placed in the area of wisdom." Therefore, taking into account Webster's idea, which does not regard making sarcastic remarks, messing with others, and bugging them as stemming from humor, we can categorize them as behaviors belonging to the others-mockery mode.

Freud, in an article regarding humor (1927), stated: Joking is the verbal and interpersonal form of the humor defense mechanism. The joke is being told when we are about to speak about the matters which speaking about them have been prohibited by society. Under these circumstances, the Superego permits the Ego to move forward with telling the joke. This way, the anxiety which Ego is expressing would decrease. An easy-going Superego would permit us to express a mild and accessible form of a joke, yet a strict Superego forms in us a sort of sarcasm and diatribe. Also, a very strict Superego would hinder the utilization of jokes of any sort.

According to Freud, humor has a useful function when we can, through its utilization, take the unbearable repressed issues which we are not aware of and move them in a tolerable fashion from the unconscious to the conscious part. Furthermore, humor has a harmful function when it takes the form of mockery or diatribe and takes the individual's "self" as its direct focus of attention. What Freud has introduced as harmful functions of humor are instances we observe in the modes of the mockery coping style (self-mockery and others-mockery modes). Furthermore, there is a slimline between humor and diatribe. Humor is considered a "useful joke" when being carried out; we do not want to turn into our already upset audience and say: "I am sorry, I was just joking!"

On the other hand, it is a reality that some individuals would even perceive humorous remarks as a diatribe. For instance, individuals with defectiveness/shame schema might personalize any form of humor and perceive it as an insult to themselves. Additionally, individuals with entitlement/grandiosity schema most often cannot take a joke, yet they easily allow themselves to make sarcastic remarks to others and make fun of them. Narcissistic individuals laugh at other's misery and harm them by mocking them. Even though the narcissistic individuals' sarcastic remarks appear as attractive to themselves, not only do they upset the ones around them, but they also push them further away. Individuals with punitiveness schema, too, respond to others' sense of humor with a very bitter diatribe on some occasions. They do so since they, due to this schema, strictly adhere to moralistic values; thus, they consider any humor as inappropriate and categorize it as a frivolous and shallow act that requires verbal punishment in order not to be repeated in the future. Misinterpretation of humor takes place significantly concerning dependence/incompetence, vulnerability to harm/illness, and enmeshment/undeveloped-self schemas. When individuals with these schemas discuss their thoughts, choices or tell others about the events which had occurred to them, their audience might mistakenly believe that they are bringing these issues up as a way of telling jokes. The more severe the schemas are in these instances, the more misinterpretation would occur. Therapists, too, should take this into account while talking with these patients that even though many of the realities of their lives sound like a "painful comedy," yet the patient is not stating them as a way for telling jokes by any means.

The difference between healthy humor (happy child mode/healthy adult mode) and mockery can be observed in their consequences. Healthy humor strengthens human relationships, decreases stress levels, boosts the individual's morale, and helps with a better understanding of challenging concepts. On the other hand, the joke coming from the mockery coping style results in tension, interpersonal problems, division, arguments, annoyance, and putting distance between individuals.

Even though humor is a trait of intelligent and creative people, schemas sometimes blind creativity; for example, patients with unrelenting standards heavily emphasize the importance of "being serious." Some managers believe that mixing up work with jokes would make the situation get out of their hands and further result in some personnel not taking the rules seriously. A manager with a mistrust/abuse schema would also avoid making jokes with employees since she worries that this would eventually bring her closer to her employees, making her more accessible to their potential abuses. Therefore she is terrified of making jokes and does her best to prevent it from happening by anyone in the workplace.

The 5th Case: The Samurai Culture

Cultural elements play a significant role in the individual's incorporation of mockery coping style. For example, the Japanese Samurais, whose doctrines still live to influence the day-to-day culture and lives of the Japanese people, never "surrender" to the enemy, never "escape" from the battleground, never "farce" and keep their equanimity and politeness in all situations. The Japanese Samurais strive to avoid "fumble" at all times by displaying honest, honorable, and grateful behaviors. Even when in captivity, they do not show signs of "indolence" (weakness and victim playing). What makes a noble military man and a martial baron from a Samurai is in his courage in engaging in a direct "fight." Therefore we observe the peak of his martial behavior after a defeat and failure. With Harakiri (honorable suicide with consent), he states that he is not to use any other styles and coping modes except for fighting and overcoming the enemy. The Samurai's life sums up in death, but he rejects the dishonor of using other styles and coping modes.

Clinical Case

During a weekend party, Eli and Sam, who had just engaged for six months, were having a conversation with their friends after the dinner they had together. When Eli left the group to use the bathroom, while passing through the hallway, she was faced with the husband of one of her friends, who was very drunk at that moment. He reached for Eli's breast and squeezed it. Eli's fiance witnessed this incident which was followed by Eli bursting into laughter. She was laughing so hard that everyone was staring at her with amazement. When Eli finally got to the bathroom, she fell on the floor and still laughed. This behavior of Eli's was so upsetting for Sam that when she came back from the bathroom, Sam had already left the party. As stated before, when in the mockery coping style, the individual sometimes tends to respond to the other's sarcastic remarks, painful behaviors or statements, strictness, being made fun of, and even sexual harassments with exaggeration and clownish behavior.

During a therapy session, Eli stated: "I just couldn't stop my laughter. I have no idea where this laughter came from! Even when I tell others the story of that night, I start to laugh even though I am deeply sad about that night and feel great anger towards my friend's husband for that incident." When Eli was informed about her reactions related to her coping mode, she stated: "I'm generally a clown since I farce in every situation I find myself in. I had no idea this coping style comes from my schemas, but I always knew there was something strange about this behavior, and I wasn't fond of it." What Sam had to say about the incident of that night was as follows: "When that incident happened, I was expecting Eli to respond to that drunk buster who just violated her with a strong slap in the face. But Eli's laughter made me think either something was going on between those two in the past, or Eli just liked what that man did to her." Therefore Sam's mistrust/abuse schema was triggered due to Eli's maladaptive reaction. Eli's reactions coming from mockery coping style in that situation as she was laughing her way to the bathroom could have taken the form of any of the other coping styles. For example, Eli could have:

- Slapped her friend's husband heavily in the face and made him understand his wrongdoing (overcompensation)
- Immediately grabbed her things and left the party (avoidance)
- Froze at her place and stared at that man (surrender)
- Said: "oh my god!" and then losing her balance and feeling on the ground (indolence)
- Made a fuss out of the situation and shout and scream so

much that the party got ended prematurely (gaucherie)

When Eli was asked what consequences mockery coping style can bear with itself, she stated: "Others are not able to understand my true feelings. For example, Sam, who is the closest person to me in my life, didn't understand how upset I am about that incident and how angry I am with my friend's husband. Also, other abusers might think that I fancy these sorts of behaviors, and they might do the same thing to me in the future." Eli added further: "I usually become a clown in most of the parties I attend to and start to play the fool. This allows others to pull out dirty verbal jokes and inappropriate behaviors with me. Now I realize this is all due to my defectiveness/shame schema. I make a fool out of myself, and when the party's over, and I get home, I heavily criticize myself for the things that I said and did. It is as if there is a huge gap between what I feel on the inside and what I display on the outside." One of Sam's traits that strongly got Eli attracted to him was his seriousness and strong self-confidence, which would not allow anyone to cross the line with him by making jokes or making a fool out of him. However, after that incident took place, Sam was out of patience and was extremely angry with Eli's farces in different situations. Eli and Sam were educated to follow the triggering course of events for mockery in that night:

Physical harassment to Eli's body by her friend's husband (triggering event)

⇩

He touched a private part of my body. I am sad and angry (abused vulnerable child mode)
He has no respect and value for me (defective vulnerable child mode)

⇩

What made Eli respond with a mockery coping style was her fear. These fears in Eli included the fear of a fight breaking out and aggression taking place (subjugation schema), and the fear of intimacy wearing off (emotional deprivation schema).

⇩

Bursting into loud laughter and falling on the bathroom floor (automatic laughter mode). With the help of this mode, Eli was trying to reduce the intensity of the sexual aggression and hostility that was happening to her.

⇩

Criticizing herself due to the inappropriate, exaggerated waves of laughter despite the incident which took place (critical/punitive parent mode).
Criticizing herself for causing unpleasant feelings in her fiancé (critical/punitive parent mode)

When the above chart was explained, Eli was faced with the details of the "automatic laughter mode" and its unpleasant consequences. She realized that she acts with the same behavior in most of her life's situations. Eli remembered that when being six years old, she was playing next to the river in the company of her mother. She suddenly fell into the river, and her mother, who was experiencing a severe depression episode at that time, made no reaction and stared at the water, which was taking Eli away in front of her eyes. Eli was telling about this traumatic memory in the therapy room with as much buffoonery as she could, and her loud waves of laughter would not stop. When the therapist asked her how she was saved, she responded:" There was an old man standing on a piece of rock in the middle of the river. When he saw me, he grabbed me by the back of my neck and pulled me out of the water." Sam stated:" When Eli tells someone about this memory for the first time, she always tells it in this way and causes the group to laugh. When most of our friends meet Eli after a while, they ask her to tell the story of getting drowned in the river once more and act it again."

This memory was so painful that with all Eli's farces accompanying it, it was truly difficult to laugh. However, in order for Eli to meet her needs from the group and at the same time does not make them upset, she made sure to tell it with as much buffoonery as she could. It was evident that the "hot spot" in that memory was that moment where Eli was carried away in the water with much horror right in front of her mother's eyes, and her mother had no reaction to the horror of Eli and her need for getting help and support. Eli said:" I have been thinking about this for years: If my mother really loved me, she could at least move a bit in her place or at least came to my rescue. She could have helped me, just the least amount of it! (emotional deprivation schema). She continued:" I still feel that I am of no value or importance to her since sometimes during our arguments she tells me it would have been better if water took you away that day" (defectiveness/shame schema). Sam turned to Eli, who still had a smile on her face, and asked her to tell the rest of the story. Eli continued:" When we came back home, and my father found out about what happened, he beat me and yelled: You are no longer allowed to go by the river and play there."

The therapist noticed that the smile on Eli's face has worn out and realized that the "abused vulnerable child mode" has been activated. The therapist asked Eli:" What did you like your father to do after he heard about this incident?" Eli responded:" I liked him to hug me and tell me that, honey, I know how scared you are; from now on, we are going to play next to the river together..." Eli had not finished her words yet as she burst into tears. Eli told us about her vulnerable child mode:" The problem started from our home where when anything went wrong, my parents used to think it was my fault. Now the problem is exactly this; I don't want my friends to do the same thing with me, and also when Sam is upset or angry with anything, I think that that's my fault." Even Though cognitively speaking, Eli knew that she is not at fault due to Sam's emotional problems, yet her guilt-inducing parent mode would repeatedly tell her: "Sam was a happy person before you came into his life, and it's your presence which makes him sad."

Since the guilt-inducing parent mode caused severe guilt feelings in Eli regarding Sam's emotional problems and bearing that situation was difficult for her, she would take help from overcompensatory mode, yelling at Sam:" I am going to end this damned relationship! You know why? Because you don't give me the importance and value that you should!" Sam has an abandonment/instability schema due to his parent's divorce in his childhood. Whenever he is faced with these Eli's threats of separation, he cries his eyes out and eventually passes out. Eli said:" But you know it's very strange. Every time we fight, Sam's interest in me grows sexually, and now I realize this is due to his abandonment/instability schema. It is as if he tries to bring back the lost intimacy with the sex, and he has always been successful."

Coping Modes in the Mockery Coping Style

Even though the automatic-laughter, self-mockery, and others-mockery modes cause laughter at the moment, they are being used, yet their effects are only short, instantaneous, and immediate, which does not result in happiness. These three coping modes are completely self-referent and form a deep semantic connection with the audience. Usually, the presence of these coping modes in interpersonal relationships leads to different and often conflicting interpretations. Sometimes the messages conveyed by these modes are so complicated and contradictory that the audience needs further examination and review of them in order to be able to make a distinction.

The Automatic Laughter Mode (ALM)

In our clinical work with some of the patients, our attention was caught by their constant fake smiles or their unrelated waves of laughter to the situation and the topic at hand. These fake smiles and irrelevant bits of laughter were related to subjugation, social isolation, self-sacrifice, emotional inhibition, defectiveness/shame, mistrust/abuse, and approval-seeking/recognition-seeking schemas. Usually, they start to laugh during the sessions when they are experiencing some psychological pressure. Also, during group therapy sessions, while all the members are serious and a topic is being discussed, which has made the members of the group experiencing feelings of sadness and discomfort; these groups of patients wear a slight smile. Sometimes during educational classes, even though nothing funny is being discussed, they chuckle. On some occasions, when the majority of participants are laughing or smiling because of a simple incident or an interesting remark, they continue to smile long afterward.

When this mode is activated, the individual is not aware of his smiling face. Individuals with this mode might wear a smile even when they are all by themselves, taking a walk on the street. The automatic laughter mode might be so persistent for some individuals that others always recall them with a smile on their faces. Having a smile on the face all the time is not an indicator of inner happiness, yet it is an indication of a strong presence of this mode in the individual. Automatic laughter mode has different functions in different schemas. For example, people with subjugation schema use the automatic laughter mode in order to protect themselves from the people they are afraid of. In an approval-seeking/recognition-seeking schema, the person tries to present herself as calm, attractive, lovable, trusting, and influential with the use of this mode. Also, individuals with defectiveness/shame schema, when being heavily criticized in a group, might automatically smirk, wear a fake smile and start glancing at their surroundings even though the incident has deeply upset them. Therefore this smile coming from the automatic laughter mode is intended to keep up the pretense. When it comes to social isolation schema, the person who is not happy with being in the group tries to respond to others' remarks by smiling. This way, he attempts at displaying his union with the group and engages in the discussions.

When the automatic laughter mode is "severely active," the person starts to farce and, by laughing, shaking with laughter, or being funny, tries to free herself from the pressure being put on her by others. In this obvious situation, detecting this mode by individuals who have been educated about the coping styles and modes is not a difficult task.

Of course, there are times where identifying automatic laughter mode for the individuals who have been educated about it is difficult as well. For example, when you tell someone a joke, it would be difficult for you to understand whether the other person truly smiles because he liked your joke or, on the contrary, he is smiling because he did not find it interesting! Just as you tell someone you are going to tell them a joke; you notice that automatic laughter mode makes them wear a smile before you tell them the actual joke. We can easily contract the muscles in our cheeks. This is just like the times we are in front of a camera and the person taking the picture asks us why we are so serious? Smile! However, according to Duchenne de Boulogne (1806 – 1875), the French Neurologist, we cannot contract the Orbicularis Oculi muscle that easily. Orbicularis Oculi is the muscle which we contract only when we are experiencing true happiness. This is why Paul Ekman has named the genuine smile after Duchenne de Boulogne, The "Duchenne Smile" (Daniel Pink, 2005). Therefore there is a close connection between the automatic laughter mode, true happiness, and the anatomy of the face.

From the evolutionary biology point of view, smile and laughter each come from significantly different descents. Smiling is the evolutionary descendant related to peace, satisfaction, and safety. First, humans experienced fullness, and a smile revealing their satisfaction came onto their faces after they had a through pleasant meal. That is because finding food and feeding themselves to an appropriate extent was the primary concern of the hunter-gatherer human. If we call that smile the "primitive smile," we can observe that happiness on the faces of ourselves and others upon our physical, sexual, and emotional needs have been met. In the traditional society of India, the guests tend to smile and belch after they eat. They do so to convey their satisfaction with the hospitality to their host. The sound of the belch assures the host that the guest has been completely satisfied with the reception and hospitality of the host.

Thus when it comes to the primitive smile, the person's physical, sexual and emotional needs have truly been met, and she is experiencing a true sense of relaxation, satisfaction, and safety. On the other hand, no needs are being met while being in the "automatic laughter (smile) mode," but the person faces a distressing situation and tension. The smile (automatic laughter mode) appears so that the person experiences the calmness from the inside and appears satisfied outwardly and keeping her safety in general. This mode in mockery coping style tended to display first humans as high in confidence in the face of the enemy and calm in the face of adversities. Thus, even though automatic laughter mode played a vital evolutionary role in the survival of the first humans, it now leads to many problems, especially when it comes to couples and interpersonal relationships.

Giti, who has vulnerability to harm and illness schema, can not stop her laughter when someone falls on the ground near her. Giti's husband has accidentally twisted his ankle or slid several times during long years of their marital life. When this incident happens, Giti's first reaction is bursting into laughter.

During one of these incidents, Giti's husband fell on the ground while he was in the bathroom. Giti overheard the sound of his fall, went to the bathroom, opened the door, and was faced with his husband on the ground as his head was broken and bleeding. She started to laugh, and in order to prevent her husband from finding out about her laughter, she ran to the kitchen, telling him she is going after the first aid kit. She spent some minutes in the middle of the kitchen, laughing out loud without having the ability to stop her laughter as she was holding the first aid kit in her hands. Finally, her husband dragged himself to the kitchen with a bleeding and broken head. Giti told us in the therapy session: "When I found my husband in that situation, on the bathroom's floor bleeding, my vulnerability to harm and illness schema got triggered severely."

Now we are aware that during that horrifying incident, the mockery coping style and automatic laughter mode significantly reduce the levels of fear and horror that Giti is experiencing. Gitti is deeply afraid on the inside, yet the uninterrupted and uncontrollable waves of laughter make the situation simple and safe for her to some extent. Giti continued: "Even though after each incident, my husband gets upset with me due to my waves of laughter, but unfortunately, I have not yet found a way to make them stop." Giti's automatic and uncontrollable waves of laughter get out of balance, and they go on until she has a sense of peace and safety. Therefore, Giti tries to control her fear and the horror of the threat by being in the mockery coping style.

An interesting point to consider here is that laughter is an evolutionary descendant from the behaviors which express anger, horror, and threat. Therefore, laughter's evolutionary descent is entirely different from the smile, which is related to calmness, satisfaction, and safety. The primitive smile can be observed in humans since their birth and after their needs have been met. This process takes place entirely out of instinct. Unlike smiling, laughter is a matter of evolution, and instincts play no role in it. Laughter is an emotion that has gradually appeared in humans during the course of their evolution. First, humans did not laugh. In case someone or something surprised them or made them satisfied, they would make a "heh" sound after taking a deep inhalation and breathing it out. Gradually this "heh" sound became "heh heh" and eventually took the form as we know it today, "hahaha." Today laughter exists in the nervous system of both humans and first primates in the form of a behavioral pattern.

Distinguishing the Automatic Laughter Mode from Other Schema Modes

Now maybe it is safe to state that there are lots of differences between real laughter (coming from the happy child mode) and the ones related to the activation of schemas (coming from the automatic laughter mode). Jacob, van Genderen and Seebauer (2015) believe that identifying happy child mode in oneself and others is a relatively easy task. The person experiences a sense of lightheartedness and happiness and laughs a lot while being playful and having fun. Generally, the person feels satisfaction, and a sense of peacefulness is spontaneous and humorous. Furthermore, due to the positive vibes that he is sending to others, often the people around gets attracted to her. The person in happy child mode is also famous for her open laughter.

Patients with defectiveness/shame and emotional inhibition schemas usually cover their faces while laughing and prevent the laughter from taking place in its usual form and manner. This might happen in these patients for different kinds of reasons. For example, the patient with defectiveness/shame schema might cover her face while laughing because she believes that while laughing, her face becomes uglier; thus, she covers it with her hands in order to prevent others from seeing it in a situation which she perceives her face as uglier. On the other hand, patients with emotional inhibition schema cover their faces during laughter in order to silence the loud voice of their laughter. People with emotional inhibition schema sometimes try to force stop their loud laughter, but they are suddenly faced with the body/emotion conversion reaction, which brings them to the "cough/laughter state." This only makes the matter worse for them as stopping waves of laughter accompanied by coughing, is a much more difficult task. In this situation, the person is experiencing a significant amount of physical/emotional pressure, which leaves the person drained when it is over. The cough/laughter state also is not related to the automatic laughter mode in any way.

Automatic laughter mode should not be mistaken with the laughter coming from the people who have difficulties controlling their laughter due to insufficient self-control/self-discipline schema. People with insufficient self-control/self-discipline schema often have difficulty controlling their laughter in formal settings such as funerals, speeches, or work meetings. They tend to excessively laugh at not rather funny subjects in these settings to the extent that they are often either asked to leave the meeting or the classroom or they make others around them uncomfortable. Also, people with this schema tend to laugh so loud due to their lack of ability to contain emotions that attract everyone's attention with their laughter.

Exercise for the Automatic Laughter Mode

1. Now that you have been introduced to the automatic laughter mode try to recall, identify and write down instances of this mode in yourself or the ones around you in daily life.
2. Considering the examples given for this mode and its

manifestations in different schemas, try to find out how this mode plays out when it comes to other schemas.

3. Find the negative consequences of this mode being at play in your marital life, interpersonal relationships, and work environment.

The Self-Mockery Mode (SMM)

During therapy sessions, we might come across instances where the patients tend to smirk while telling stories about the things they have done in the past or mocking themselves for their behaviors. The self-mockery mode is another mode related to the mockery coping style. It is usually connected to defectiveness/ shame, subjugation, self-sacrifice, failure, dependence/ incompetence, approval-seeking/ recognition-seeking, punitiveness, vulnerability to harm and illness, and insufficient self-control/ self-discipline schemas. For example, the patient with defectiveness/shame schema who hates his face's shape makes faces that give it an ugly appearance. He does so while in the group, thus mocking himself in other's presence. Another case is a patient with a dependence/ incompetence schema who tells stories of her incompetencies and failures in carrying out simple tasks and mocks herself in front of others. Also, a patient with insufficient self-control/self-discipline bursts into laughter as he calls himself a stupid wacky after telling a story about how his car ran out of gas again, and he was left all by himself in the middle of the road. Another patient with vulnerability to harm and illness schema was mocking herself by laughing out loud during the therapy session as she was telling us how every time she experiences a simple headache, she thinks it is related to a tumor in her brain.

This mode is observed more frequently among the individuals who have learned to play the role of the mood-lifting mascot for other family members since their childhood. These individuals usually grew up with depressed, aggressive, or addicted parents. Thus, they were used to repeatedly coming up with funny subjects just like a comedian to ease the tense situation they were facing or boost their parent's mood. Also, they might have played the role of someone who tried to ease or end their parents' conflicts. One of the patients stated: "Whenever there was a huge fight breaking out between my parents, I used to run in the middle of their fight and started to somersault, thus attracting their attention to myself. When they started to pay attention to me, they would have stopped their fight. Thus I had learned always to play this role in my family. Now that I'm married, every time there is a fight between my wife and me, I start to make her laugh by mocking myself. This way, I manage to put an end to our fight."

In the self-mockery mode, the person tries to end the difficult situation and the tension she is experiencing by mocking herself. Thus in distressing situations, the person's self-mockery causes others not to take her seriously and stop being hard on her. This helps the person shape a safe atmosphere for herself with the aid of the mockery coping style. Therefore the person covers her negative emotions, including fear and sadness, with the self-mockery mode. This mode prevents the individual from being in touch with their true feelings and experiencing them. The patient in self-mockery mode tends to make fun of herself in front of others by finding and exposing her weaknesses, shortcomings, and deficiencies.

The patient in self-mockery mode is on the lookout for finding the data that would help him make others laugh to free himself from the psychological tension and pressure. The individual takes advantage of verbal communication and makes fun of himself in a playful manner while in a way that both ends of this communication have accepted their roles. In the more advanced form, the person makes fun of the ethnicity, language(accent), race, and the culture in which he grew up. This advanced form consists of the jokes that the person tells about his language, cultural and social background, making others laugh. Therefore, the person tries to come up with multifaceted jokes and speaks ironically about the region's language, cultural and social structure. He does so by attempting to change the normal, ordinary, and reasonable situation of that region into an anomalous, abnormal, and unreasonable one. Even though self-mockery mode might help to form closer connections with others in this situation, it might affect and weaken the person's self-confidence and self-esteem.

Exercise for the Self-Mockery Mode

1. Now that you have been introduced to the self-mockery mode try to recall, identify and write down instances of this mode in yourself or the ones around you in daily life.
2. Considering the examples given for this mode and its manifestations in different schemas, try to find the manifestations of this mode for other schemas.
3. Find the negative consequences of this mode being at play in your marital life, interpersonal relationships, and work environment.

The Others-Mockery Mode (OMM)

While being in the others-mockery mode, the patient tends to make fun of others by giving offensive remarks, displaying exaggerated behaviors, making faces (mimicking), moving hands or other parts of the body exaggeratedly, sending others up, etc. Most of the time, when the patient is experiencing significant levels of tension and psychological pressure due to activation of his schemas by another person, he tends to mock and make fun of the other person with the use of his others-mockery mode in order to reduce the effect of experienced negative emotions. For example, a patient with entitlement/grandiosity schema who can not stand news of her colleague's financial successes expresses her "anger" by making fun of her colleague's face and appearances. Another patient with unrelenting standards/hyper-criticalness schema who had just lost the game to his opponent in a sporting event would cover his sense of "incompetence and despair" by making fun of his opponent's ethnicity and accent. Another patient with approval-seeking/recognition-seeking schema who had no luck gaining others' attention while being in a party would leave the place being "sad." Later on, when it is only her and the person who accompanied her at the party, she would imitate and make fun of how the host and other guests talked, walked, and laughed.

Even though the others-mockery mode is deeply connected with the three conditional (compensatory) schemas above (entitlement/ grandiosity, unrelenting standards/ hyper-criticalness, and approval seeking/ recognition-seeking schemas), yet it can be observed among other unconditional (core) schemas in other forms. For example, a patient with defectiveness/shame schema would try to do leveling by making fun of others to reduce his feelings of worthlessness.

This mode is more commonly observed compared to the other two modes of the mockery coping style (automatic laughter mode and self-mockery mode). This mode can even be observed among the children population when their peers have hurt them, or their needs have been frustrated. Children learn the act of making fun of others from their parents, peers, and others around them through observational learning. *Mockery* is a negative behavior that can be picked up quickly by children.

When the parents make fun of others, children learn as well to mock others when they are facing tension. They do so to calm themselves.

There is a high chance for children who get ridiculed by their parents while growing up to make fun of others with the others-mockery mode in adulthood. These individuals are usually very sensitive to any kind of jokes and humor of others. They tend to personalize these instances and get hurt instantly. In other words, they are touchy, and they cannot take a joke, yet they easily permit themselves to make fun of others.

Even though since the advent of human history, especially in most of the religions, cultures and recently in the modern education systems, ridiculing others is considered as abnormal behavior, and since the beginning years of childhood, the parents and teachers have tried to prevent children and adolescents from making fun of each other; still, the behavior of mocking others remains intact today.

Probably most of us have either read, heard the story, or watched the movie, cartoon, and many plays which are created around the world based on the story of The Ugly Duckling written by the Danish writer, Hans Christian Andersen (1805 - 1875) and published in 1843. A duckling hatches an egg and emerges from it on a farm, and due to his different appearance, he gets ridiculed and mocked by the other animals of the farm. Finally, when he reaches puberty, he turns out to be a beautiful white swan, making all other animals surprised and ashamed. What made other animals make fun of the duckling? The answer, according to the writer of the story, was duckling's ugliness. Was being different from other ducklings further made things worse for the ugly duckling? The answer is yes. Even though people make fun of each other based on ugliness/ beauty or similarities/ differences standards, yet the issue is deeper and more complex than these standards. People who make fun of the ones who are different from them or are not consistent with their definitions of aesthetics probably have severe entitlement/ grandiosity and unrelenting standards/ hyper criticalness schemas. These instances are observed much frequently in the issues regarding racism. Racists believe that we are superior, and since you do not look like us, so you are ugly, retarded, and stupid. Thus the "others-mockery mode" tends to make fun of others based on aesthetics, ethnicity, culture, and language. It is important to note that racism does not end with mockery; sometimes, people tend to take a step further and intimidate, threaten or get aggressive with other races and strangers with their bully and attack mode.

The mockery coping style utilizes the others-mockery mode, which appears to be a primitive behavior in order to put behind psychological tension and pressure. Primitive behaviors are entirely based on instincts, and their function is to act as a response to life-threatening situations as a reaction pattern since the early years of human development. Hiding and covering are other examples of primitive behaviors. We also know that children enjoy immensely playing hide and seek with their parents and peers. Also, sometimes when teachers are about to ask questions in the classroom, some distressed students tend to hide behind the classmate who is sitting in front of them. According to Phylogenetics, the source of these behavioral patterns is probably the Autonomous sections of the brain.

The feelings of jealousy cause severe emotional pain for the individual. Thus the jealous person seeks help from the mockery coping style to protect himself from the suffering stemming from jealousy. Since the primary purpose of all coping modes is to protect the individual from the distress and the painful emotional experiences, the others-mockery mode functions outside of the individual's awareness and starts to make fun of others. As an example, patients with approval-seeking/ recognition-seeking schemas grow highly jealous of the ones who win their colleague's admiration and praise. They tend to make fun of their appearance, race, accent, age, personal life, and behaviors in their mockery coping style (others-mockery mode) in order to reduce the emotional pain they are experiencing from their jealousy. Sometimes mockery coping style might not be all that is needed to reduce the emotional pain. Thus the patient with approval-seeking/recognition-seeking schema might get into an overcompensatory coping style and flagrantly devalue the admired accomplishments of the other person by relating those successes to chance or favoritism or a result of having a sexual relationship with the superiors or juries.

The feeling of frustration is among the other issues that cause the individual deep levels of suffering. The others-mockery mode might begin to operate outside of the individual's awareness to make fun of those who have caused the frustration. For instance, a patient with abandonment/instability schema whose wedding is called off by her fiance might start to make fun of her family, social status, job, or income.

Often, the others-mockery mode would start to mock and ridicule others when faced with symptoms and clinical manifestations of other schemas. For example, a patient with a dependence/incompetence schema might be made fun of with the label of "the burden" since the person is incompetent in handling his day-to-day personal affairs or is not able to manage his finances effectively. Also, a patient with enmeshment/undeveloped-self might get ridiculed because of being a "mamma's boy," a patient with defectiveness/shame because of being "shy," a patient with emotional deprivation due to being "too romantic," a patient with vulnerability to harm and illness schema due to being "precautious" and a patient with insufficient self-control/self-discipline because of being "dumb and wacky." Therefore it is safe to state that the symptoms and clinical manifestations of schemas are good subjects for the others-mockery mode to make fun of others.

Since the healthy adult mode never makes fun of others because of their negative features and considers mockery as dysfunctional behavior, there is a high chance that the others-mockery mode gets activated in individuals who themselves were struggling with the symptoms of that schema in the past to an extent and experienced great levels of sufferings from it.

For instance, a person who used to surrender to his subjugation schema in the past, when faced with someone who is currently surrendering to her subjugation schema, might make fun of her "being a yes-woman" in his others-mockery mode. He has now overcompensated to his subjugation schema and makes fun of others being a yes-man or a yes-woman. Thus not only this person's difficulty with his subjugation schema is not resolved, but also due to overcompensation coping style, he is taking revenge on the emotional pain of his schema from others by causing others emotional pain with being disobedient and aggressive (bully/attack mode).

In some societies where the people are faced with economic difficulties, political disagreements with the government, and a probable war breaking out, the others-mockery mode operates like a mockery generating machine and manifests itself every day through collective lampoon literature, especially in social media. Making fun of famous figures, sarcastic remarks on the differences between the promised actions and current statistics and the reality of people's everyday living, and bitter laughter at daily events and incidents are among the examples of the actions taken to discharge anger, sadness, distress, and contempt. Mocking attacks on the legends of a nation, humiliating strangers, and breaking taboos are among the newer forms of behavioral components in mockery coping style with others-mockery mode.

Exercise for the Others-Mockery Mode

1. Now that you have been introduced to the others-mockery mode try to recall, identify and write down instances of this mode in yourself or the ones around you in daily life.
2. Considering the examples given for this mode and its manifestations in different schemas, try to find the manifestations of this mode for other schemas.
3. Find the negative consequences of this mode being at play in your marital life, interpersonal relationships, and work environment.

Personality Disorders and the Modes of the Mockery Coping Style

There is a close connection between many of the personality disorders and the mockery coping style. The table below lists the modes which have been observed more frequently among each one of the personality disorders.

Table 4-1: Personality disorders and the modes of the mockery coping style

Person-ality Dis-orders	**Modes of the Mockery Coping Style**	**Unhealthy Way of Expressing Emotions and Meeting Needs**
Histrionic	A. Automatic Laughter B. Others-	A. Gains other's "attention" by out of the context's waves of laughter.

	Mockery	B. Takes over the control of the group by making fun of others.
Narcis-sistic	Others-Mockery	Feels “better or superior” by teasing or ridiculing others.
Avoidant	Automatic Laughter	Shows him/herself as a calm and positive person by wearing a constant smiling mask in order to avoid “criticism, humiliation, and disapproval.”
Dependent	Self-Mockery	Makes fun of the self in order to “attract others’ help.”
Schizoid	Automatic Laughter	In order not to be labeled as isolated or shy by others, displays him/herself as a fan of jokes and jests in inappropriate ways.
Passive-aggressive	Others-Mockery	Discharges “anger” experienced from others, especially the superiors, by giving sarcastic remarks, sneering, or making fun of them.
Obsessive compul-sive	--------------------	Behaves in a serious, formal, and rigid manner and strongly believes in moral principles and interpersonal respect. Therefore the modes of the mockery coping style are rarely observed among them.
Antisocial	Others-Mockery	“Enjoys” teasing others in groups, pulling pranks, or messing with people.
Borderline	A. Self-Mockery B. Others-	A. Tries to reduce the amount of “experienced negative emotions” by making fun of the self.

	Mockery	B. Expresses "feelings of disgust and hostility" by ridiculing others.
Paranoid	A. Automatic Laughter B. Others-Mockery	A. "Pretends to be in friendship" with the other person by wearing a fake smile. B. Somehow "takes revenge" by mocking others whom they perceive as enemies.

Even though the above table does not explicitly mention any of the three coping modes of mockery coping style for the obsessive-compulsive personality disorder, yet there is a probability that individuals with this disorder might use others-mockery mode when faced with others who do not attend to the job and do the things consistent with their standards. Nevertheless, this issue requires further review in the future. The others-mockery mode is frequently observed among the histrionic, narcissistic, passive-aggressive, antisocial, borderline, and paranoid disorder populations. Therefore, this mode is the most used mode among the modes of the mockery coping style.

Final Words

Generally speaking, the utilization of the mockery coping style can have its roots in the cultural and social history of different races and nations. The mockery coping style is often used by people when there is immoderacy presenting itself in any given issue at hand. For example, in societies where tyrannical rulers have ruled with cruelty and injustice for centuries over people, this style is more popular among the people in their day-to-day political/social conversations. Also, the mechanisms of mockery coping style are more evident among the families and societies where sexual issues are severely considered taboo. Furthermore, in societies where strict rules have been legislated and are set to be carefully followed, the utilization of mockery coping style by people facing the rules occurs. Also, extremism in educating and following religious practices might activate the use of this style in religious contexts. The excessive usage of mockery coping style results in mass production of mocking products, and even though these products are among the most democratic forms of cultural productions, they are not sufficient for healing the sufferings of the people in the long run.

Furthermore, since the truth is not compatible with reality and people are not free enough to express their emotions and speak up their minds, they would turn into the mockery style in order to meet their needs. This way, they are actually expressing themselves in two different ways and conveying two different messages. In fact, in this situation, the individual states something, yet he draws another meaning from what he has stated.

During difficult economic and social times, the mockery coping style starts to be taken advantage of as a new behavioral/cognitive and emotional constellation to heal the unsolvable sufferings that have no end to them. The style temporarily makes the frustrations and unfavorable events of the days more bearable. When the situation has gotten too worse, and the individual lacks the ability to make any changes happen, he would turn into clownish behaviors in order to control the environment and enhance the existing conditions to a small extent. Mockery on one end and domination on the other end are always two sides of the same coin. When the individual finds himself in a difficult situation, and the domineering party tends to exert force, clownish behavior comes of the situation. People not only tend to be mocking in the face of domineering individuals, but they also tend to make fun of the weak and dominant ones as well. Considering the reward-pleasure that the person takes from the mockery coping style, this style is entirely self-sufficient. In other words, this style temporarily reduces the interpersonal pressure, political/social issues, sexual subjects, legal concepts, and religion and does not point out anything outside its own context. Therefore, the use of this style, even though it might result in laughter but is not being solely used for making the self or others laugh. It is being used for bringing a change into an existing situation, gaining one's authority over self, others, or the environment.

Just like other styles, the mockery coping style is a method for making unbearable situations bearable. Today the outputs of mockery can be observed easily in social media. A vast and massive collection of repetitious, obscure, and vain idle talks which more and more are being added to them every day. None of the other coping styles have been equipped with the state of the art technology as much as mockery has been so far. The daily consumption of mockery products in social media has reinforced the presence of people due to the reward-pleasure system and is one of the reasons for long hours of internet and cell phone usage during days and nights. *Mockery* is a coping style which even though it is capable of temporarily reducing the psychological pressures, frustrations, and tensions of daily life, is incapable of changing the existing reality by any means.

CHAPTER FIVE

THE GAUCHERIE COPING STYLE

In this chapter:

- Gaucherie Coping Style Explained
- Behavioral Components in Gaucherie Coping Style
- Cognitive Components (Creativity, Problem-solving, Decision making, and Reasoning)
- Emotional Components in Gaucherie Coping Style
- The Controversial/ Troublemaker Mode (CTM)
- The Misguide/ Misdirect Mode (MMM)
- The Obstructionist/ Saboteur Mode (OSM)
- Personality Disorders and the Coping Modes in Gaucherie Style

In this coping style, the individual, despite being well aware of the issues, problems, and dangers associated with doing certain things, still moves forward with doing them, which results in damaging himself or the ones around. He might also risk losing the people close to him or even losing his job or social credibility. *Gaucherie* is a coping style associated with the fumble reaction and carries many negative consequences for the individuals engaging in it. Many examples of the gaucherie coping style related to each schema have been pointed out in chapter two. It is important to note that people might exhibit behaviors that resemble gaucherie due to lack of experience or their incompetence; therefore, the therapist should conduct a more accurate analysis of the observed behavior based on the patient's schemas and modes. If gaucherie is the dominant coping style for most of the patient's schemas, making mistakes and causing trouble would be significantly evident in her behavior. This has happened to the degree that the patient has lost her credibility and reputation in the eyes of others.

In Persian poetry and literature, many poems point out to gaucherie. This is also the case in other cultures and world literature, where many instances of gaucherie in humans can be found. In fact, incorporating this coping style has its historical roots in our ancestors as well. Mohtasham Kashani (1500-1588), the Persian Poet in his book of poems (ghazal number 428), highlights the inconsistencies between the thought and the individual's action due to gaucherie, which ultimately results in mockery and being ridiculed. Pay attention to how the poet draws attention to the "gaucherie in being tactful" in the following verses:

Where is the tenderness brilliance trance of love *** That last night they took me out of there not yet drinking the wine

Wisdom began to laugh seeing the gaucherie in my reason *** As it observed how your fire brought me to boil

Indeed, gaucherie results in a lack of tactfulness. The tactless person does not think through the activities which he carries on and ignores their consequences. Unquestionably, there is a need for contemplation, attention, and precision before carrying out any task or activity. The patient in the gaucherie coping style does not seek advice before making important decisions, is tactless while carrying out different tasks, and lacks the ability to develop appropriate solutions and make necessary arrangements when an urgent situation is calling for them. Due to schema perpetuation, the patient in the gaucherie coping style does not foresee the consequences of her behaviors; she is accustomed to transferring the negative consequences of them to others, thus avoiding responsibility.

Behavioral Components in Gaucherie

There are lots of instances in patients' daily life which indicates their lack of responsibility. For example, consider a person in love with someone, yet due to her abandonment/instability schema, she is afraid to reveal her true feelings to the person she is secretly in love with. Therefore she is afraid that her feelings might get rejected. On the other hand, the beloved is not aware of the lover's feelings for himself and what is going on in her heart. Therefore the lover waits patiently for an extended period so that one day she tells her beloved about her feelings towards him. This delinquency and hesitation ultimately result in losing the beloved. Nizami Ganjavi (1141-1209), the Persian Poet in his main poetical work, The Khamsa (in the 52nd section of Khosrow and Shirin, where Khosrow Shapoor is being sent asking for Shirin), thinks of the behaviors of the person who is in love as mostly being in the surrender coping style (the state of restlessness for the beloved) rather than the gaucherie coping style.

Patience while being in love is gaucherie *** The foundation of love is impatience

Patience is far from the manners of love *** The one who is patient is not in love

According to Nezami Ganjavi, the excessive patience of the lover is a gaucherie behavior that results in the vanishing of love. Even though "patience with problems" is considered one of the traits of the healthy adult mode, the other person, the situation, and the duration are all essential aspects to consider if being patient is going to be the chosen way forward. Due to the immense love that they are experiencing, most lovers do not possess the tolerance required for being patient. Therefore they become impatient, and their sole demand is to get to their beloved as soon as possible. In case the lover has chosen someone as their beloved who is either excessively cold towards him or does not love him back at all (the surrender coping style to the abandonment/ instability and emotional deprivation schemas), he tends to suffer from this situation constantly and gets restless. Now, if the lover has chosen someone who has the potential to love her back, yet due to the gaucherie coping style attends to "excessive patience," she might lose her beloved as well. This excessive patience might take the form of waiting for an incident or finding someone that helps her reveal her feelings to the beloved or even the beloved stepping forward himself. It is difficult for the lover to "take responsibility" for her negligence, procrastination, and hesitation. Thus she ignores her role in all this and holds others or the universe accountable for what happened to her love story!

Accordingly, one of the leading behavioral aspects of the gaucherie coping style is the individual's lack of responsibility while her schemas are being activated. The individual refuses to accept responsibility for her actions by holding others accountable for the consequences of her own actions. Hence, in this way, she can ignore her negligence to a somewhat acceptable degree. Consider a person with a social isolation schema. When behaving according to the gaucherie coping style in response to his schema, he gets in a fluster and acts clumsy while being on his first dates. His strange behavior surprises his date. Due to his social isolation schema, he has kept so much to himself and kept so much distance from others that he finds it difficult to even act according to basic social manners.

On the one hand, his anxiety grows worse due to his misbehaviors and mess-ups, and on the other hand, he does not want his date to find out about his anxieties while being on a date. This intense and increasing tension and uneasiness makes him behave carelessly or clumsy while being on the date. Ultimately he opts for finding a way to leave the situation. He regrets his decision later and eventually tries to go back to the person he was dating. Therefore the gaucherie coping style makes him lonelier and even more isolated after a period of trying to find a way out of isolation. Saib Tabrizi (1592-1676), Persian Poet, in his book of poems (ghazal number 1786), states:

Those curls got all garbled over hearth's anguish *** This branch's fruit got spoiled over gaucherie
Saib, how can I be safe over hearth's anguish? *** As for thousands of times, the glass broke next to me

Therefore the person with social isolation schema tells herself:" No one likes me on a first date. That is because I am not attractive, beautiful, rich, educated, and successful enough." She puts the responsibility of failures on her" self" and arbitrarily puts herself down while not being aware that it is her increased levels of anxiety due to her social isolation schema, which causes her to not even carry on her daily routine behaviors. Thereupon, she is unaware of the fact that her mess-ups take place as a result of her gaucherie coping style. So she continues to denigrate herself, which further pushes her towards self-isolation, thus helping with schema perpetuation.

Gaucherie; Temperament or Behavior?

It is interesting to know that around 850 years ago, Khaqani (1120-1190), the Persian poet and prose-writer in two separate verses, indicated that gaucherie is somehow related to the temperament (individual's nature). This demonstrates that since past centuries, the sages, poets, and philosophers were well aware of the significance of the gaucherie issue, yet they could only attribute it to a kind of a temperamental trait (nature) in the individuals and did not elaborate further on this subject. Khaqani, in his ballades (number 77- in admiration of king Shervan), states:

I whimper at her way over her nature's gaucherie *** Only if the gossipy watchman let me to

Also, Khaqani, in his book of poems (ghazals, ghazal number 105), states with utmost elegance that how his nature has contributed to gaucherie. Therefore, no matter the shape of the violence, it always destroys the self and the other person.

Gaucherie not diminished from her nature *** Burned is my chest, her eyes not wet

Hence, according to Khaqani, gaucherie is considered a feature of nature or temperament (physiological temperament), affecting the behavior. Nevertheless, based on the new coping styles, we now know that no one is born with nature or temperament, which carries gaucherie. It is the maladaptive schemas that take advantage of the gaucherie coping style in order to perpetuate themselves. While taking into consideration the beliefs of Nizami Ganjavi regarding the "indolence temper" (as was referred to in chapter 3) and Khaqani's beliefs regarding the "gaucherie temper" in this chapter, it becomes apparent that somehow the previous centuries poets and sages did pay attention to the behaviors which they observed from other people and they tended to correlate them to the person's temper or nature. It is important to note that only Nizami Ganjavi pointed out the adverse effects that gaucherie has on the next generations in his book Khamsah (section "Haft Peykar" Seven Beauties, part 16, the letter of Iran's king to Bahram Goor). He associates gaucherie with the "behavior," which somehow identifies it with the transgenerational patterns of schemas and maladaptive coping styles.

The true heir to this estate is you *** This kingdom your royal heritage
Yet due to your father's gaucherie *** The shadow of the umbrella went away from you

Cognitive Component in Gaucherie

Without a doubt, the patients' thoughts in the gaucherie coping style are more complex and rigorous compared to the other coping styles. In this style, the patient loves the mistakes that she makes and even confesses to loving them and making them happen again. By intentionally not learning from past mistakes, the patient deliberately sets for absolute indiscretion and ineptness. The therapist quickly identifies the shallow and simplistic thoughts while speaking with these patients. Even if the patient is doing well intellectually (scoring high on IQ tests), gaucherie portrays him as a naive and foolish person who lacks the ability to make sound judgments and cohesive decisions.

In the gaucherie coping style, the person feels no need for accurate thinking, maintaining foresight, and utilizing problem-solving skills since it is others who are going to suffer from the weight of the troubles that they cause. The war general commander, who issues an attack order without a prior accurate analysis of the battleground's situation and foreseeing all the aspects of such an attack, only sends his young soldiers to death while ironically remains intact himself. No one would pay for the incorrect economic decisions of a politician who drags his country into inflations and financial bankruptcy but the citizens of that country by facing poverty and misfortune. There is no doubt that the job credibility and social status of that commander and politician get affected significantly, yet the damage that they have done to others and the society is far greater than the damage that they did to themselves. Thus, as long as their gaucherie coping style stays dominant, they keep causing minor damage to themselves and a severe one to others no matter which position they take. Here it must be said: Hey gauche! How long are you going to go on with a lack of wisdom?

In a critical match of soccer, the player who has just

scored a goal turns to the fans present at the stadium and performs a celebration by dragging his eyes to the sides with the help of his fingers, which closely resembles the eyes of the Eastern Asians. When the match ends, the federation's Disciplinary and Ethics Committee bans the player from playing in any matches for six months due to his racist behavior. The player states that he was not meant to do any racism, and he was only joking with his nephew, who happens to have slanted eyes. Regardless of this player's true intentions, whether they might be intentional racism or an innocent joke made with his nephew, there is no explanation for this behavior at this level of professionality except for a gauche behavior which has caused trouble for the club manager, the coach, his teammates, and the fans. However, the main gaucherie takes place after his six-month suspension from playing in any matches becomes approved and finalized. Many players, singers, actors, and other celebrities started to publish pictures of themselves mimicking the exact behavior of the suspended player, slanting their eyes with the fingers on social media in order to express their support of that player. This time they insisted on doing that behavior even though they knew the whole world considers it racist behavior.

Now the question is, why do they repeat the racist behavior even though it is considered as wrong behavior? The answer to this question is simple. While in the gaucherie coping style, people love making mistakes; they enjoy them. Hence they repeat them. For instance, if you stick your tongue out at a child and the child likes this behavior, the child would do the same thing after a short while, Even though he is aware that this behavior is considered impolite. Therefore this behavior (sticking your tongue out) gets repeated between you and the child many times. Both you and the child enjoy it despite both of you being aware that it is considered impolite. Therefore, a limited form of stubbornness, affront, and disrespect forms between you and the child. Breaking social etiquette and destructive behaviors of this kind carry a pleasurable experience with themselves which when it comes to gaucherie coping style, the person repeats this pattern to gain pleasure. The commander-in-chief who orders the attack despite knowing there is a slight chance of success in the battleground proceeds to do so because commanding is a very pleasurable act. The politician who insists on his policies and procedures to be taking place despite being aware that he lacks the necessary knowledge of economics causes lots of trouble for the country's economic structure. He insists on doing so since the pleasure of power and being the person in charge is far superior for him compared to other consequences and aspects of his decisions. When gaucherie reaches behavior (action) from thoughts, it leaves many damages behind with cruelty.

Creativity is defined as the ability to build or make something new. Without a doubt, creativity is humans' most significant capability in innovation, invention and is considered the essence of civilization's building blocks. Despite all this, there are far fewer people who harness their creativity in their career and daily life than those who show no signs of being creative. In the gaucherie coping style, the person blindly follows, obeys, and imitates others' creative ways. Thus, gaucherie steals individuals' opportunities in being creative talents. For example, the individual with gaucherie coping style to her failure schema does not tap into her creative abilities at all. She carelessly imitates the successful people and their ways and thoughts without taking her situation and existing conditions into account, which ultimately results in her failure. She continuously follows the updated plans and procedures of the successful people or organizations but neglects the fact that if they update their plans, they do so based on a felt need. A need which their own unique experience of carrying out procedures made them aware of. In this situation, blindly following the patterns of the plans and behaviors of others and carrying out the same procedures as they do only results in more failures. Gaucherie gets the individual occupied with the issues of others to the extent that he will not be able to identify and develop his own capabilities and inborn talents.

Problem-solving is another cognitive process that takes place in the mind or cognitive structure of the problem solver. This phenomenon requires manipulating the existing knowledge to reach a goal that is not easily accessible. While in the gaucherie coping style, identifying the main issue goes wrong and laying out the procedures, plans, and existing information regarding the issue go sideways as well. As an example to further illustrate this point, consider a person with unrelenting standards who insists on being skillful in a vast number of diverse subjects. In a world where specialists are valued far more, this person calls himself a jack of all trades. When his washing machine is broken, he opens up the device without having the necessary knowledge and tools to do so. Long hours of trial and error wastes time and energy, and in the end, not only the washing machine is not fixed, but also it is in a worse condition than it previously was. The person with unrelenting standards, if not the gaucherie coping style is his way of coping, will not act gauche and would seek help from the best professional who is qualified enough to fix the machine. He would do so despite believing that he is perfect. Therefore, gaucherie not only does not solve any problems but also adds to them. The person with unrelenting standards and in gaucherie coping style has heard this sentence from authorized service centers many times:" since you have opened up the device yourself, it is out of warranty." When the therapist asks the patient about the reason for these behaviors, the patient states:" I enjoy it so much when I myself get involved with solving the problem which has occurred to the device And if I get to solve it, I experience a sense of superiority." Here in this instance, too, one should not neglect the critical role gaining pleasure plays in the gaucherie coping style.

Decision-making is another cooperative process that involves choosing a single action among a set of alternatives. While in the gaucherie coping style, the person who is trying to make a decision faces challenges regarding the timing (urgent vs. timely), the complexity (complicated or straightforward), and the basis of thinking (emotional, logical, Cooperative) and makes the worst decision. A case example for this subject would be a patient with severe emotional inhibition schema who stated:" while being in college, I grew feelings for one of my classmates. I was just struggling with myself to express my feelings to her. Expressing my feelings to others has always been an issue for me. In the end, I decided to seek help from one of my friends and asked him to talk with that girl on my behalf." His friend stepped forward and talked with the girl; she said:" I don't fancy men who are shy and a coward. If he had something to tell me, it would have been better if he stepped forward himself. I'm sorry, but I'm not interested!" Without a doubt, asking others to do things on our behalf, the things which require the expression of emotions by the person himself, is sort of gaucherie in decision making. Despite lots of gaucheries taking place in the animal world, you can never find a male who asks another male to step forward and try to attract the female on his behalf during the mating season! You understand how flawed this way of decision-making is when you have an emotional inhibition schema, imagining asking someone else to whisper romantic things in your partner's ear on your behalf.

Reasoning is another cognitive process where the mind connects several subjects to draw conclusions based on the discovered connection. In the gaucherie coping style, the patient cannot discover unknown and unidentified subjects based on the already known and familiar subjects. For instance, the person with vulnerability to harm and illness schema is always highly occupied with the economic situation, his job, and other threats such as a war breaking out and getting homeless. He is also afraid that reaching his elderly years, the health insurance and the quality of medical care might not meet his needs. In the gaucherie coping style, he would plan to immigrate to one of the already developed countries without taking the entire aspects of such a decision into consideration beforehand. His course of reasoning for going forward with such a decision would be that as soon as he gets to the destination country, everything would be ready for him; thus, he can spend the rest of his life being in peace and full of joy. He has already heard many positive reviews about the high quality of life in those countries, and he has already imagined them as well. Since this person is in the gaucherie coping style, he leaves his home country illegally by giving money to human traffickers. He dreams of having a better life, but unfortunately, he gets drawn in a sea, or the best-case scenario, he will get arrested by the police force and gets forced to live in a migrant detention center.

When it comes to cognitive concepts, other examples can be discussed as well. Nevertheless, what is important is that after studying what has already been discussed so far, one gets to be able to identify the cognitive components (creativity, decision making, problem-solving, and reasoning) of each schema in each patient for their gaucherie coping style.

Emotional Components in Gaucherie

With regard to the overcompensation coping style, patients tend to cover the unpleasant feelings of each schema with the opposite feelings of that kind. For example, the feeling of power covers the feeling of weakness, and the feelings of pride take over the feeling of humiliation. Despite all this, in case of compensation meets with failure, unpleasant feelings will follow back (van Genderen, Rijkeboer, Arntz 2012).

However, when it comes to the gaucherie coping style, the patient tends to create a new unpleasant feeling instead of an already existing one in order to feel relieved. This way, she no longer experiences previous unpleasant feelings and starts to experience another one. Even Though both of these feelings are unpleasant, yet they each carry different emotions, which make them separate from each other. As an example, a lady who has just recently lost her husband in an airplane crash and is experiencing severe sadness and grief, before going through her grieving period and reaching a position where she can have some acceptance for that unfortunate event that took place, starts to date one of her previous pursuers. Not only did she not have any feelings for that guy, but she also hated him. Even though meeting with that guy was disgusting and hurting for her, yet at that time, she preferred to experience the unpleasant feeling of disgust over experiencing the unpleasant feeling of sadness (grief) without even being aware of it. In response to the therapist's question of how could you stand these disgusting dates, the lady stated:" I don't know! It's complicated, but it's good. At least I find something to entertain myself with." There is no evidence of entertainment here since entertainment causes happiness, and the happy child mode should be activated for a while during and after each date. When the happy child mode is not observed in the relationship with the old pursuiter, the romantic relationship does not follow a correct path, and the emotional growth does not take place. The emotional content of these dates circles around two main topics, the man, while displaying signs of dissatisfaction, repeatedly talks about his difficult life after the lady rejected him previously, and the lady talks about the sudden and shocking news of her husband's death and the feelings that she is experiencing because of misbehaving with him while he was still alive. Indeed, the discussed topics are not pleasant and satisfactory for both parties, and the relationship comes to an end after a while.

Opening up a New Window

Item One: Inherited Monarchy

The king wanted his eldest son to rule the country among his other sons, yet the son had no interest in accepting this responsibility. He was mostly into painting, music, and sculpture. His artistic nature and gentle spirit stopped him from accepting the role of the king, yet on the other hand, he was not that dissatisfied with the proposal offered to him. Even though after facing the father's request and some pressure from others around, he wore the crown, soon after the father passed away, the royal family and the officials realized that appointing him as the king was a grave mistake. The burden of the many responsibilities that the young king faced prevented him from pursuing his artistic endeavors. Despite the country he was ruling had many foreign enemies, instead of conducting peace negotiations, he reduced the military budget and increased the artist's fundings as his first order. This order left the army officials severely unhappy, and the enemies taking advantage of this situation attacked the country. As the war suddenly broke out, he started issuing strange commands and expected everyone to follow them. Soon, the country was occupied, and the kingdom was overthrown. He was placed under house arrest and spent many years attending to his artistic activities. Without a doubt, heredity monarchy has been one of the most gauche forms of ruling in the history of humankind. The firstborn son of the ruling king gets to rule over the people of a country. This is nothing but a gaucherie coping style to entitlement/grandiosity (narcissism) schema. It only suffices to go through the pages of history and review the history of different nations to realize how this form of gauche appointment has made the empires collapse after a while. The narcissistic king assumes his right to rule over a nation. He assumes this right for his family as well and believes his intelligence, talents, and capabilities are far superior to others. Therefore in order to keep his name immortal and his position intact while being in the gaucherie coping style, he announces his eldest son, the new king. Even though this appointment reduces the future anxieties of the king for a while, this gaucherie eventually costs them the monarchy itself. It is important to note that according to schema therapy, the coping styles lose functionality after a while and lead to maladaptiveness.

Item Two: Military Rules

There is an unspoken rule in the military that states: "punishment for all, encouragement for one!" Indeed, there are many problems with this rule when being examined psychologically, yet what is the reason that the commanders insist on this illogical rule while dealing with their soldiers? The commanders believe that conducting this rough rule over their soldiers makes them understand that their individualized actions and behaviors impact the group and that the group's fate depends on every one of them. For example, if the soldier taking the watch falls asleep, the enemy might penetrate from that spot and arrest or kill the rest of the unit. The enemy always takes advantage of this point since they are well aware that there is always someone who will eventually make a blunder in each unit. If we take a closer look around ourselves, we can always find some people among our relatives, friends, neighbors, colleagues or other people whom we know, that due to being in gaucherie to their schemas, they have caused a great many troubles for themselves, us and the others. There is usually no end to these troubles, and only their shape and context tend to change. As a first taught, the more distance we can keep between ourselves and the person who causes many troubles due to being in gaucherie to her schemas, the better. Yes, sometimes this person might be so close to us that keeping distance from her might not be that easy of an option.

Clinical Case

Aisa is a 48 years old accountant who works for a clothing company. Due to her vulnerability to harm and illness schema, she has acquired lots of information regarding traditional and modern medicine. She always wanted to be a doctor. A dream which never became an actuality, yet when someone is faced with health difficulties, in a gaucherie coping style, she tends to step in and conveniently prescribes herbal remedies, distillates, and teas. Even though Aisa never threatens the well-being of the patients around her with her prescriptions, she strongly believes in herself and discourages others from seeking help from health professionals. She believes that doctors lack the necessary knowledge required for treating their patients and usually misdiagnose their patients and cause them irrecoverable physical damages in the long run by prescribing them unnecessary amounts of medicine. Aisa's treatment of her patients usually starts with humorism and continues with the prescription of different mixtures of herbal distilleries, massage, and eventually cupping. She has many friends who are health professionals, and they do not approve of Aisa's procedures in any way. Usually, long arguments dispute between them. In case one of Aisa's patients' health conditions does not improve despite following her advice, she always refuses to accept responsibility and makes up different excuses for the treatment going wrong. Aisa believes that by following her traditional medicine guidelines, she never had to seek help from a health professional.

The main difference between the overcompensation and the gaucherie coping style in vulnerability to harm and illness schema lies in how individuals deal with illness. In the overcompensation coping style, the patient does risky and careless behavior; for example, he self-prescribes medicine without consulting with a doctor, which results in physical damages or drug dependency. That is why many of the companies in the Pharmaceutical industry state in their brochures:" The sale of this drug without a prescription is prohibited," and the pharmacies are told a statement:" Use this drug according to prescription advice." However, when it comes to the gaucherie coping style, the patient does not self-prescribe medicine and believes that taking drugs in any form has many side effects and is hazardous to their health. Like Aisa, many of them believe that chemotherapy and radiotherapy are not effective in treating cancer and cause people their lives. People like Aisa insist on curing cancer with the help of their traditional interventions, which include taking rest and going on a vegetarian diet. As Jeffery Young and his colleagues (2003) have stated before, one of the difficulties with patients with "vulnerability to harm and illness schema" is that they are terrified of putting aside their old ways of coping with the schema through avoidance and overcompensation coping styles. This holds for the patients with gaucherie coping style as well. They refuse to stop their gaucherie coping style, and it makes them highly anxious if they were not to follow their traditional ways of treatment. They use up lots of their financial resources on purchasing herbal goods. These herbal goods are not usually accessible to everyone since some tend to grow in only certain remote places. The main features of Aisa's gaucherie coping style to her vulnerability to harm and illness schema includes: giving wrong advice to others regarding their treatment plans, prescribing ineffective distilleries instead of guiding them to seek effective interventions, preventing others from visiting health professionals, hesitation in visiting the doctor during emergencies, Intervening in medical subjects without having the necessary specialization, not believing in modern forms of treatment, etc.

These days we witness the peak in the COVID-19 pandemic. Unfortunately, some people lose their lives due to getting infected with the Coronavirus. Some people "overcompensate" and try to put a brave face on and do not take the issue seriously (dangerous behavior), they do not keep themselves quarantine (high-risk behavior), they do not wear a mask when leaving the house, and they do not do social distancing (severe high-risk behavior). Some others try to treat this severe illness with home remedies and traditional interventions, which is considered "gaucherie." they lose out on the incubation period and the golden window at which they have a shot at seeking treatment from doctors. They only visit the hospitals when the symptoms are pretty severe, they have difficulties in breathing, and their lungs are seriously damaged; and unfortunately, this is too late.

Coping Modes in the Gaucherie Style

The coping modes of the gaucherie style include: controversial/troublemaker modes, misguide/misdirect mode, and obstructionist/saboteur mode. Arntz and Jacob (2013) believe that patients utilize coping modes in order to experience a sense of relief and alleviation. In fact, these modes keep them away from negative feelings or guide them to engage in exciting or soothing activities. This holds for the coping modes which belong to the gaucherie style. The patient experiences a sense of temporary relief for witnessing "somebody was served right." Therefore, the patient tries to achieve this sense of relief by utilizing the coping modes of the gaucherie style, which requires less energy instead of engaging in a direct fight (overcompensation coping style). Playing tricks on others, putting others off for some time, sneaky behaviors, mischief-making, giving someone or something a runaround, putting a spanner in the works all are behavioral features of the gaucherie coping modes which are discussed in detail in the following segments. Even though these three coping modes, just like the rest of the coping modes, manage to keep the patient away from negative feelings for some time, yet these modes cause so many troubles and distresses for the patient in the areas of intimate relationships, social interactions, and career-wise with lasting destructive effects in the patient lives as well.

The Controversial/ Trouble-maker Mode (CTM)

The patient gets involved in events and incidents which are not of high importance and emergency and causes trouble for himself and others around. The patient causes trouble for himself and others by exhibiting unpredictable behaviors, excessive gossiping, talking behind other's back, spreading rumors, making up stories regarding others, getting involved in unnecessary issues, intrusion and interference in others business, going after others belongings and things without asking for permission, asking inappropriate questions, giving controversial statements and forming close relationships with problematic individuals. This mode in the patient is capable of making a huge fuss out of a relatively minor issue. It seems as if the patient does not have the tolerance for living a quiet, peaceful life! She cannot stand witnessing the passage of life in tranquility and without experiencing any distress by any means. The patient experiences inner insecurity. She tries to extend this insecurity into her whole environment and the lives of the others in it as well. She does so with the aid of her controversial/troublemaker mode. Since the patient lacks inner peace, she would cause trouble even if she is surrounded by quiet people in a safe place. This mode makes others keep their distance from the patient as much as they can afford to. This mode sometimes causes the patient to get fired from his job or makes him enemies among the relatives, colleagues, or neighbors or even facing legal challenges with them.

The controversial/troublemaker mode has a variety of manifestations among different schemas. For example, in the Approval-Seeking / Recognition-Seeking Schema, in order to "get noticed" in social media, the patient engages in unnecessary arguments with famous people. Even though he gets recognition for this, he might face legal issues as well. When it comes to Entitlement / Grandiosity Schema, the individual fakes academic degrees or job resumes in order to "show off and feel superior to others." Of course, this might cause her troubles due to being inconsistent with reality in the long run. In unrelenting standards/hyper criticalness schema, the person faces challenges with others due to "lack of forgiveness and flexibility," and when it comes to Abandonment/Instability schema; the person faces issues with others and does not do well in the area of interpersonal relationships because of "jealousy."

Therefore the controversial/troublemaker mode can cause certain troubles for the patient when it comes to each schema. In fact, in the gaucherie coping style and its modes, the individual is trying to meet his needs but in the wrong way. In some cases, the person might consciously make the wrong choice while making decisions, and in some other instances, this might take place out of the patient's awareness.

The Controversial/Troublemaker Mode in Personal Area

Case One: Davood

Davood is a 36 years old martial arts coach who teaches Kung fu in a sports club. He started learning Kung fu as an adolescent, and now after many years of practice and getting an education has become an experienced and recognized coach who has many students of his own. He has traveled to the Shaolin temple in China several times and has even taken photographs with the temple's main building. His students love and respect him. The problem for Davood started when he published an announcement on his website and his Instagram account where he mentioned that he had taken specialized training courses in Kung fu in the Shaolin temple. In one segment of his announcement, he stated that the great martial masters and Buddhist monks of the Shaolin temple had acknowledged and formally appreciated him due to his extraordinary capabilities in martial arts. This was the start of a movement where many coaches and students from the country of Iran sent him messages requesting him to publish the images of the certifications and acknowledgments he received in the Shaolin temple. These requests increased day by day, and even his students started to doubt him. Davood was in real trouble.

On the one hand, he did not have any proof of his claims, and on the other hand, he could not answer any of the requests in a convincing way. He was in real trouble, and some of his students even left the club. Meanwhile, he published some statements and announcements on his Instagram to win over the public's trust, but with each announcement, he was in more trouble.

Davood had always experienced feelings of worthlessness since childhood due to his defectiveness/shame and emotional deprivation schemas. This always made him go to great lengths to look for ways to experience feelings of value and worth. Thus he had overcompensated for these core schemas of himself, and now entitlement/grandiosity was his most significant schema playing out itself in his life. Even though Davood had managed to get himself to a recognizable place in the world of Kung fu, yet in a therapy session, he stated his use of gaucherie coping style as following: Day after day, I was witnessing how my physical power was degrading, and my students were becoming more powerful and skilled. Sometimes this even made me afraid of conducting a practice fight session with them. This made me make up the Shaolin temple's story to create a glorious position for myself and almost unreachable for everybody else. This alone caused serious troubles for me, which cost me my reputation, which I fought tooth and nail to get for myself during my career.

The table below states how an unmet emotional need (feeling worthy), due to a schema (entitlement/ grandiosity) in a particular coping style (gaucherie) based on a mode (controversial/ troublemaker) has adverse effects on the professional life of an individual.

Table 5-1: controversial/ troublemaker mode and negative consequences

Core Emotional Need	Maladaptive Schema	Controversial/ Troublemaker Mode	Cause (unrecognized need)	Negative Consequences
Feeling worthy (secure attachment)	entitlement/ grandiosity	Presenting a fake academic, or work resume	Showing off and feeling superior to others	Will get caught, and his reputation gets questioned

In this case example, the troubles that the controversial/ troublemaker mode causes for the individual himself were stated. However, on many occasions, the controversial/ troublemaker mode does not solely cause trouble for the individual; it puts others around him in trouble too. The following case examples, number two and three, point out these instances.

Case Two: Dorsa

Dorsa is a 26 years old young woman who recently got divorced from her husband and lives in a small rented apartment by herself. She also recently got fired from her work because she was gossiping about her boss and her colleagues. She was referred to the therapist on the court order due to the charges filed against her by her neighbors. She was used to turning up her music at night and when the neighbors were supposedly taking rest which caused them serious discomfort. Furthermore, she left her thrash in inappropriate places to make the common areas of the apartment messy and smelly. One of the other complaints came from another neighbor who stated that she was intervening in their private life. She was used to making up rumors about neighbors' private matters and sharing them with the rest of the building neighbors. All this caused her to receive several warnings from the building manager and other neighbors, which all proved ineffective. One last scene that seriously caused her trouble was her friend, who was addicted to Methamphetamine. Dorsa was trying to help her friend to quit her addiction. She took the friend over to her home. The friend who started to experience withdrawal symptoms started yelling, breaking the windows, and trying to find a way to escape Dorsa's apartment. This caused a physical fight to break out between Dorsa and her friend. The noises made the neighbors call the police. The police forces arrived at the scene, found some drugs, and took Dorsa and her addicted friend into custody.

Dorsa, due to her Insufficient Self-Control / Self-Discipline schema, could not adhere to realistic limits regarding the privacy and citizenship rights of others. Thus by getting into the gaucherie coping style, she refused to accept responsibility for her inappropriate behaviors and, with her controversial/troublemaker mode, caused serious troubles for herself and others. Further, she was trying to help her friend who was struggling with addiction due to her self-sacrifice schema but being in gaucherie coping style, instead of referring or taking her friend to a professional, getting her hospitalized in a hospital or rehab, she decided to take her friend to her small apartment, and on the third day of withdrawal, when the withdrawal symptoms were at their worst, she and her friend were in serious trouble.

Case Three: Ailin

Ailin and her husband, along with some of their friends, took a trip to a jungle wilderness area on the new Year holidays. There was a wooden cottage in the heart of the jungle, which the group used as a place for their stay and taking rest. Ailin's husband, who was seeing his friend after a long time, started to talk with them, and together they brought up and reviewed their shared past memorable and happy memories. Ailin felt she was left out due to her emotional deprivation and abandonment/instability schema and started to get upset and bored. Thus she made several attempts to make her husband pay attention to her as well, all of which turned out to be futile. Ailin's vulnerable child mode was deeply affected by being in that place and witnessing her husband's lack of attention to her. Being in the gaucherie coping style and controversial/troublemaker mode, she quietly left the cottage and started to take a walk around the area without notifying anyone about her departure. Not after long, her husband noticed her absence at the cottage. He started to search the nearby area for Ailin without success in finding any traces of her; he rushed back in and told others that she had disappeared. This time, The whole group came out and started looking for Ailin. As the time passed, their anxiety grew, and as it got dark, they called off their search and returned to the cottage in horror and desperation. It was several hours that Ailin went missing, and they decided to call the police on this matter. Ailin's husband burst into tears while he was giving the missing report to the police station over the phone. Just before the police officers arrived at the scene, Ailin came back. She told the group that she was bored and, out of curiosity, started to take a walk around the area and fell asleep near the river. Her husband lost his temper, and after a serious argument and fight, he decided to put an early end to their trip and get back home.

Exercise for the Controversial/ Troublemaker Mode

1. Now that you are familiar with the controversial/troublemaker mode, try to identify instances of this mode in yourself or the ones you know in daily life and write them down.
2. Considering the examples given for this mode and its manifestations in different schemas, try to find the manifestations of this mode for the rest of the schemas.
3. Try to find the negative consequences of this mode in marital life, intimate relationships, interpersonal relationships, and the workplace.
4. Ask the patient to fill in the rest of the schemas and modes activated due to controversial/troublemaker mode in the table.

The Misguide/Misdirect Mode (MMM)

In this mode, the patient sometimes without being aware and sometimes intentionally guides others in the wrong direction or causes others to make mistakes by giving unsound and emotional advice without taking all the aspects of the issue into full consideration. While being in misguide/misdirect mode, many patients comment on topics they have no sufficient knowledge or the necessary and comprehensive information. It should be noted that this mode costs the misguided people around the patient lots of troubles and challenges, and eventually, it makes others question his credibility and reliability. Usually, this person is left with fewer people who prefer to ask for his advice or value his opinions and viewpoints in the long run.

The following sections point out several case examples of

the misguide/misdirect mode related to each schema:

Case 1: Mr. A, due to his unrelenting standards/ hyper criticalness schema, highly insists that his only daughter should study hard in order to get into one of the highly recognized and competitive universities. The daughter has failed to pass the entrance exam for these universities for several years now and is in deep despair and confusion. Due to her repetitive failures, she tends to function well below her potential when attending an exam session. Despite all this, Mr. A still insists on his opinions regarding his daughter's education path and believes the only path for gaining success and happiness in life lies in getting into one of the top universities.

- Negative consequences: The young girl has been worn off due to studying repetitive lessons and courses. She does not attend any other activities such as playing sports, nor does she engage in activities of artistic or leisure nature. Her primary activity revolves around studying. Considering her mood, she is highly depressed.
- Mr. A's reaction: He believes his daughter is not putting the necessary effort into following her studies. According to him, his daughter's main reason for not getting accepted into one of the top universities is her laziness and lack of competence.

Case 2: Due to self-sacrifice schema (an overcompensation for emotional deprivation schema), Mrs. B is mostly surrounded by broken, poor, and diseased people. Mrs. B spends most of her time listening to their problems and being in the gaucherie coping style, giving them advice on various topics without having any skills and knowledge of counseling and psychotherapy. Her counsels cover a wide variety of issues, from medical interventions to encouraging others to get married and having children, lessons on children's upbringing, and communication with adolescents. Most of the time, being in misguide/misdirect mode, she only makes matters worse for the ones around her by giving them unsound advice.

- Negative consequences: People who are already in trouble follow her fallacious advice, thus making wrong decisions; they fall from the frying pan into the fire!
- Mrs. B's reaction: She usually gets surprised when she witnesses that the people who followed her advice end up in more trouble. She refers to the unfortunate events as some things that fate had in store for them and was unavoidable. After each damage that she does, she still goes on with even more fallacious advice until she destroys the other person's life.

Case 3: Mr. C lives in a city where attracts many tourists, especially over the weekends and holidays. Mr. C believes that these tourists overwhelm his town by disrupting its order and safety, and cleanness. Thus he highly disguises them and is angry with the stranger travelers. Due to his entitlement/grandiosity schema, he stated: If the matters were in my hands, I would have stopped the tourists from entering the city altogether, or I would have made sure to cause them some sort of trouble so that they would have left this city with bad memories. Usually, when tourists ask him about an address of a popular place in the city to visit, he being in the misguide/misdirect mode, directs them so that instead of getting to the destination, they end up at the routes which take them out of the city!

- Negative consequences: The tourists having wanted extra fuel and causing traffic, get back to their initial location with anger and frustration. The tourists overgeneralize this behavior of Mr. C to the whole population of the city.
- Mr. C's reaction: He believes that the people of his town do not have any needs for the tourists. They are doing well financially, and tourists bring them nothing but misery

and disorder.

Case 4: Mrs. D got divorced from her ex-husband many years ago and now lives with her son. Due to her mistrust/abuse and enmeshment/undeveloped-self schemas, she repeatedly cautions her son to be on the watch for other's deceptions, especially the ones from other women. When her son meets someone, she usually advises him not to share anything about their family's past, assets, and information regarding details of his job. She also advised him not to get close to the other person emotionally, and she encourages her son to test the other person in different ways and on many occasions in order to gain evidence that the other person is worthy of their trust. Mrs. D's son always follows her mother's suggestions, which has always caused him to fail in his relationships.

- Negative consequences: Even though Mrs. D's 26 years old son feels an intense need for a romantic relationship as well as a sexual one with a potential partner, he hasn't managed to enter a healthy romantic relationship and to form a separate individual identity of his own which suit his needs yet due to following her mother's orders (enmeshment/undeveloped-self schema). He has lost his self-confidence and deeply feels lonely.
- Mrs. D's reaction: She states that she prefers her son to be alone instead of getting trapped in a cunning and predator woman's trap. She points out to a couple of men she knows, and their wives have emotionally or financially abused them all.

Case 5: Mrs. E's abandonment/instability schema usually gets activated when she encounters single men and women. Being in the gaucherie coping style and misguide/misdirect mode, she tends to advise them to get married as soon as possible so that they do not wind up alone during their elderly years. She usually starts her advice with the following statements: You should get married before you get old even if you are not doing well financially or don't have a paying job. After you get married, everything will get fixed on its own. The more you put off your marriage, the more difficult it gets for you to find an appropriate partner for your life. Just remember, it's almost impossible to be all by yourself when you are old. So, get married as soon as possible and bring as many children as you can to not ever be alone.

- Negative consequences: The married couple cannot afford their life's expenses. Financial difficulties dispute many arguments and fights among them. Their married life eventually ends with a divorce due to economic poverty.
- Mrs. E's reaction: She feels sorry and sorrowful upon discovering the news of the couple's divorce. She believes that today's young generation is not as patient as the previous generations were and that they do not have what it takes to tolerate all the different difficulties that life brings with itself. She brings up memories of the dire economic situation about the time she was young and how she and others from her generation put up with those difficult conditions.

Indeed, the misguide/misdirect mode causes serious damages to the lives of others. The harmful and undesirable impacts of these damages can have long-lasting effects on the psychological well-being of individuals. If the psychological damage is severe, it may take a very long time for the damaged person to be able to fix it, and it is not going to be an easy process. The severity of the damages that this mode causes to others covers a broad spectrum, starting with slight and ending with severe. It is also a subject to different areas such as academic, financial, social relationships, family, marriage, bearing children, and immigration.

Throughout history, humankind severely felt the need to consult others and ask for their opinions, ideas, and advice whenever they were faced with a problem or a dilemma in any given period of their life. Also, others' experiences were a priceless gem when it came to choosing the right direction in life, and everyone not only needed it but also tried to make the best out of it. There were usually wise, experienced men and women in each tribe whom youngsters would go to in order to ask for advice and get a consultation. Today those wise individuals who gained their knowledge through experiments and experiences they had in life have given their place to educated professionals. What is of utmost importance in today's modern and complicated world is that the healthy adult should not neglect seeking consultation from qualified and competent individuals when about to make any of the important life decisions, including choosing the field of study, career, getting married, having children and immigration. This is important since many of the problems people have to deal with daily are due to getting misguided or receiving lousy advice. Thus people might guide us to a completely wrong path due to their schemas and while being in their misguide/misdirect mode either intentionally or unintentionally. It's our healthy adult mode's task to identify the schemas of the important people of our life based on which they tend to misdirect us and cause us to make faulty decisions when being in the gaucherie coping style with the help of a therapist. The more the healthy adult mode is developed in a person, the less likely it is for her to be under the influence of people who have had a long history of misguiding and misdirecting others.

Exercise for the Misguide/ Misdirect Mode

1. After being familiarized with the misguide/misdirect mode, try to identify and write down instances of this mode in yourself or the ones around you in daily life.

2. Considering the examples given for this mode and its manifestations in different schemas, try to find the manifestations of this mode for the rest of the schemas.
3. Find the negative consequences of this mode being at play in marital life, interpersonal relationships, and work environment.

The Obstructionist/ Saboteur Mode (OSM)

In this mode, the patient intentionally or unintentionally tries to disrupt and interfere with the plans and activities of others in a way that others fail to recognize his role in the disruption. The patient does this in different forms, including engaging in obstructing activities, stopping progress, continuously creating complications and difficulties, causing states of disarray in the system, making a fuss and complicating the situation, and preventing activities from making progress. Actions such as causing disarray in the organization (in subjugation, self-sacrifice, entitlement/ grandiosity, and mistrust/ abuse schemas), not giving clear responses (in defectiveness/ shame, failure and dependence/ incompetence schemas), causing delays and procrastination (in insufficient self-control/ self-discipline and unrelenting standards schemas), destroying documents and evidence (in entitlement/ grandiosity, punitiveness, and mistrust/ abuse schemas), blocking (vulnerability to harm and illness, punitiveness, mistrust/ abuse and abandonment/ instability schemas), placing obstacles in the way of progress (in unrelenting standards, entitlement/ grandiosity, punitiveness, negativity, and emotional deprivation schemas), causing interruptions (in subjugation, self-sacrifice, mistrust/ abuse, and social isolation schemas). Blocking technology, destroying others' works and artifacts, destroying evidence, damaging others, etc., are also accounted as behaviors that stem from this mode.

The Obstructionist/Saboteur Mode in the Area of Children and Adolescents

The obstructionist/saboteur mode is a primitive mode. This means that this mode can be observed even among one-year-old newborns. By observing the behaviors of children, too, one can become aware of the presence of this mode. As an example of this case, consider ten years old boy whose father just sent him shopping for some bread and milk from a nearby supermarket while the boy was busy playing video games. Obviously unhappy with the situation, the boy left the house, nagging and saying: "You always ask me to do difficult things when I am playing." The boy started to go up on the street, and just as he passed their house, he suddenly noticed the beautiful viola flowers in the neighbors garden. He entered the neighbors garden, picked a handful of them for himself, ruined a couple of them while he was walking in the garden, and started to amuse himself with the flowers he just picked for himself. The boy spent so much time in the garden that the worried father had to come out and start looking for him, only to find the boy in the neighbors garden busy with subversion. The obstructionist part of this mode reveals itself in the boys amusing himself in playing, delaying, and ultimately refusing to do the shopping his father asked of him to do. The saboteur part of this mode also lies in ruining and picking up the viola flowers of the neighbors garden. The obstructionist/saboteur mode easily causes trouble for oneself and the others around. The boy took the blame and got reprimanded by the father for his actions, and the father also had to pay the neighbor for the damages that his son caused to the garden and its flowers. If this becomes a habitual behavior where the boy causes trouble for the neighbors more than often and engages in vandalism, this behavior can be considered part of the controversial/ troublemaker mode. That is when he will be known as the troublemaker among the neighbors. The modes of the gaucherie coping style are similar in how the child tries to meet her needs. When the child's core emotional needs are not being met, she will express her anger, sadness, and frustration through the controversial/troublemaker or obstructionist/saboteur modes. If the boy in the case example learns that he can avoid "responsibility" by behaving in the obstructionist/saboteur mode, this mode becomes reinforced. In other words, if the boy realizes that his father is not going to send him shopping anymore because this time not only did he not do the shopping but also damaged the neighbor's garden, he would repeat this behavior next time as well if faced with the same situation. Therefore he might "avoid responsibility" with this mode. As mentioned earlier, the main reason for using the gaucherie coping style is "avoiding individual, family, and social responsibility." The child has no interest in doing anything else but to continue with her playing (the need for spontaneity and fun) or resting while she is engaged in either one of them. Asking the child to do something and giving her responsibilities while she is playing or resting disturbs the child's emotional need (playing), resulting in her dissatisfaction, sadness, and anger. Thus, the obstructionist/saboteur mode gets activated in these instances and causes trouble for the child or the ones around her.

The Obstructionist/Saboteur Mode in Group Therapy Settings

After the first couple of sessions where the group leader and his assistants educated the group members about the schemas and modes, the members gained a noticeable awareness of these concepts in schema therapy. As a part of a self-knowledge exercise, the members started to reveal instances of their obstructionist/saboteur mode in the group's safe environment with the direction of the group therapist and the help of his assistants. The group therapist asked the members to identify their obstructionist/saboteur mode related to their schemas in different situations.

One of the members stated: Due to my social isolation schemas, whenever my husband intended to invite his friends or family to our house, I would prevent him from doing so by making up different excuses such as I have a deadline at work which is close and I don't have time for this. Another member stated that: Because of my emotional deprivation schema, I excessively try to have my husband's attention, especially when he is playing video games. This has made me hide his games or lose them on some occasions. A father stated: When my daughter got accepted into a well-known university, she was thrilled, and she had to leave our small town and move to another city far from home. I cleverly and without getting noticed, managed to cause troubles in her plans which ultimately prevented her from leaving home (obstructionist/saboteur in abandonment/instability). A woman stated every time I have an achievement in work or my studies, my husband's defectiveness/shame schema gets triggered severely, and in his obstructionist/saboteur mode, he causes me many troubles by not being cooperative or acting indifferent when it comes to our children issues or house chores. A managing director of a government organization stated: Due to my entitlement schema, I put an end to all the long-term projects which the previous managing director had started.

Furthermore, I wanted my performance to get noticed,

so I started a couple of similar projects but with different project names in other locations. This way, everyone knew that I was the one who started these projects and not the previous managing director. Another member said: because of my mistrust/abuse schema when it comes to financial matters, and I'm planning to buy or sell something, I either hesitate so much or postpone the meetings that either the deal were canceled or the other person got too close to calling off the deal. A soccer player who wasn't getting paid by his club for several months and had already asked for his salary said: Since the coach and the club manager refused to pay my salary despite my repeated inquiries, I decided to take soft revenge against them by slacking off during training sessions, putting less effort in the matches and losing scoring chances (obstructionist/saboteur mode in punitiveness schema). A university student stated: due to my subjugation schema, I didn't dare to ask for more time from my professor in order to finish and hand in my dissertation. So I finally ended up handing it in without appropriately editing it first while it contained errors and copyright violations. The last member of the group was a retired university professor who said: When I was the person in charge of the committee overseeing the research plans and projects, I deliberately rejected most of them since I didn't want my colleagues to accelerate in their academic successes and wanted to stay ahead of them (obstructionist/saboteur mode in the unrelenting standards/hyper criticalness schema).

Next, the group therapist asked the members to find the problems and the "negative consequences" of this mode in their marital life, social interactions, and work environment. The member with the social isolation schema stated: finally, my husband grew tired of my excuses for refusing to have his friends and family over. Being hurt, one day he made reservations at a luxurious restaurant and invited all of his friends and family there and told me: If you found free time you can join us! The woman who used to hide her husband's computer games said that my husband grew suspicious of me after a while since his video games were getting lost. He eventually found out that I was the one who hid them, and not only did this not make him pay more attention to me, but also he was not on talking terms with me for some time. The worried father told the story of how his daughter got relocated to the new city: When my daughter found out about my subversions, she got frustrated and told me: "You are afraid to lose me. That's why you don't want me to go to another city to continue my studies. You really are damaging my future! "The father continued: I asked her to let me go with her to the new city, which she refused. Due to my abandonment schema, as soon as she got settled in the student dormitory, I rented a house nearby. After a couple of days, I went to her university campus and met her there. She got severely frustrated because of my behaviors and refused to see me or return any of my calls for several months. Now I'm fully aware of my misdoings and how this mode resulted in me being abandoned by my daughter. The managing director stated: Due to my sabotage, the previous director's projects didn't come to an end. This also didn't mean that my projects were successful. It makes me sorry to know that this mode and my entitlement schema prevented a big organization from making progress. The other member with mistrust/abuse schema stated: My obstructionist/saboteur mode has cost me a great deal of my credit in my line of work which is heavily involved with making deals with others and making purchases or selling things. This mode prevents people from keeping their words whether they are the buyer or the seller in a given transaction. On one end, I aim to make a profit from a deal, and on the other end, by repeated mess-ups, I somehow get the profitable deal to be called off. Once, one of my friends told me: "I will never make any deals with you because you don't keep your word!" It has happened numerous times where due to my procrastination, the other party has called off the deal and has even sued me after a while to get me to compensate for their losses. Before today, I kept thinking to myself that my intuitions were always right, and these people wanted to abuse me from the beginning. Now I get to understand that those people were not ill-intentioned from the beginning, and it is this mode that puts me in conflict with others. The soccer player, being sad and frustrated, stated: after putting out my worst game at a couple of matches, the coach benched me, and after showing up late at the training sessions, I finally got fired.

The university student sighed and told the group in a state of sadness: As I entered my dissertation advisors' office, I was faced with his face burning with anger. My whole body was shaking out of fear. He yelled at me, pounded the dissertation on the table, and told me:" You are going to stay here for another semester, and you are going to write this again from the beginning!" My unacademic behaviors, which were from my obstructionist/saboteur mode, perpetuated my subjugation schema. The retired university professor stated: This mode made interruptions in the process of accepting new research plans, delayed some of them, and prevented new researches from making progress. This made other university professors object to my performance, and ultimately I lost my position. Due to my unrelenting standards schema, status-seeking and being achievement-oriented had always been a priority for me, and losing that position was a huge setback for my state of achievement. It was such a loss that I had to deal with depression for a rather long period of time.

The Obstructionist/Saboteur Mode in the Individual Setting

Helen is 36 years old who went to see a therapist because of her dissatisfaction and problems in her romantic relationship as well as her work. She was extremely unhappy with remaining as an entry-level employee in a commercial firm with a low salary and no promotions after many years. On the one hand, she needed the job's money, and on the other hand, she was extremely angry with her managers. As a result, she was used to intentionally getting some of the firm's letters lost and not following up on some of the others. Also, while dealing with clients, she would try not to give them clear answers and instructions, thus putting off the clients and making interruptions in their work as much as she could. This way, she got the clients to question the firm's credibility. She told the therapist: "Every day, I enter the firm thinking about new obstructions and sabotages in my mind. Even though I am embarrassed with my behavior, it is as if I have no power in dealing with this mode of mine." She also shared with the therapist how in her relationship with her husband, when she is not feeling like having a sexual encounter with her husband, she prevents him by making up excuses. Therefore, Helen's most significant schema was subjugation while being in the gaucherie coping style, and with the obstructionist/saboteur mode, she engaged in unreasonable behaviors.

The therapist asked Helen to write down the negative consequences of her obstructionist/ saboteur mode and how this mode activated her other modes and schemas at her work as in the table. She filled the table in with the help of the therapist as following:

Table 5-2: Other schemas, modes, and negative consequences related to the obstructionist/ saboteur mode

NO.	Other Maladaptive Schemas	Other Modes	Negative Consequences
1	Defectiveness/ shame, Failure	Guilt-inducing Parent Mode	I don't attend to my responsibilities at the firm. I violate the client's rights on purpose. Now when the time comes to

			get that minimum salary, I intensely feel guilty.
2	Defectiveness/ Shame, Failure	Vulnerable Child	The managers don't put me on serious tasks since they think of me as a dysfunctional employee. This alone has prevented me from making progress.
3	Negativity/ Pessimism	Detached Protector	Maybe at the beginning tearing the letters made me feel better but eventually, after a while, that lost its effect too.
4	Vulnerability to Harm and illness, Emotional Inhibition	Vulnerable Child	I severely disguise myself because of all these wrongdoings, making a fool of myself and always being afraid. Neither I dare to leave this job nor dare to express my feelings and ask for a promotion.

Exercise for the Obstructionist/ Saboteur Mode

1. Now after being familiarized with the obstructionist/ saboteur mode, try to identify and write down instances of this mode in yourself or the ones around you in daily life.
2. Considering the examples given for this mode and its manifestations in different schemas, try to find the manifestations of this mode for the rest of the schemas.
3. Find the negative consequences of this mode being at play in marital life, interpersonal relationships, and work environment.
4. Ask the patient to fill in the table with other schemas and modes that get activated due to obstructionist/ saboteur mode.

Personality Disorders and the Modes of the Gaucherie Coping Style

There is a close connection between personality disorders and the gaucherie coping style. Listed in the table below are the most frequently observed new modes among each personality disorder.

Table 5-3: Personality disorders and the modes of the gaucherie coping style

Personality Disorder	Modes of the gaucherie coping style	Description

Histrionic	Controversial/ Troublemaker	Easily gets into trouble and, by telling exciting stories about the troubles faced, gains others "admiration, attention, empathy, and approval."
Narcissistic	Misguide/ Misdirect	Since thinks knows best, likes to give comments on every issue. Gives comments on the upbringing, educational, financial, martial, and other issues. This way directs others to a wrong path and usually will not accept the negative consequences of his/her mistake.
Avoidant	Obstructionist/ Saboteur	When faced with adversities, remains completely "silent" or does not speak up about the issue in the hope of prematurely ending the tension and returning to the safe spot. This inappropriate keeping of silence either results in intensifying the tension, or the problem remaining unresolved forever.
Dependent	Controversial/ Troublemaker	Since is not able to take care of him/ herself or appropriately undertake the daily routines, makes naive decisions or does things that either causes trouble for the self and the ones around or damages them in minor or severe ways.
Schizoid	Controversial/ Troublemaker	Has not learned the necessary communication skills due to constant isolation from society and always being by him/herself. Thus when it comes to social relationships, gets involved with unwanted sufferings and difficulties.
Passive Aggressive	Obstructionist/ Saboteur	Responds to orders from superordinates or expectations of the ones around in specific indirect ways such as deflecting, wasting time, stubbornness, and intentional forgetfulness or incompetence. Sometimes asks for more responsibilities in order to do more severe damage.

Obsessive Compul-sive	A. Misguide/ Misdirect B. Obstruction-ist/ Saboteur	A. Encourages and directs others into taking difficult paths to reach their dreams, success, and attain their goals instead of more accessible paths since believes facing hardships broadens the mind. These unrelenting bits of advice increase the chances of others' failure. B. Might disapprove of others' work and constantly reject them due to being a perfectionist. This causes a sense of failure and dissatisfaction in others.
Antisocial	Misguide/ Misdirect	By being silver-tongued, deceit others and encourages them to engage in illegal acts. Enjoys from giving others false information and watching them getting hurt. Sends others down the well with his/her rotten rope and gains satisfaction from observing their misery and suffering.
Borderline	Controversial/ Troublemaker	The patient faces many challenges due to having conflicting encounters, stressful relationships, and distressing choices with others while not having clear goals for the future. When out of control, lacks empathy, and is not aware of the damages, stresses, and pains that are causing others. If getting rejected causes dangerous and strange troubles for the self and the other person.
Paranoid	A. Misguide/ Misdirect B. Obstruction-ist/ Saboteur	A. If suspects others have ulterior motives against him/her, prevents the perceived threat by giving them false information, thus confusing them. B. If becomes afraid of someone, stonewalls in order to prevent the friendship relationship from making progress or causes interruptions in the work affairs. Does not allow others to get close or penetrate.

As we know, a personality can either be adaptive or maladaptive. We refer to a condition as maladaptive when the individual lacks the ability to adapt her thoughts and behavior to her environment and the changes taking place in her surroundings. The gaucherie coping style contributes to a significant degree to making an individual maladaptive with his environment. Therefore the degree of adaptiveness and maladaptiveness can be correlated with the degree to which the gaucherie coping style is being used. The stronger the healthy adult mode becomes in an individual, the less are the chances of using the gaucherie coping style. Maladaptive individuals display gauche behavior when faced with situations that require them to make changes and correct decisions.

Final Words

In this chapter, topics were discussed, which in the future require more discussion and review in human relationships. Gaucherie is a new coping style along with its modes, namely Controversial/ Troublemaker, Misguide/ Misdirect, and Obstructionist/ Saboteur modes. After learning and becoming familiar with this coping style, its modes, and concepts, one can find many instances of it in his clinical work, private life, and surrounding environment.

Reaching the final section of this chapter, an important question has yet remained unanswered. A question which addressing it is of utmost importance. Why should we consider gaucherie as a coping style? The answer lies in the Mysteriousness and subtlety of the human mind. The surrender, avoidance, and overcompensation styles are the least complicated and most accessible forms of copings for humans. The complex mind does not always surrender, escape or fight! Sometimes when the mind finds itself in trouble or is faced with an unresolvable issue, it chooses to bring chaos into the lives of others and the environment as well. This way, not only its troubles are not being noticed as significantly as before, but it can also get along with its own troubles way easier while observing plenty of troubles in others. When the person states that everyone has their own issues, it brings her a sense of relief, and when she observes someone who is carefree and in peace of mind, it severely makes her anxious and angry. An alcoholic would encourage others to abuse alcohol (Misguide/Misdirect Mode) as well in order to normalize a behavior (alcohol addiction) that has caused him many sufferings and has cost him his reputation in society. Gaucherie is a coping style in which the individual does not try to improve her condition, yet she would state: I'm not the only one who is not doing well, take a look around, and you see no one is doing well! While in this mode, the patient avoids responsibility and moves in the direction of intentional or unintentional destruction. The dissatisfied worker who is not happy with his minimum wage, which he gets from his boss, would throw a spanner in the works (obstructionist/saboteur mode) and state: If I'm not going to do well financially and be prosperous, nor shouldn't my boss! Like other coping styles, gaucherie and its modes not only do not resolve the existing issues but also add to them. The person who has failed to gain his favorable social status due to his schema-driven behaviors would enter conflicts (Controversial/Trouble-Maker) with credible and respectful people on mundane subjects. This way, he assumes that their position and status are being damaged. Thus the patient in the gaucherie coping style, instead of making an effort to bring positive changes into his own life and taking responsibility for his own problems, prefers to bring himself a temporary sense of satisfaction and relief by bringing chaos into the order and peacefulness of others lives and the environment.

CHAPTER SIX

THE HEALTHY ADULT MODE (HAM)

In this chapter:

- Getting to know the Healthy Adult Mode (HAM)
- Introducing the manikin figure
- Getting focused on the cognitive and behavioral aspects of the healthy adult
- Learning the attached/assertive behavior
- The Happy Child Mode (HCM)
- Introducing the seven appropriate grounds for the healthy adult
- The healthy adult mode checklist

The healthy adult mode, just like a kind and strong guardian, constantly looks for empathic statements and narratives for our thoughts and behaviors. This mode prevents the parent modes from continuously blaming, humiliating, or punishing us, or brutally making us feel guilty and afraid, or becoming so demanding that we feel tremendously being under pressure. The healthy adult mode helps us love and support ourselves and come to terms with our weaknesses and strengths. David Bernstein has recently (2020) pointed out 48 features of the healthy adult mode in the Bernstein List of Strengths (BLS) and has formulated appropriate statements to assess the healthy adult mode. Some of these features include: self-controlled, self-confident, creative, physically fit, playful, spiritual, responsible, empathic, assertive, kind, funny, understanding, wise, patient, grateful, realistic, and flexible.

The individual with a weak or under-developed healthy adult mode does not know himself, has no idea about how his emotions get triggered or where his feelings have their roots. He is unable to identify the reason for other's inappropriate behaviors with him. He is still puzzled when it comes to his parents, their role, and their position in his life. He has got no way of thinking to himself, thus accepting what others believe in as absolute facts. He has no control over his future and sometimes thinks that fate and destiny have handed him the horrible situations he is dealing with due to unclear reasons. This person is not aware that if he behaves too submissively in the face of the authority figures, he might rebel against them one day. In fact, for an extended period, his way of living closely resembles the one of a slave, only which suddenly turns into a full-blown rebel.

Reaching balance in life takes place with the development of the healthy adult. During the course of therapy, some of the patients worry that if the balance is achieved in their life, they might miss out on the successful future they have been eagerly expecting to arrive. On the contrary, the healthy adult does not have excessive or high-risk ambitions, yet he is aware of the correct means through which the proper forms of progress and advancement are achievable. The healthy adult tells us that if something gets broken, it can be fixed and changed; if a difficulty arises, it can be resolved, if there is a wound, it can be healed, and if a sentence has been written wrong, it can be rewritten. The healthy adult is not worried about getting failed, yet he constantly is searching for the reasons for the failure and striving to carry on a new plan. In fact, this mode inwardly consulates us in the face of adversities and encourages us with much praise to endure and be resilient in the face of frustrations and failures.

When it comes to interpersonal relationships, each instance of conflict makes the healthy adult strengthen and develop its creativity, initiative, ways of resolving conflicts, and individuality. The healthy adult is well aware that he should not idolize anyone since after each period of idealization comes the degradation phase. Therefore the healthy adult is always looking for equal, friendly, intimate, and safe interpersonal relationships. With this mode, we can accept the people around us with all their strengths and flaws, knowing that no one is one hundred percent perfect. For example, narcissists are among the most challenging population with regard to communications.

Wendy Behary (2013) has stated seven gifts that can be utilized while communicating with individuals with a narcissistic personality disorder. It appears that these seven gifts are not only effective methods when it comes to communicating with narcissists but are also applicable concerning all interpersonal interactions. There are countless arts of communication, yet the following seven are the ones that Behary has discussed, and they have applications for the healthy adult mode in general as well. Each gift is associated with a specific form of artful communication, which are as follows:

1. The art of mutual respect is an expression of the gift of generosity.
2. The art of self-disclosure is an expression of the gift of courage.
3. The art of discernment is an expression of the gift of truth.
4. The art of collaboration is an expression of the gift of shared effort.
5. The art of anticipating clashes is an expression of the gift of foresight.
6. The art of apology is an expression of the gift of responsibility.
7. The art of reflective listening is an expression of the gift of balance.

When the therapist speaks with the patient about the schema and mode that the patient possesses and unravels and explains the coping behaviors of the patient, the most crucial question that the patient brings forth is this: Now that I know all this, how should I behave? The answer lies in the strengthening and development of the healthy adult mode. The aim is to behave like a healthy adult. Farrell and Shaw (2012) believe: "We see the executive functions of the Healthy Adult mode developing throughout the lifespan beginning in childhood." Therefore, considering the temperament of each given individual and the conditions of the environment they grew up in, the development rate of the healthy adult differs from person to person.

The healthy adult mode is among one of the main modes in schema therapy. This mode reflects psychological well-being, maturity, and a good sense of judgment. Furthermore, this mode accurately works on the structure of psychological flexibility (Brockman, 2013; from Roediger, Stevens and Brockman 2018) and can be primarily described and addressed using the concepts and strategies of acceptance and commitment therapy (ACT; Hayes, Strosahl, & Wilson, 2012; same source). The components of the healthy adult mode are described in figure (6-1) based on the concepts offered by schema therapy, acceptance and commitment therapy (ACT), and mindfulness. One reason for coming up with a picture describing the healthy adult mode was the patients who asked different questions about the shape or appearance of the healthy adult mode. By designing a manikin figure with five heads rather than one head who spends her day to day time on seven grounds (education and learning, social interactions, altruism, sense of aesthetics, spirituality, sexual relationship, and body exercises), many patents found an answer to their question. The other reason for designing such a figure was that since the healthy adult mode is the orchestrate who oversees the executive functioning duties of the other modes if being presented by a figure with specific and certain components would be more memorable for the patients. As the therapy sessions continued, the patients were asked to place the figure of the healthy adult mode in an appropriate location so that they can observe it several times during the day. These groups of patients came back with positive feedback. Some of them reported that after looking at the figure, they could better connect with their healthy adult mode, thus making correct decisions regarding the issues at hand. Also, another group reported that while facing difficulties, they could take better care of themselves by looking at the manikin figure.

Detailed explanations of each of the healthy adult modes' cognitive and behavioral components are presented in the following sections.

Figure 6-1: The manikin; components of the healthy adult mode

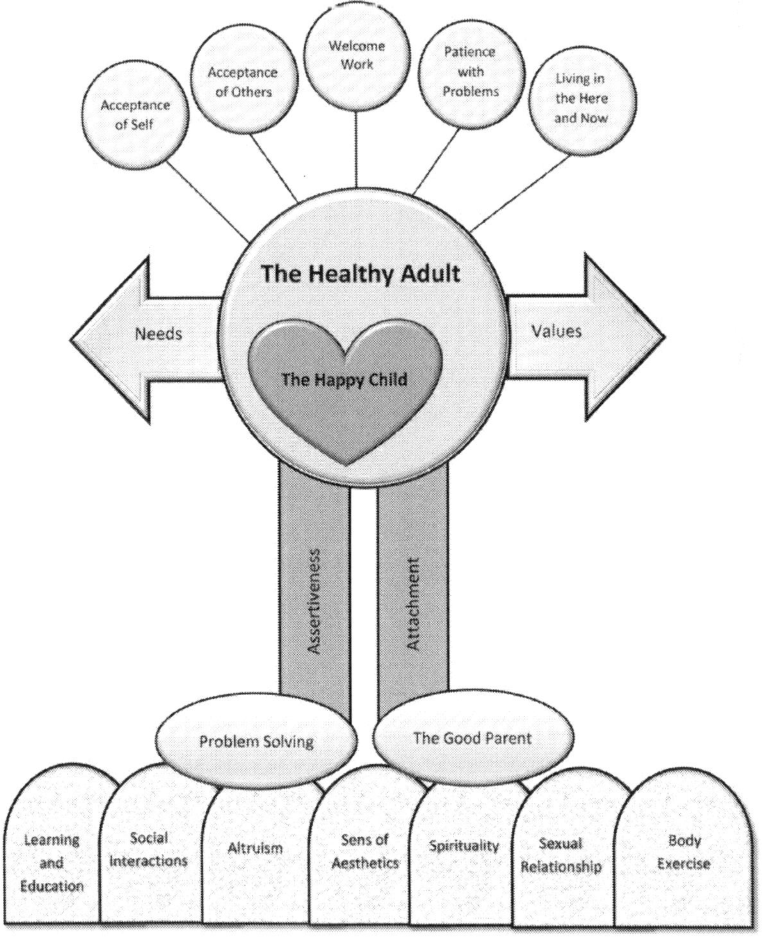

Acceptance of Self

When the time comes that we come to terms with a bitter reality, the amount of pain and suffering we experience gradually decreases, and we gain peace to some extent. Let us recall the moment when we found out about the amount and severity of our early maladaptive schemas for the very first time. At that moment, we realized that many of our sufferings we went through our entire lives were direct results of our maladaptive schemas. The reason for many separations, losses, abstentions, lonelinesses, failures, and betrayals were our schemas and modes which we had no awareness of their presence. Our pain and suffering reached their most when we realized that the cause of all these schemas forming in us were our parents or early caregivers in the first place. They were supposed to play the role of a good enough caregiver, providing us with nurturance, yet unfortunately, this was not mostly the case for us. At that moment, we were left with only two choices: Either we could account our parents as the forever guilty and blameful figures, thus refusing to accept the responsibility for healing our sufferings, still taking the path which further perpetuated our schemas, and we could never have witnessed even the slightest happy part that life has to offer us, Or on the other hand, we could grief over all the damages, frustrations and difficulties that we had gone through our entire childhood with the help of a therapist, vent our anger, try to heal our wounds and in the end accept them completely.

Furthermore, we could accept all the hurtful shortcomings, incapacitations, and limitations that we had experienced and aim to modify our schemas. Even though not all individuals yet, most of them choose to proceed with the second option. Acceptance of self means to accept ourselves as worthy human beings despite all the wrong schema-driven choices that we have made our entire lives. Individuals with the healthy adult mode accept themselves with all the unfortunate incidents that have happened to them in their childhood and try to modify their schemas and bring changes into how they make decisions regarding the important matters in their lives. Acceptance of self helps us to accept and love ourselves with all the weaknesses and shortcomings that come with us. If acceptance of self has been achieved within an individual to a high degree, the person would bring less attention to the negative aspects of her life and become more self-compassioned than in the past.

Acceptance of Others

Around us are people whose psychological structure might collapse upon the slightest difficulty taking place. According to Sigmund Freud: "The scope of one's personality is defined by the magnitude of that problem which is capable of driving a person out of his wits." There is no doubt that all of us are vulnerable on some level when it comes to difficulties, yet the reactions that we exhibit differ from an individual to the other. Individuals with entitlement/grandiosity schema taking the "I am the wise one" stance believe that others should follow whatever solution they propose for overcoming the problem at hand. Individuals with vulnerability to harm and illness, dependence/incompetence, failure, mistrust/abuse, and defectiveness/shame schemas grow increasingly anxious upon facing a new problem and do not find the necessary strength within themselves to tackle the problem. If we are to accept that all human beings are different from each other, even the identical twins differ from each other in many aspects, we would find ourselves in a more convenient position to proceed from. Therefore it would be better to accept that different individuals exhibit different behaviors from each other and from us under different circumstances that are not necessarily aligned with our interests or perspective. It is utterly domineering of a person if she expects others to behave according to her views, standpoint, and interest. In fact, no one is able to permanently change others by being forceful and putting pressure on them. Thus, if a father attempts to force his son or daughter to a particular way of living, the way he himself approves of, then that father has failed to accept his son or daughter.

The reality is that the people around us have many weaknesses as well as strengths. They drastically differ from us on many issues, such as thinking, taste, the view on life, interests, behaviors, and personality traits. Unfortunately, domineering individuals fail to accept viewpoints different from their own, and this lack of acceptance of others yields many interpersonal problems among them and the ones close to them. On the other hand, individuals with a developed healthy adult mode hold much respect for these individual differences and accept others as they are. Individuals with a healthy adult mode are well aware of the reasons lying underneath inappropriate behaviors of others, understand them, and are flexible toward them as long as no harm is coming their own way. This comes from a principle which states: "Only after we have accepted ourselves we are to accept others since the person who has accepted himself is well aware that others too, have gone through their own pains and sufferings in the past and the reason for many of their behaviors are their activated schemas and modes. This person can understand others and all the faults that come with them."

Welcome Work

Work can act as a miracle that saves human beings from depression, suicide, addiction, and physical illnesses and guarantee the individual's mental health. On the other hand, "working excessively" can be accounted as a sort of addiction that can hide the existing depression and lead to physical and psychological damages and drug abuse. In fact, not working and putting lots of time into working are both harmful in their own way. The healthy adult keeps "balance" in her work. Individuals with unrelenting standards and entitlement/grandiosity schemas are usually prone to workaholism. Individuals with failure, dependence/ incompetence, defectiveness/ shame, enmeshment/ undeveloped-self, and insufficient self-control/self-discipline schemas usually either stick with types of works that are way below their capabilities or have experienced long periods of unemployment throughout their life. Also, change of jobs is observed frequently among them. Individuals with self-sacrifice and subjugation schemas put too much into their work which ultimately results in their burnout. The ones with a social isolation schema favor solo works, and they fail to shape and form a network of working relationships that is necessary for making progress. Individuals with mistrust/ abuse schemas avoid forming working partnerships as far as they can, and they rarely make sound investments. Thus, schemas play an important role when it comes to financial and career disarrays. That is why recently, a workgroup called "Schema Therapy for Organizational Development" has been formed to address these issues.

Naturally, the famous rule of 888 can be used in order to bring balance into life. (dedicating approximately eight hours to sleep, eight hours to work, and eight hours to leisure, nutrition, shopping, cleaning, and other life activities). It appears so that putting forty hours of work each week is balanced and normal to a great extent if the income and expenses are compatible. Now in case, someone is forced to put in long hours of work or working more than one job, she should expect the negative consequences, physical and psychological illnesses in the near future.

If a person is working too much, yet his salary and incomes do not meet the expenses of his life, then the two major reasons are at play: schemas and the economic state of the country he is living in. Working has many hidden angles to itself, one of which is the age at which the person starts to work. For example, one of the issues in Iran's society these days is an increase in the child Labor rate in big cities. Before turning 18 years old, individuals are going through their childhood and adolescent years, and besides attending school, their need for play and spontaneity should be met sufficiently. 18 to 28 years old is the period best suitable for "specialized education," which usually takes place at universities, and 28 to 38 years old is the period where "gaining experience and creativity" takes place in the desired job or profession. Finally, during the 38 to 48 years old period, individuals, after gaining specialized education and sufficient experiences, reach the important stage of "production." Since production is accounted for as a difficult process, in this age period, the individual can start to produce as an energetic middle-aged man or woman by utilizing what he or she has learned and experienced in the previous stages. The 48 to 58 years old period is dedicated to "development and expansion of productions," where the individual introduces his earlier productions and expands upon them. Last but not least, 58 to 68 years old is the most suitable time period for providing the youth who are seeking to know their own interests, talents, and capabilities and enter the job market with "guidance and advice." After the age of 68 years old, "retirement" can be experienced gradually.

People usually experience peacefulness due to their successes which outweigh their failures. If military service is an obligation for men or both sexes in some countries, two years can be added to each one of these age periods. If a person has accepted the employee's life, it would be difficult to categorize him according to the system mentioned above. Furthermore, the retirement age for men and women is different in some countries. Thus we can change these numbers accordingly. Carl Young has stated an agreeable proposition; if someone has failed to find the path of his life until the age of 35, it would be difficult for him to do so afterward.

If upon reading these statements you feel sorry in your mind, it is better to bear in mind that according to the healthy adult viewpoint, nothing exists as "the perfect life," and everyone is capable of designing and coming up with the best path that is suitable for them and certain exceptions due occur among human beings.

Patience with Problems

Patience is a mandatory element in the life of a human being, yet since thousands of years ago, unaware humans who refused to be patient were used to turn to magic, spells, and amulets. Since those days also a group of abusive individuals has exploited the unaware population with magical spells, witchery, and amulets. Unfortunately, still to this day, traces of witches and fortune-tellers can be witnessed worldwide, especially in the parts where ignorance is bolder. The person with a failure schema who repeatedly fails in her endeavors at reaching her goals prefers to spend significant amounts of her money on magical spells so that the black magic is being removed from her life; thus, she can reach success. She does so instead of thinking through the reasons which have brought her the failures in the first place. A person with an emotional deprivation schema who has fallen in love with a cold and distant person reaches out to a fortune-teller and asks for a magic spell that would turn her cold beloved into a warm and passionate lover. She does all of so without thinking about the reasons that made her choose that person in the first place. For individuals with a weak and underdeveloped healthy adult who are not primarily interested in thinking, superstitions have always been the most convenient solution to their problems. In a relatively new form of superstition, a given individual with a dependence/incompetence schema waits for the universe and the consciousness governing it to provide him with a convenient way forward and a solution to his problems without himself having to put in any effort. The healthy adult does not waste his time fantasizing about having an easy life, yet he has accepted that life is difficult, and in order to have tolerance for the problems and challenges and to overcome them, he goes after gaining the set of skills that can empower him in this process.

Many patients complain about the goals that they have set for themselves previously yet have failed to reach them. This has made them sad, and they feel humiliated. In today's competitive world, reaching big goals is usually a difficult task that requires much patience. Patients think that they can only experience happiness after they have reached their goals. Patients with a failure schema have a low chance of reaching their goals unless they address and treat their schema. Patients with vulnerability to harm and illness schema exhibit lower levels of acceptance and resilience when being faced with common diseases such as cold, during their recovery phase. Askari, Madgaonkar and Rowell (2012) have indicated that the partners of the patients diagnosed with cancer are at an increased risk of contracting depression and severe anxiety. The higher the levels of resilience in those partners are, the better primary caregivers they would be as well as decreasing the risk of contracting depression and severe anxiety. Also, patients with unrelenting schema are not happy when they have reached their goals since they believe they have not done anything of significance. Therefore reaching or failing to reach our goals can not be a reason for our happiness, yet the healthy adult experiences happiness for what she is and what she is currently doing. While being in the healthy adult mode, the person tackles the problems one by one with much patience, has no rush in reaching the goals, calmly and slowly solves the problems, and ultimately reaches her goal which in turn is happy for. On the other hand, a lack of ability in being patient might lead to weak decision-making since the person has made those choices while being in a state of restlessness, anxiety, and disturbance.

Now the most significant form of patience is "Sahya" while dealing with the individuals who give you pain and suffering due to their own schemas. If you are a therapist, then certainly you have many experiences and memories of the sufferings you had gone through because of your patients. This sacred suffering requires something more than patience which in the Sanskrit language is called "Sahya" (Amir Askari's personal interview with L. Sam S. Manickam). Therapists are well aware of the fact that the treatment is a long and time-consuming process that requires Sahya so that the patient (for example, a patient with a borderline personality disorder) gradually gets her needs met through the therapy relationship and comes to terms with its real limits. Sam Manickam (2004) believes that sahya is one of the characteristics of therapists, along with warmth, acceptance, positive non-judgemental attention, and empathy, which are all of high importance. Furthermore, the failure to paying attention to Sahya can result in premature termination of the therapy relationship. According to Sam Manickam, what Mahatma Gandhi and Swami Vivekananda (1863 – 1902), Indian Monk meant by "perseverance for what is demanded" in their political, social, and cultural activities was Sahya.

Living in the Here and Now

Living in the present moment is a preventive method against psychological pressures stemming from day-to-day conflicts. Living in the here and now prevents the mind from escaping into the future, which results in anxiety. Also, it prevents the mind from regressing into the past, which is a contributing factor to depression. Many patients find themselves helpless when it comes to experiencing "being in the present moment"; thus, they are faced with a decrease in their day-to-day functioning. When you are able to engage in doing an activity, and you find yourself capable of bringing your attention to it and enjoying it at the same time, you are experiencing living in the present moment. Individuals with a healthy adult mode utilize "mindfulness techniques" in order to experience living in the here and now. Continued practice of mindfulness exercises brings awareness and non-judgemental view into the present moment. In case the patients are regretful about their past behaviors or grow highly anxious about the unknown events which are yet to take place in the future and they have a difficult time managing their unpleasant inner experiences due to the activation of their schemas and modes, then it is suggested that the therapist educates the patients about mindfulness by introducing self-help books. The therapist can further ask the patients to discuss their experiences from doing the exercises in the therapy session. These exercises aim to prevent patients from wasting their golden time on the events that have already taken place in the past and also the future which is yet to come. The aim is to help patients experience the universe firsthand so that their behaviors become flexible and according to their values. Ultimately the present moment is all that we have; thus, if we were to bring our awareness into another time or place, we certainly have missed the present moment. As Omar Khayyam puts it:

O friend, for the morrow let us not worry *** This moment we have now, let us not hurry
When our time comes, we shall not tarry *** With seven thousand-year-olds, our burden carry.

The Needs

It is of high importance for a given individual to be able to reach a balanced state between meeting her own needs and the ones of others. The needs hand in the healthy adult mode helps the person to first meet her own emotional needs. This mode connects the needs hand and the values hand, which in return results in connection with emotional well-being. Coping modes prevent our emotional needs from being met; hence since many of our needs are met while being in contact with others, we ought to express these needs clearly while communicating with them. Even though this is a relatively tricky task and might push the person toward avoidance, we can exercise our freedom in expressing our needs by utilizing the assertive leg. The assertive leg helps us with expressing our needs directly and asking them to be met. Jeffery Young and colleagues (2003) believe that human beings have five basic emotional needs. An individual with psychological well-being manages to meet these needs adaptively. These needs include 1. Secure attachment with others, 2. Autonomy, competence and identity, 3. Freedom in the expression of the healthy needs and emotions, 4. Fun and spontaneity, 5. Realistic limits and self-control.

The Values

In order to reach a rich, mature, worthy, and meaningful life, moving towards individualistic values is a principle that bears utmost importance. Even Though personal values are somehow different from person to person, moving in the direction of personal values is not possible without "action and movement." "Action" is what makes the person seek his life values and brings in the sense of satisfaction within the individual. Even Though many people correctly mention marriage, parenting, family relationships, staying healthy, etc., as their personal values yet the healthy adult mode also chooses higher personal values such as entrepreneurship, producing wealth, and making investments in order to fight poverty, participation in citizens activities, protecting the environment, cooperation in crisis management and natural disasters, engaging in civic activities, seeking justice, etc. As an example, many people do not consider the protection of public capital resources, conscientiousness towards nature, and biodiversity protection as their personal values due to cultural and educational poverty. Thus today, we witness the destruction of the environment and natural resources taking place relatively easily in different places worldwide. Many trees are being cut, the jungles shrinking in size every day, giving their place to houses in the heart of the jungles. For the healthy adult who accounts her identity as part of nature and believes that nature plays a vital and significant role in her life, a single tree is not just a tree but a breathing green. A strong, healthy adult can understand and identify different threats such as water pollution, the problems with the ozone layer, the polar ice melt crisis, the destructive effects of leaving plastic in nature, and the danger of extinction of the rare species.

Furthermore, she can try to prevent any of these crises from taking place as much as she can afford to. However, many people are entirely incapable of understanding a threat since they assume that the effects of an environmental threat are going to happen somewhere far from their own place of living. Thus they neglect its negative consequences thinking the destructive effects will not have any impact on their own place of living. Frederick and colleagues (2002) state: "People tend to underestimate the threats which have a negative effect only to take place in the far future. This tendency towards short-term thinking probably has its evolutionary roots in our human ancestors. Their survival lied in overcoming immediate threats, and often they did not live long enough to take benefit from their long-term considerations." Suppose we were to expand upon the protection of the environment as one of the examples of personal values. In that case, we could name values such as economizing (bringing balance into the usage of materials that are harmful to the environment), foregoing aggressiveness, or Ahimsa (not damaging plants and animals), foresight (respecting the precautionary principles concerning the environment), appreciation (respecting and loving the nature) and royalty (preserving all parts of the environment) (Clayton and Myers, 2009).

Most individuals have learned their values through their verbal social interactions. Values are highly personal, and the values of one individual can not be passed by another since the evaluator should undergo that evaluation in the context of his own values. Thus it is only natural that what is of value to some person might not be valuable for the other one. Since there exists no golden rule for the values, thus they can not be judged by others (Bach and Moran, 2008).

The Happy Child Mode (HCM)

This mode can act as the beating heart of the healthy adult, and it is accounted as a functional and healthy mode. Jeffery Young and colleagues (2003) have described the activation of the happy child within the individuals experiencing states of love, belonging, bonding, contentment, and satisfaction. Furthermore, they have stated that this mode is not linked to any of the early maladaptive schemas since the emotional needs are met adequately while being in this mode. In addition to the characteristics mentioned above, Arntz and Jacob (2013) have introduced the following features for the happy child mode as well: Feel contented, connected, satisfied, fulfilled, protected, praised, worthwhile, nurtured, guided, understood, validated, self-confident, competent, appropriately autonomous or self-reliant, safe, resilient, strong, in control, adaptable, optimistic, and spontaneous. Whenever individuals experience these feelings, the happy child mode has activated in them.

Farrell and Shaw (2018) have suggested exercises for owning and enforcing the happy child mode in patients, which include: playing video games, watching cartoons or movies, doing favorite sports, activities with friends, listening to music, playing with pets, etc. They believe "patients have not experienced a playful and spontaneous environment while growing up as children or due to their patent's neglect, competitiveness, perfectionism and holding a grudge against entertainment, they were not familiar with any sort of pleasurable activities and had no idea how to come up with a fun and entertaining activity as children."

In schema therapy, we come to learn that fun, playfulness, and spontaneity are among the basic emotional needs of humans, and we try to meet this need in different ways throughout our life from childhood years up to the elderly days. Any culture or school of thinking that disapproves of having fun or limits it to the children is completely wrong. Having fun brightens the human's life and brings joy into it; hence it is better to be included in day-to-day activities. A small group of patients even have problems accepting the principle of spontaneity and playfulness as a need, yet a bigger group of patients do not have any problems with approving of this need, but they prioritize it after everything else. There exist another group of patients who have waited years until the time comes when they finally go to that party, picnic, or vacation.

Furthermore, it is essential to notice that the happy child mode does not engage in abnormal behaviors and breaking the norms while having fun. Some of the patients believed that they could only gain pleasure from a particular situation where they have broken some norms. Indeed, this type of pleasure or happiness is not healthy since it might result in damage to the self, others, or the surrounding environment.

Some of the patients grow anxious from the idea that their happy child mode gets activated. They hold this compulsive and superstitious belief that if they were to be happy for an extended period of time and being extremely joyful, then trouble, conflict, or challenge would come in their way. This dysfunctional belief which can be traced back to the vulnerability to harm and illness schema prevents the person from engaging in fun activities.

From the evolutionary perspective, the human mind has evolved over thousands of years to survive in a world full of different threats. It has not evolved to be playful or experience happiness. The minds of our ancestors were constantly occupied with overcoming different threats, and engaging in fun and playful activities would have distracted them from the vigilance required for their survival. Many parents, teachers, and managers believe that their children, students, or employees should not witness them in their happy child mode since they would no longer respect them or take their words seriously. Indeed, this type of thinking is pathologic which requires modification and adjustment.

Assertiveness

Even Though it is a bitter truth, yet the reality is that humans get sick first in their families and later on in society. Gradually over the course of time, people close to an individual have pushed him towards weakness, humiliation, irresponsibility, laziness, sensitivity, weariness, worthlessness, etc. The patient has become someone who is defined by others. Now comes the hopeless patient who does not see within his power the ability to bring change into his life. The therapist encourages the patient to make changes in his life by reinforcing his assertive spirit and the ability to grow. The therapist teaches the patient how to say no to others, directly expressing his needs and respectfully preventing others from insulting him. The therapist helps the patient change his opinions despite living in a domineering environment and putting aside the fears he experiences regarding others. The patient thus learns a healthy behavioral method through which he can meet his needs. The therapist further utilizes self-disclosure (appropriate closure) as an assertive role model and teaches the patient how to deal with and overcome the obstacles others have brought into the patients' life. As the patient feels more in control, he believes that he is capable of overcoming the challenges of his life. As this sense of being in control increases, the patient's feelings of helplessness gradually fade away, and the patent decisively takes over his life.

Attachment

Maladaptive schemas attract us to people with whom we would experience intense psychological and emotional damages. However, a developed healthy adult would choose people with whom she can experience a deep state of attachment. Attachment brings about a rich life in relation to others. Thus the individual finds the chance to improve, adapt and solve problems. Few human beings have received so much affection and love that they just act caring and loving toward others without wanting anything in return. Thus, loving and receiving love and affection can take place in our relationship with the safe people of our lives. The healthy adult appreciates the kind and respectful behavior of others and the good deeds and favors others have done for him with his attachment leg. Furthermore, the healthy adult is well aware that when the time comes to use his assertive leg, it would be better to use his attachment leg both before and afterward in order to take the possible tension out of the given situation.

Good Parent

Rumi turned to Shams Tabrizi and asked him: "Then what happens to our wounds? Shams replied: The passage of light is through these wounds."

The healthy adult mode is completely aware of the activation of all the other modes throughout the day. The healthy adult mode engages in self-observation, recollects the reasons that caused the mode's activation and plans, and meets the frustrated needs with having the future in mind. Since the process of answering the needs is very delicate and important, it is the good parent who takes over this procedure. For example, the individual does those activities with her good parent, which bring a sense of being understood, loved, and worthy to her vulnerable child mode. The good parent attends to her vulnerable child's needs with compassion, kindness, respect, validation, admiration, and approval, which she feels towards herself. The good parent does the same for the angry child mode but with a slight modification. For example, she first sets limits, then hears out the angry child mode and validates the anger which is being expressed maturely.

Problem Solving

Laozi, the Chinese philosopher, and founder of Taoism, in his book Tao The Way, states: "I have three treasures which hold dearly and cherish. The first one is compassion, and the second is contentment, and the third one avoiding being the number one in the world." Compassion with other human beings empowers us with the courage to live with contentment, our resources never cease to exist, and if we never strive to be the number one, we would eventually find ourselves in that position. Like Laozi, many philosophers have suggested different behavioral rules to address the problems of humankind throughout history. Many of these behavioral rules either came from the person's own lived experiences or have been passed along as advice from the master to the next student and so forth until it has reached us. The healthy adult mode utilizes the learned lessons and the collective wisdom in order to come up with solutions to the complex issues in life. Problem-solving becomes relevant when the person has no idea on which path she must take in order to navigate her way from a certain situation to the other one. Many patients get to know the methods with which the therapist solves the problems and the distinctive ways of thinking of the therapist throughout the therapy process. They gradually come to realize how to make the best decision in the face of adversities and complicated situations. One of the patients stated: "During one of my triggering situations, I thought to myself, what would my therapist do if she found herself in this situation? How would she behave? Suddenly an idea struck me and I went on accordingly. After a couple of days, I met with my therapist, told her about the situation and my reaction, and she appraised and admired my reaction."

It is only through gaining awareness that the healthy adult mode becomes capable of solving a problem. When we have grown up holding dysfunctional beliefs, molded incorrect thoughts, outdated customs, bad habits, and unsound traditions, also in a family environment full of tension to complicate the matter further, we have got maladaptive modes and schemas which not only do not provide us with any ability to solve any problems in life but also turn the slightest challenges into big tragedies thus throwing bigger challenges back at us. Schemas and modes pull us toward the deepest states of unawareness. This process takes place in a way that when the individual is about to tackle a problem, she will do so without feeling the need for giving the issue any precise thinking, thus moving forward being unaware and without having taken the necessary measures. Maladaptive schemas, along with their dysfunctional coping styles, have pretty much pre-determined the reactions to the problems in particular and the way of life in general. They dictate to us the good and bad in life, refusing us any sign of disagreement. Schemas and modes prevent the individuals from making an effort to think about the solutions to a given problem which is, of course, a rather difficult task.

The meaning which living an aware life carries is this: the

maximum utilization of the healthy adult mode's capacity while dealing with the issues regarding the triggering situations. Individuals living an aware life observe the events as they really are and, by constantly holding their healthy adult mode as their frame of reference, aim for analyzing the problems and issues in a correct manner. Individuals living an unaware life do not think about their issues, and they leave them to the voice of their schemas that they hear and the reactions from their modes to solve. On the other hand, individuals living an aware life deeply think about their issues, examine the danger signals, consider the emotional needs, and behave "attached/assertively."

The Seven Grounds for the Development of the Healthy Adult

In this section, the seven grounds on which the healthy adult mode spends her daily time and engages in them are examined. It is a high expectation if we demand ourselves to include all seven of these activities in our daily routine every day. However, if the individual manages to dedicate his daily time to these seven grounds, he, therefore, has placed himself on a correct way of living. These activities are timeless and are not bound to any specific locations. In other words, the wise humans of the past have done them, and the smart ones of the future will continue to do so.

1. Education and Learning

Schema therapy helps us to reassess our thoughts, behaviors, and emotions. In order to build a better life in the future, we are required to find out the reasons for the wrong choices we made in the past. Furthermore, we should be careful not to repeat the same mistakes again in the future. This can be achieved with two concepts of education and learning. When it comes to education, we first learn about the concepts of schema therapy, including the childhood origins all the way to the signs of the schemas and their coping responses. We then learn about how we should modify our schemas utilizing cognitive, behavioral, and experimental techniques. Furthermore, we learn from our therapist as a good enough model on how to replace our inappropriate behaviors with the proper ones in different situations. The healthy adult mode usually develops through education, modeling, and in the process of treatment through accessible patterns. The individual gradually takes responsibility for the different roles she has accepted and learns how to act accordingly. The patients with a weak healthy adult would face problems while playing their social, career, family, and marital roles. As an example, as regards the issues among couples, since the partner with an emotional deprivation schema has not received the necessary education and proper treatment regarding her schema, she has high expectations of her partner. In fact, she does not know where the line is drawn when it comes to having expectations from her partner.

Individuals with healthy adult mode strive for learning and getting educated regardless of their age and the period they are in. Furthermore, they teach others about what they have learned. The behavior of individuals who get educated and learning does not concern them, regardless of their age, is immature compared to the ones who take these two issues seriously. Some of the individuals with dependence/ incompetence, failure, and enmeshment/ undeveloped-self schemas have realized that the more immature behavior they exhibit, the more their needs would get met. Thus the person with a dependence/ incompetence schema does not show any interest in learning and exhibits behaviors that are relatively immature concerning his age in order to get his needs met. This person might even attend therapy sessions or skills classes, yet he refuses to act according to what he has learned since his gains and benefit lie in behaving dependant and incompetent. Hence, education and learning are necessary for life, but it is not sufficient by any means. We should be able to act according to all the things that we have learned; otherwise, we have turned into a "richly informed- poorly capable" person.

2. Social Interactions

Human beings are entirely social creatures by nature, and keeping their fellowman at a distance would cause them various problems. The avoidant and Schizoid personality disorders directly concern the weakness in social interactions. Among schemas, the social isolation schema points out the person's maladaptiveness with regard to her social interactions. Individuals with his schema are not comfortable being in groups and prefer to avoid attending parties and gatherings. Individuals with a mistrust/abuse schema are not comfortable being around others since they worry about others' abuses, humiliations, or ulterior motives. People with defectiveness/shame schema are not confident while being in a group and grow increasingly anxious when they want to talk. Individuals with self-sacrifice schema put others first to the degree that after a while, they grow tired and burned out due to their social interactions.

People with approval-seeking/recognition-seeking schema only attend in the groups where they get recognized, approved, and admired. The same goes for individuals with entitlement/grandiosity schema. Furthermore, they tend to take advantage of others to the degree that they are ultimately left alone. People with unrelenting standards schema are so occupied with their work and daily chores that they never find the time to socialize with others. Individuals with a punitiveness schema tend to punish others for even their slightest mistakes.

They have done so rather frequently that even their own family members avoid them. Therefore social interactions are a need of great importance, which schemas prevent them from getting met. Each one of the schemas disturbs our social interactions in their own way. This issue has caused individuals not to be able to have healthy social interactions the way they should. Nevertheless, the reality is that individuals with the healthy adult mode put a great emphasis on social interactions. Today's world is the world of communications, and the more the individual is capable of communication skills, the more social capital he poses. It is not to mention that social capital is more beneficial to us compared to financial capital. With regard to the therapy process, too, many patients have found their group therapy sessions of more benefit to them even compared to their individual therapy sessions. We can form appropriate social interactions by modifying schemas and developing the healthy adult. Achieving a healthy adult mode without having to form close connections with others, where mutual intimacy is at the heart of the connection, is not possible.

3. Altruism

Individuals with a developed healthy adult mode are always found at the heart of the society dealing with the problems of their own and the ones of other people. These people are well aware that in order to overcome the problems of the social life, they have to step forward as a volunteer, harnessing their knowledge, skills, and resources. Many of the altruistic experiences are results of the active participants of the individuals in their humanistic society, which bear many lessons to them. Problems of other people do not concern the individuals with entitlement/grandiosity schema. Most often, they act as if society owes them something. They raise this question: What has society done for me ever? A Socratic answer to this question would be: What have you yourself ever done for society? Also, individuals with self-sacrifice schema tend to be altruistic while they have difficulties in meeting their own needs in the first place. For this group, it is recommended that they attend to their own needs in the first place since true altruism takes place only when we have met our needs first and then have put our focus on the needs of others. Consider a poor country whose own people are starving, yet this country decides to send food packages to their neighbor country, which is also dealing with famine. This behavior is not considered altruism by any means. It just reminds us of the Persian proverb, which literally states: "A blind man is carrying another blind's cane." Individuals with approval-seeking/recognition-seeking schema take advantage of altruistic behaviors in order to gain popularity, fame, and attention from others.

Auguste Comte (1798 – 1857), the French Philosopher, was the first person who mentioned the concept of altruism. He believed that there exist two separate forces (motives) within each individual. One of the forces is directed toward the individual herself (selfishness), and the other one is directed toward others (altruism). According to Comte, altruism is considered the building block of living in society (Scott and Seglow, 2007). According to Emile Durkheim (1858 – 1917), the French Sociologist, altruism is more than just a favorable embellishment to social life, yet it forever remains the main basis of living (Piliavin and Charng 1990). Alfred Adler has pointed out the concept of "social interest" as well. According to him, the first task of life that we are faced with is forming connections with others. The individual is forced to collaborate with society and participate in it to achieve her personal and shared goals. Adler has further emphasized the point that lack of altruism results in a vast majority of evil acts, from wars to racism and even alcoholism (Schultz and Schultz, 2016).

4. Sense of Aesthetics

Aesthetics are in close and direct contact with art. Since art reflects the knowledge, thinking, and creativity, it results in the further enhancement and development of cognitive capabilities. Sense of aesthetics lies within the human's nature and profoundly impacts her psyche as well as her view on life. Consequently, the healthy adult mode engages in activities that are concerned with the philosophies of aesthetics, such as comprehending the beauty which lies within a phenomenon (like a painting), analyzing the elegant aspects of a living creature (like a flower), helping with the development of the aesthetics (such as preserving and caring for historical artifacts), helping others with developing their own sense of aesthetics (encouraging a talented person to learn how to play the piano) and thinking about the reasons which bring about a sense of beauty (like love).

Even though individual's opinions of aesthetics might differ from each other, it is crucial that they utilize this sense of theirs through their daily activities. The healthy adult mode enjoys both the aesthetics found in nature and the ones coming from artistic artifacts. Individuals with this mode enjoy the most while visiting museums and historical sights and artifacts; they go to painting galleries, visit modern and postmodern art exhibitions, show interest in carpets and rugs booths, and spend their time observing and viewing different sculptures. They never miss a chance to go to a music concert, a theater or go to the cinemas. Exploration in nature is another interest of theirs. Jungles, mountains, deserts and seas, each hold their own unique beauty. Thus an individual with a healthy adult mode spends a segment of his income and dedicates part of his time in order to visit artistic places and take a trip to the areas with beautiful natural views.

Art activates the sense of aesthetics and forms a mutual dialogue with the mind. The mental challenges stemming from nature push the person toward analyzing the universe. While being in the healthy adult mode, the individual might face unexpected events which would stir a sense of amazement and surprise in her.

It appears that the individuals with an unrelenting standards schema never find the time nor the opportunity to attend to their sense of aesthetics and regard those activities as pointless and a waste of time and energy. Individuals with a negativity/pessimism schema show a little interest in the sense of aesthetics as well. Others with vulnerability to harm and illness schema rarely go to nature, take fewer trips, and won't spend their money and time on satisfying their sense of aesthetics. Individuals with social isolation schema show little interest in attending crowded places such as concerts, theaters, museums, and exhibitions. People with emotional inhibition schema find themselves incapable to an extent when it comes to expressing their sense of aesthetics while being faced with a beautiful phenomenon or creature. Individuals with defectiveness/shame schema have a difficult time with regard to displaying their own made art pieces, and their sense of aesthetics gradually fades over time. Therefore schemas prevent individuals from being in touch with those parts of themselves which are concerned with the sense of aesthetics. These parts are actually within the elements which constitute human nature. When it comes to the couple's relationship, the partners considering each other's sense of aesthetics and supporting its further development can dramatically impact the quality of the relationship.

5. Spirituality

Today's world is filled with mass media and social networks. These mediums constantly broadcast news regarding the details of the intimate lives of the cinema celebrities, words of the unwise controversial politicians, costly parties of the famous models, and romantic relationships of the popular athletes. They also constantly keep advertising the "how to" s and directions on how to use different products, consumer goods, and foods high on calories, and take part in bet websites to accumulate more wealth. In this new world, filled with these media, the need for spirituality and the lack of it is being felt more than ever before. Furthermore, the world is changing at an increasingly unbelievable rapid pace. The pace indeed has not been ever observed before in the life of humans. Therefore, these are the times where humans are in need of spiritual experiences more than ever. Spirituality is of great help when it comes to dealing with the rapid pace of changes occurring in life as well as the chaos that it brings with itself. Without a doubt, spirituality fills a significant portion of people's lives and plays a vital role with regard to their psychological well-being and welfare.

While being in healthy adult mode, individuals put great emphasis on their spiritual dimension. This is due to the fact that having a mission and a calling in life is part of having a sense of duty and commitment. This goes hand in hand with holding an image of a better world for oneself and all other people, finding a meaning and a goal in life to fill the extension holes that can be found within us. All of these matters help with regard to reducing the real sufferings. Thus seeking a sense of spirituality in individuals leads to a change in their views on life and their ways of living it.

One of the methods that help with developing the spirituality dimension in individuals is engagement in daily meditation. Meditation is a simple method in order to protect the psyche in the face of daily mental challenges and distresses. Furthermore, therapists need daily meditations more than others due to the psychological pressures that they experience while dealing with their patients and as a means to prevent their career burnout. Claxton (1996) believes that meditation results in gaining more insight, awareness, equanimity, and magnanimity. Furthermore, he states that every therapist who fails to develop these qualities in himself would not be able to justify and explain his approach to treatment. Rumi (1207 - 1273), Persian poet and Sufi mystic, has stated the necessity for spirituality and being in touch with the universe in the following verses:

If it is with the sea, a drop is a sea *** Otherwise, the drop is a drop, and the sea is the sea

6. Sexual Relationship

Even today, talking about sexual relationships is considered taboo in many cultures. This is in contrast with the fact that "sexual health" is one of the most significant factors contributing to the individual's quality of life and psychological welfare. Some of the horrible sexual events in childhood play an important role in the formation of maladaptive schemas. These schemas have a negative impact on the children's sexual well-being continuing to adulthood years manifesting themselves in the form of complex and difficult to overcome sexual disorders and Paraphilias. For example, through the Repetition pattern, individuals who have been subject to sexual abuse in their childhood develop certain schemas such as mistrust/abuse schema. On many occasions, individuals with the pedophilic disorder have stated that they themselves have been sexually abused as children. Also, with regard to Vaginismus, vulnerable child mode plays a significant role. Herby different instances of the vulnerable child mode related to Vaginismus disorder are being stated: Abandoned vulnerable child mode: "I'm not sure whether after having the sexual relationship, he won't abandon me." Deprived vulnerable child mode: "I only hand in my virginity to someone who is truly in love with me. I'm not yet sure of my husband's love toward me." Defective vulnerable child mode: "If I lose my virginity, I would lack something; I would become flawed and defective." Abused vulnerable child mode: "My husband forces sexual relationships on me; he appears as scary as if he doesn't understand anything in those moments!" Indeed, the sexual need has formed an inseparable part of human nature as a natural and instinctive need for gaining pleasure, peace, and reproduction. On the other end, some of the schema modes play an important role in decreasing, disturbing, or even completely stopping this activity by stirring up feelings of guilt, fear, anger, and disguise. Furthermore, many of the cultural attitudes have an impact on the individual's healthy sexual functioning. Polygamy, female circumcision, or holding women solely responsible for unintended pregnancy are among these instances.

Individuals with a healthy adult mode emphasize their sexual relationship and intimacy as a means of meeting their emotional/sexual needs. The healthy adult pays attention to "sexual ethics," which is based on sexual equality, sexual responsibility, and acceptance of differences. Furthermore, individuals with a healthy adult mode are constantly trying to increase their "sexual knowledge" in order to enhance the quality of sexual relationships.

Bearing children does not happen by accident and unintentionally for a healthy adult. In contrast, healthy adults have children with prior planning when both parents find within themselves a pure and shared motive and eagerness to experience the incredible feelings associated with being a mother and father. For humans as social creatures, forming realistic limits and self-control with regard to sexual behaviors is of utmost necessity.

7. Body Exercise

Any regular daily activity which is meant for protecting physical fitness, well-being, happiness, and general health is called body exercise. The proverb "A sound mind in a sound body" signifies the importance of daily body exercises as a part of the human's healthy lifestyle.

Each nation holds a history of a national sport. For example, ancient Iranians were much interested in playing Chovgan, attended "Pahlevani and zoorkhaneh rituals," and since the old days, wrestling has been the national sport of this land. According to Iranians, a "Pahlevan" or hero is a person with a sturdy, muscular physique who is courageous, assertive, fair, humble, and very kind, among other positive characteristics. In this regard, Pahlevan has many differences from a champion; most notably, the Pahlevan emphasizes moral principles over physical strength. This ancient ritual considers selfishness, arrogance, and pride as the most incorrect characteristics of individuals. Ferdowsi (940 - 1019), Persian Poet, in Shahnameh tells the stories of the ancient legends of Iran. Among these legends are many Pahlevans, yet Rostam is being referred to as the Pahlevan of the universe. Ferdowsi describes Rostam as a wise Pahlevan whom just any other human being can get hurt and bears his own wounds. In Hinduism culture, too, people hold much respect for Yoga exercises. Yoga is a set of physical activities, mental exercises, and spiritual concepts dating back to ancient India. Yoga, along with its healthy diet, takes up part of the Indian's daily life along with many people from all over the world.

Individuals with a healthy adult mode put much emphasis on regular body exercises. This is due to the fact that doing regular body exercise results in an increase in the quality of sleep, energy levels and flexibility, and happiness, a decrease in overall stress levels, enhancement of heart's well-being condition and body's immunity system, and prevention of diabetes and obesity. Therefore it is recommended that individuals with a healthy adult mode assign 30 minutes to an hour every day to walking. Furthermore, it is suggested that they do different sports such as swimming, hiking, or cycling for one to two sessions each week as it favors them.

The Healthy Adult Mode Checklist

Roediger, Stevens, and Brockman (2018) believe that many of the techniques coming from mindfulness, flexibility, and building a life worth living which have been invented by the third wave therapies such as the ACT, Compassion-focused therapy, and Dialectical behavioral therapy (DBT) have many applications for shaping a proper healthy adult mode. Thus the healthy adult mode checklist, which is composed of the elements from the combination of the third wave therapies, is being introduced here. This checklist is an easy-to-use tool for self-assessment of the healthy adult mode based on individuals' beliefs and activities.

Taking the topics being discussed thus far in this chapter, assign a rating from 1 to 6 to each item in the below table, considering the current circumstances in your life. This checklist helps you realize the strength of your healthy adult mode. Rating 1 indicates the presence of the given item as very low, and rating 6 would mean very high, respectively. Please choose ratings for each item as best it describes it in your current life, not how you wish that item had played out itself. Furthermore, do not assign higher ratings to an item just because it is a good and important feature to have but rate it based on how much it holds true regarding your current affairs. In the third column, briefly explain your rationale for each rating, whether that rating being high or low.

Item	Rating (on the scale of 1 to 6)	Explanation or Elaboration
Acceptance of self		
Acceptance of others		

Welcome work		
Patience with problems		
Living in the here and now		
Assertiveness		
Attachment		
Learning and education		
Social interactions		
Altruism		
Sense of aesthetics		
Spirituality		
Sexual relationship		
Body exercise		

Final Words

Both the therapist and the patient do their best to develop and reinforce the healthy adult mode during the process of treatment. The healthy adult mode development process takes place rather slowly in most patients, yet the therapist can gradually come to identify its signs in the patient. No one can be in healthy adult mode all the time; thus, it would be very demanding of the patients if we were to expect them never to leave their healthy adult mode. All of us have to deal with different problems throughout our lives, and we cannot find anyone who has never been through a problem. When we come up with a smart, creative, and realistic method to address our problems, we find ourselves in our activated healthy adult mode. Jacob, van Genderen and Seebauer (2015) mention these features as the qualities of the healthy adult mode:

- "Healthy ego functioning"
- Realistic judgment of situations, conflicts, relationships, yourself, and other people
- Minor problems do not trigger overwhelming negative emotions.
- You sense both your own feelings and needs and those of other people.
- You can balance your needs with the needs of others.
- You can make commitments, take responsibilities, and comply with your duties.
- You find constructive solutions for problems.
- You enjoy adult pleasures and interests (sports, culture, sex, etc.)

"Awareness" of the basic emotional needs means knowing and gaining experience from what has not been provided to us previously and what shortcomings we have had. For example, a person who is emotionally deprived and feels severely lonely is well aware that she needs a kind and committed companion. However, if her healthy adult mode is not developed enough, she would not know why she is afraid of getting close to others and forming intimate relationships. She acts as if she needs a relationship, yet she refuses to do so in practice! This person comes to realize that she has an emotional deprivation schema during the course of therapy and that she has chosen avoidance as her primary coping style without being aware of it. Now she has reached some degree of awareness so that when she experiences feelings toward someone else or has given a proposition for having a relationship, she considers those instances first before making an unaware decision. Usually, these are the situations in which schema modes get activated. Roediger and colleagues (2018) believe that: "The healthy adult mode manages to overcome the effects of the other problematic modes when it becomes aware of their activities. Thus, it is necessary to become aware of these modes, and the healthy adult mode is self-aware."

On the other hand, there is a risk that many clients might confuse the healthy adult mode with the Over-controller mode. Clients might go through the motions of carrying out rational activities that are considered healthy on a superficial level (e.g., attending the gym, eating the right foods) with a sense of efficiency rather than self-compassion. Thus it is important to develop the healthy adult mode to have a keen awareness of the needs of the vulnerable child mode as well. The healthy adult mode should be able to prioritize its own needs and the needs of the vulnerable child over the competing demands and needs of others (Simpson and Smith, 2020).

What usually takes place in the group therapy sessions is that the person himself is not aware of the activation of his modes, yet the group leader and some of the members identify his activated modes. Indeed, the healthy adult mode of each individual realizes his activated modes before others become aware of their presence. In case an individual manages to become aware of his modes in each given instance deeply, he has reached a level of deep self-knowledge.

Finally, we should acknowledge the fact that the more developed the healthy adult mode becomes in an individual, she would face unpleasantness while dealing with others who possess lower levels of awareness. This is because an aware person has an influential power over others, whether this influence is intentional or unintentional. It is to state that she would also go through lots of suffering in her attempts at opening up the doors of awareness for others. All in all, the healthy adult mode is a comprehensive, influential and active mode.

APPENDIX A

Tehran - Schema Mode Inventory (T-SMI)

Amir Askari © 2020

Full Name:
Age: Gender:
Education: Occupation:
Marital Status:

Instructions

Instructions for The Tehran - Schema Mode Inventory (T-SMI): Please read each statement carefully and answer every 45 questions below honestly. In case you choose "never" as your answer, you will receive 1 point, and in case you choose "always," you will receive 6 points accordingly. Your answers can be based on how much you believe in the given statement or how frequently it has occurred to you. The aim of this questionnaire is the assessment of 9 schema modes.

Never = 1 Rarely = 2 Occasionally = 3

Frequently = 4 Most of the time = 5 Always = 6

No	Statement	1	2	3	4	5	6
1	If my interests are not met, I will stop the plan from progressing by deliberately creating obstacles.						
2	If faced with a conflict, I swear						

	up and down until I get my way. I expect others to back down when they hear my swearings.						
3	Issues that are not of much importance turn out to be great headaches for me.						
4	When under psychological pressure and intense distress, I start to laugh with no apparent reason.						
5	During a period in my life, I have spent my days picturing an imaginary love.						
6	I make fun of my face, body, appearances, taste, or beliefs.						
7	I find great						

	ability in teasing others in myself.						
8	I can play the role of a poor and miserable person in order to achieve my desired outcomes or goals.						
9	Even if I lack the required knowledge and necessary background on a given topic, I will go on giving my remarks.						
10	In case I don't like someone, I tend to make fun of him/her in front of others.						
11	It has happened to me that if I wanted something or someone from the bottom of my heart, I got						

	to them in my dreams.						
12	Even though I don't like troubles at all, yet I easily find myself in one.						
13	In order to prevent others from making progress, I take or destroy their resources or essential documents.						
14	When arguing with someone or being told something that upsets me or makes me angry, I tend to smile.						
15	If someone asks me for directions, I will point them to a route even if I have no clue.						
16	If someone						

	hurts me, I will let that person know about the karma of his/her action or the curse I will make for the harm going their way.						
17	When being asked questions by authority figures, I act hasty and as being flustered so that they let go of me.						
18	If someone messes with me, I would go along despite it being hurtful.						
19	It brings me solace that I'm able to make bully and dominant people pay for what they did to me in my imaginations.						

20	By fudging and delaying others' works, I keep them from reaching their goals.						
21	I tell others about my ridiculous mistakes. This way, I entertain them and make them laugh.						
22	I constantly keep reminding others how my previous advice that I gave them has saved them a day.						
23	Due to some of my remarks or behaviors done to others, a new challenge or brawl is being made.						
24	If I feel someone is more successful than me, I try to						

	misdirect him/her by feeding them misinformation.						
25	I am highly capable in playing the role of a sick patient having heart or digestive problems or even faking being depressed.						
26	Whenever an incident occurs to someone such as falling on the ground or getting burned in my presence, I can't stop my laughter at that moment.						
27	I take the weaknesses of a person and turn them into topics for others to laugh at.						

28	Due to putting my nose in others' business and interfering in their personal matters, I run into conflicts with them.						
29	It is my duty to give advice to others, especially when it comes to important matters in their lives.						
30	When I discover a way that can result in making progress, I won't share it with others. In case I'm being asked about it, I would direct them in the opposite direction.						
31	I have a high tendency to make fun of the people who are						

	more popular or successful than me.						
32	By daydreaming about whatever I can't achieve, I make myself happy and satisfied.						
33	I put on a confused, groggy, or slow-witted act in order to make my way through difficult situations.						
34	On some occasions I take the role of the clown of the group.						
35	Others know me with my constant smile on my face.						
36	By breaking my promises and not keeping my words, I disrupt other's plans.						

37	I tell others jokes about the ethnicity, language, or culture I come from.						
38	It doesn't bother me at all when others keep drinking from my Kool-Aid.						
39	I grow fond of the ones who listen to my advice and recommendations.						
40	I have the ability to exaggerate my feelings of sadness, distress, anxiety, and physical weakness.						
41	When in a quarrel with someone, I mimic his/her behavior or voice mockingly.						

42	I spend lots of time in my imaginations thinking about love, wealth, status or traveling every day.						
43	By troubling the situation and making a mess, I attempt to fish in troubled waters.						
44	Whenever I'm talking about a topic, lots of uncontrollable waves of laughter accompany my speech.						
45	Some of my efforts or relationships get ruined as some of my exaggerations or lies get revealed.						

Scoring Tehran - Schema Mode Inventory (T-SMI)

No	Schema Modes	Questions					Total
1	Distressed/ Helpless Mode	8 =	17 =	25 =	33 =	40 =	
2	Hesitant Imagined Mode	5 =	11 =	19 =	32 =	42 =	
3	Moral Preacher Mode	2 =	16 =	22 =	29 =	39 =	
4	Automatic Laughter Mode	4 =	14 =	26 =	35 =	44 =	
5	Self-Mockery Mode	6 =	18 =	21 =	34 =	37 =	
6	Others-Mockery Mode	7 =	10 =	27 =	31 =	41 =	
7	Obstructionist/Saboteur Mode	1 =	13 =	20 =	36 =	43 =	
8	Misguide/Misdirect Mode	9 =	15 =	24 =	30 =	38 =	
9	Controversial/ Troublemaker Mode	3 =	12 =	23 =	28 =	45 =	

Interpreting Tehran - Schema Mode Inventory (T-SMI)

Five statements have been assigned to each mode. The highest score for each mode is 30, and the lowest score is 5. For examining the result, the examiner adds the scores of the test taker. The higher the subject's score is from 13, the more inflexible that mode is in the test taker. Scores lower than 13 are indicators of normality, and relatively high scores (scores close to 30) are indicators of strong governance of the mode on the structure of information processing in the individual. Considering the quickly changeable nature of modes during different treatment sessions, it is recommended to ask the patient to answer this questionnaire twice, with one month in between, for achieving more accurate results.

REFERENCES

Arntz, A. (2012). Imagery rescripting as a therapeutic technique: Review of clinical trials, basic studies, and research agenda. Journal of Experimental Psychopathology, 3(2), 189-208.

Arntz, A., & Jacob, G. (2013). Schema therapy in practice: An introductory guide to the schema mode approach. Chichester, UK: Wiley-Blackwell.

Arntz, A., & van Genderen, H. (2009). Schema therapy for borderline personality disorder. Chichester, UK: Wiley-Blackwell.

Askari, A, Hakami, M. (2012) Couples-Based Coping Training on Thought Control Strategies of Spouses of Cancer Patients, South Asian Academic Research Journals. ACADEMICIA: An International Multidisciplinary Research Journal (SAARJ), Vol. 2, Issue 11, ISSN: 2249-7137

Askari, A., Madgaonkar, J.S, Rowell, R.K (2011) Assessing Thought-Control Strategies: Cancer and Family, Asian Journal of Development Matters 4: 13 - 19

Askari, A, Madgaonkar, J S; Rowell, R K. (2012) Current Psychopathological Issues among Partners of Cancer Patients, Journal of Psychosocial Research; Vol. 7, Iss. 1, 77-85.

Atkinson, T. (2012). Schema therapy for couples: Healing partners in a relationship. In: M. van Vreeswijk, J. Broersen, & M.M Nadort (Eds.), The Wiley-Blackwell handbook of schema therapy: Theory, research, and practice (pp. 323–335). Chichester, UK: Wiley-Blackwell.

Bach, P. A. & Moran, D. J. (2008) ACT in Practice, Case Conceptualization in Acceptance and Commitment Therapy, New Harbinger Publication.

Behary, W. T. (2013). Disarming the narcissist. Surviving and thriving with the self-absorbed. Oakland, CA: New Harbinger Publications.

Bernstein, D. P. (2020) Bernstein List of 48 Strengths (BLS) & Bernstein Strengths Scale (BSS), www.i-modes.com

Blomqvist, C., Mello, I., Amundin, M. (2005) An Acoustic Play-Fight Signal in Bottlenose Dolphins (Tursiops truncatus) in Human Care. Aquatic Mammals Journal.

Clayton, S., Myers, G. (2009) Conservation Psychology, Understanding and Promoting Human Care for Nature, Wiley-Blackwell.

Claxton, G. (1996) Therapy and Beyond: Concluding Thoughts, in G. Claxton (ed.), Beyond Therapy: The Impact of Eastern Religious on Psychological Theory and Practice. Dorset: Prism.

Davila-Ross, M., Allcock, B., Thomas, C., Bard, K. A. (2011) Aping Expressions? Chimpanzees Produce Distinct Laugh Types When Responding to Laughter of Others. Emotion: Publisher: American Psychological Association, 11(5):1013-20

Erickson, E. H. (1963) Childhood and society (2nd ed). Newyork: Norton.

Farrell M. J, Shaw A. I (2012). Group schema therapy for borderline personality disorder: A step-by-step treatment manual with patient workbook. Chichester, UK: Wiley-Blackwell.

Farrell, J. M., & Shaw, I. A. (2018). Experiencing schema therapy from the inside out: A self-practice/self-reflection workbook for therapists. New York: Guilford.

Farrell, J. M., Reiss, N., & Shaw, I. A. (2014). The schema therapy clinician's guide: A complete resource for building and delivering individual, group, and integrated schema mode treatment programs. Chichester, UK: Wiley-Blackwell.

Frederick, S., Loewenstein, G. & O'Donoghue, T. (2002). Time discounting and time preference: A Critical Review. Journal of Economic Literature 40, 351-401.

Freud, S (1927), Humor, International Journal of Psycho-analysis, 9, pp. 1-5.

Genderen, H. van, Rijkeboer, M.M., & Arntz, A. (2012). Theoretical Model: Schemas, Coping Styles, and Modes. In: M. van Vreeswijk, J. Broersen, & M.M Nadort (Eds.), The Wiley-Blackwell handbook of schema therapy: Theory, research, and practice. Chichester, UK: Wiley-Blackwell.

Hayes, S. C., Strosahl, K. D., & Wilson, K. G. (2012) Acceptance and Commitment Therapy: The Process and Practice of Mindful Change (2nd ed.). New York: Guilford Press.

Jacob, G., van Genderen, H., & Seebauer, L. (2015). Breaking negative thinking patterns: A schema therapy self-help and support book. Chichester, UK: Wiley-Blackwell.

Karpman S.B (2014) A Game Free Life, Drama Triangle Publications. ISBN 978-0990586708

Lobbestael, J., Van Vreeswijk, M., & Arntz, A., (2007). Shedding light on schema modes: a clarification of the mode concept and its current research status. Netherlands Journal of Psychology, 63: 76-85

Manickam LSS (2004) Sahya: The concept in Indian philosophical psychology and its contemporary relevance. Journal of Consciousness, Indian Psychology, and Yoga, pp. 426-35.

Piliavin JA, Charng HW (1990) Altruism: A Review of Recent Theory and Research, Annual Review of Sociology, 16: 25-65.

Pink, D. H (2005) A Whole New Mind, Moving from the information age to the conceptual age, Penguin Publishing Group.

Roediger, E., Stevens, B. A., & Brockman, R. (2018). Contextual Schema Therapy. An Integrative Approach to Personality Disorders, Emotional Dysregulation & Interpersonal Functioning. Oakland, CA: New Harbinger Publications.

Schultz, D. P. & Schultz, S. E (2016) Theories of Personality, 11th edition, Cengage Learning, ISBN 978-1305652958

Scott, N., & Seglow, J. (2007) Altruism, New York, Mc Graw-Hill.

Shammi, P., Stuss, D.T (1999) Humor Appreciation: A Role of the right frontal lobe, Brain; vol. 122, 663.

Simeone-DiFrancesco, C., Roediger, E., & Stevens, B. A. (2015). Schema Therapy with Couples. A Practitioner's Guide to Healing Relationships. UK: Wiley-Blackwell.

Simonet, P., Versteeg, D., Storie, D. (2005) Dog-laughter: Recorded playback reduces stress related behavior in shelter dogs, 7th International Conference on Environmental Enrichment.

Simpson, S., & Smith, E. (Eds.). (2020). Schema therapy for eating disorders. New York: Routledge.

Vaillant, GE (1992), Ego Mechanisms of Defense: A Guide for Clinicians and Researchers, Washington DC, American Psychiatric Press.

Van Vreeswijk, M., Broersen, J., & Schurink, G. (2014). Mindfulness and schema therapy: A practical guide. Chichester, UK: Wiley-Blackwell.

Webster, J.D. (2003) An exploratory analysis of a self-assessed wisdom scale. Journal of Adult Development. 10(1), 13-22.

Young, J. E., & Klosko, J. S. (1993). Reinventing your life: The breakthrough program to end negative behavior and feel great again. New York: Plume.

Young, J. E., Klosko, J. S., & Weishaar, M. E. (2003). Schema therapy: A practitioner's guide. New York: Guilford Press.

LITERATURE SOURCES

Anvari, Divan: A Pocket Book for Akbar, Publisher: Metropolitan Museum of Art, 2012, ISBN 978-0300193053

Hafiz, Divan-i-Hafiz, Translated by Henry Wilberforce-Clarke, Ibex Publishers, Inc., 2007, ISBN 0-936347-80-5

Khaqani, Selected Poems, Translated by Paul Smith, CreateSpace Independent Publishing Platform, 2012, ISBN 978-1479391936

Khwaju Kermani, Three Poems, Namly Homay o Homayun, The Kamal-Nameh & Raudat ul-Anwar, Iranian Academy of Arts, 2014, ISBN 978-9642322077

Mohtasham Kashani, Divan-e Mohtasham, Edited by Ahmad Baharvand, 2004, Negah Publication.

Nizami Ganjavi, The Emperor Akbar's of Khamsa, Publisher: British Library Board, 1995, ISBN 978-0712303927

Omar Khayyam Neyshaburi, The Rubayat of Omar Khayyam, translated by Edward FitzGerald, 2011, Dover Publications. ISBN 978-0486264677

Jalal al-Din Rumi, The Essential Rumi, Translated by Coleman Barks, 2004, HarperOne, ISBN 978-0062509598

Saadi, The Divan, Translated by Paul Smith, CreateSpace Independent Publishing Platform, 2014, ISBN 978-1500252427

Saeb Tabrizi, Divan-e Saeb-e Tabrizi, Edited by Parviz Natel Khanlari, Volumes 1 & 2, 2004, Negah Publication.

Shaykh Farid Al-Din Attar Neyshaburi, Asrar Nameh, Parvan Publication, 2009, ISBN 978-9648333268

Ubayd Zakani, Poetry, Prose, Satire, Jokes, Ribaldry, Translated by Paul Smith, CreateSpace Independent Publishing Platform, ISBN 978-1512182965

Made in the USA
Columbia, SC
11 February 2022

55961097R00170